THE BROKEN IMAGE

Pat Collins CM

The Broken Image

REFLECTIONS ON SPIRITUALITY AND CULTURE

the columba press

First published in 2002 by
ᴄhe ᴄoʟᴜᴍʙᴀ ᴘʀᴇss
55a Spruce Avenue, Stillorgan Industrial Park
Blackrock, Co Dublin

Cover by Bill Bolger
Origination by The Columba Press
Printed in Ireland by Colour Books Ltd, Dublin
ISBN 1 85607 356 4

Contents

"Whatever its source, truth is of the Holy Spirit"
St Thomas Aquinas, *ST* I-II, 109, 1 ad 1.

Introduction

The authors of secular fiction write either novels or collections of short stories. The authors of spiritual works do much the same. They either write thematic books that expound a particular aspect of the Christian life, such as prayer, or they put together a collection of different but loosely related topics. This book, like *Spirituality for The Twenty First Century*, is a collection of such reflections. Most of them have been published in Irish magazines and journals over the last few years. I am grateful to all those editors who printed the various articles I submitted for publication. In doing so they provided me, as they do for so many others, an invaluable forum for creative reflection on a range of subjects. I'm grateful to those editors who also gave permission to reprint articles, some of which have been modified since they first appeared. The chapters entitled 'Envy: Cancer of the Soul', 'Experience and Belief in Theological Reflection', 'Sacred Violence Unveiled' and 'Thérèse of Lisieux: A Saint for our Times' began life either as lecture notes or as personal attempts to clarify my thinking on those topics.

The nineteen chapters cover a fairly wide range of subjects. Some are relatively short, others much longer. Some are relatively simple, while others, such as the ones on petitionary prayer and atheism, are more difficult and academic. They reflect my overlapping interest in subjects such as psychology, spirituality, philosophy, science, and the need for effective evangelisation in the contemporary world. When I looked at the different chapter headings, I decided, a little arbitrarily, to arrange them into three sections.

The first section contains chapters which look at Christian issues with the help of modern psychology. Perhaps it would be more accurate to say that they examine a number of very different issues mainly from a psycho-spiritual point of view. The second section deals with mainly spiritual topics. The third section contains reflections which are broadly speaking, to do with evangelisation and mission. I'm aware that the different chapters are peppered with many quotations, some of them lengthy. When I'm teaching in college I like to quote what the people I'm referring to, actually said. I could summarise their thinking but usually prefer to quote their exact words. Apart from that, I like quotations myself. When I'm reading a book, I look out for them in particular. That said, I'm aware that they can be used as a convenient refuge for a lazy mind, a plagiaristic substitute for original reflection and personal expression. I hope that is not the case here.

I expect that, like me, you sometimes enjoy reading relatively short pieces on different issues rather than long reflections on single topics. In a fast changing world it is good to have, at least, a passing familiarity with a range of ideas. This book is written for those who, like me, have intellectual curiosity of the eclectic kind, and who enjoy reflecting on a variety of contemporary subjects. Perhaps there is something typically postmodern[1] about this kind of approach. Instead of looking in the mirror of overarching theories and symbols[2] as heretofore, people in postmodern culture tend to content themselves with shards and fragments of truth. Hence the title of the book. It is written as an aid for thoughtful pilgrims in a fast changing culture and is dedicated to four of my priestly relatives, Joseph Collins OP, Bernard Collins SJ, and James & Neil Collins who both ministered in the archdiocese of Sydney.

CHAPTER ONE

Intimacy and Christian Maturity[1]

The Church, like secular society, is in a crisis of change. It will lead to either growth or decline. The choice is ours. To choose wisely, we will have to identify the basic issue that lies at the heart of the often bewildering and disconcerting changes of recent years.

I have believed for some time that the interpretative key to this complex phenomenon is that the *centre of gravity in modern Catholicism is shifting from the experience of religious authority to the authority of religious experience.* As a result increasing numbers of people accept the authority of church teaching in so far as it is meaningful and relevant in their lives. Although many Catholics may be aware of a tension between their personal experience and the teaching of the church, both factors are important. While dogmatic faith unsupported by personal experience is moribund, personal experience unrelated to the faith of the church is blind. If this shift is the interpretative key to the religious crisis of our times, the experience of intimacy is the interpretative key to most forms of religious experience.

The word 'intimacy' is being used in its etymological sense, meaning, 'to publish, to hint at, or to make known that which is inmost'. Religious experience as conscious relationship with God involves three interrelated forms of intimacy. Firstly, self-intimacy whereby I get in touch with what is innermost in my own heart. Secondly, intimacy with other people, whereby I reveal my true self by means of self-disclosure and pay sustained, empathic attention to what is inmost in another. Thirdly, there is intimacy with God. It is a heart-to-heart conversation with him by whom we know ourselves to be loved. Not only do these three forms of intimacy facilitate a person's human development, they enable him or her, like Jesus, to speak and act with the kind of inner authority that is rooted in the depths of his or her personal experience. In the future, the bishop, priest or lay person who substitutes the authority of objective religious truth for the authority of subjective, but orthodox religious experience, will contribute by default to the decline of the church.

Self-Intimacy

There is something paradoxical about self intimacy. While it is the *sine qua non* of interpersonal intimacy, and intimacy with God, it is at the same time dependent upon both. Self-intimacy is the point of intersection where these enriching intimacies meet. In this connection it is important to appreciate the much neglected distinction between *self-knowledge* and *self-awareness*.

Self-knowledge refers to a way of looking at oneself; it leads to knowledge about myself. For example, in recent years many priests and religious in English-speaking countries have used personality tests for this purpose. For instancee, there is the Myers Briggs Personality Type Indicator (based on Jung's monumental study *Psychological Types*, 1920) which suggests that there are sixteen basic personality types.[2] The Enneagram is another test, of Eastern origin, that focuses on nine personality types. They turn the spotlight on the main compulsion that is characteristic of each personality type with a view to helping the person to grow in self-awareness, inner wholeness and freedom.[3] There are many other tests of this kind.[4] While taking such a test may increases knowledge about the self, it takes time and reflection to use them as an aid to the kind of self-awareness which is in touch with the deeper things of the heart.

Self-awareness is a way of going beyond the narrow and arbitrary confines of the conscious ego and its roles, to get in touch with the hidden self which is pre-conscious, and the unknown self which is unconscious. The most important way of doing this is to get in touch with one's feelings. A person can have an emotion such as anger or grief and not be aware of it. But a feeling is an emotion that has articulated itself in a conscious way. Feelings are revelatory because they tell us what we *really* perceive, believe, think and value, as opposed to what we *imagine* we perceive, believe, think and value. In that sense, feelings never lie. If there is anything 'wrong' with our feelings it is because there is something wrong with the way in which we perceive the world and ourselves. To have a healthy emotional life, we need a healthy outlook. To grow in emotional self-awareness three things are necessary – to recover, understand and express our feelings.

a) Recovering feelings

As we have seen, a person can have an emotion, e.g. anger or grief, and not be consciously aware of it. This is usually because it was buried alive in the unconscious, either because it was too painful or thought to be inappropriate for one reason or another. To recover lost feelings a number of things are necessary. Firstly, we need to stop all activity in order to have an appointment – free from distractions – with ourselves. Secondly, we need to relax our bodies as much as possible. There are many recognised ways of doing this.[5] It is only as we relax physically that our feelings begin to emerge from the shadows of anonymity to declare themselves. Thirdly, we need to pay attention to our bodily sensations because all our emotions express themselves physically, e.g. a headache, or an upset stomach could be due to repressed anger or resentment. We can dialogue with our bodies, letting images float freely into our minds. Often the unconscious will suggest some symbolic representation of a repressed emotion. As we savour the image, we may find that we begin to get in touch with its associated feeling. Fourthly, we can recall our dreams and reflect upon them. So often these letters from the unconscious remain un-opened and un-read. In fact they are psycho-dramas which are symbolic representations of our deepest feelings. Usually the main feeling in the dream is one that was evoked during the previous day or two, but went un-noticed. Frequently feelings like these will also be related to emotionally charged memories from one's earlier life. We cannot go into the subject of dream interpretation here.[6] Suffice it to say that usually everyone and everything in a dream is a personification of some aspect of oneself.

b) Understanding feelings

According to Ellis, our feelings are not directly evoked by people and events, but rather by the way we perceive them. Our

perceptions are coloured by a unique cocktail of our values, beliefs and past experiences. For example, a man hates being
licked by a dog. He feels disgust, aversion and fear. Because he
had no animals at home, he has grown up with the questionable
belief that dogs are dirty and liable to attack for no good reason.
So when we want to understand a feeling we can ask ourselves
three important questions: What thought or belief evoked my
feeling? What in my earlier life conditioned my attitudes, values,
beliefs and perceptions? Are they realistic and Christian?

c) Expressing feelings
We can appropriate our emotional life by expressing our feelings verbally. We will examine the dynamics and effects of such
self-disclosure a little later. But self-awareness can also grow by
means of 'journalling', i.e. not only recording external events in
a diary, but also one's subjective reactions to them. As one layer
of feeling is recognised and expressed in this way, another is
likely to float into consciousness, and so on. Not only that, previ-
ously unrecognised emotional patterns can come to light as one
re-reads the journal every now and then.

Nowadays an increasing number of people are growing in
emotional self-awareness as a result of receiving counselling,
therapy, spiritual direction or by attending group dynamics and
human development courses. Self-awareness can have an important religious dimension. Among other things, it enables one
to get in touch with two spiritual realities. Firstly, one can become more aware of the negative impulses of the human heart.
As Jer 17:9-10 says: 'Who can understand the human heart?
There is nothing else so deceitful; it is too sick to be healed. I the
Lord search the minds and test the hearts of people.' As Deut
8:2-3 indicates, the Lord often does this by means of adversity
and affliction. Secondly, we can become more aware of our positive impulses, what spiritual writers have called 'holy' or transcendental desires. These longings, as distinct from merely
physical or psychological ones, are initiated by God in our souls,
i.e. in that part of us which can only be satisfied by conscious
relationship with God. As a result it could he said that the dynamics of our spiritual lives are rooted in holy desire. No wonder
St Ignatius says that all prayer begins with the question: what do

you want? To be out of touch with one's God-prompted desires for God (cf. Jn 6:44) is to be absent from the first and foundational way in which we experience the action of the Holy Spirit within.

Self-intimacy enables us to reflect on our relationship with God. This kind of reflection is a *sine qua non* for the examen of consciousness, which enables us to discern the origin and orientation of thoughts, feelings, impulses, etc. Did they come from God, or from myself or even from the evil one? Inspirations that come from God and tend towards God will be associated with on-going consolation, i.e. feelings of peace, joy, hope, etc. Those that are not from God will be associated with desolation, i.e. feelings of agitation, sadness, morbidity, aridity, etc. As St Vincent de Paul once observed, 'a mark of illusions and false inspirations is that they are persistent and troublesome and make us uneasy.'[7] Self-awareness, then, is a prerequisite for discernment of Spirits.

Interpersonal Intimacy

From the 1960s onward the developmental psychology of Erik Erikson has exercised increasing influence. It maintains that the life of men and women involves a succession of stages, each one of which is characterised by a specific developmental task. For example, while one attains a sense of identity in adolescence, the basic challenge of early adulthood is to develop a capacity for intimacy with another person/s. It involves an ability to go beyond one's public *persona*, which is made up of roles and masks, in order to increasingly reveal one's true self to a trusted confidant or friend. This will only be possible to the extent that we are in touch with our own inner lives. Erikson maintains that our sense of identity is actualised and consolidated through self-disclosure. When it is absent we feel isolated, lonely and dispirited.

Robert J. Sternberg has suggested that there are three main components involved in adult relationships: intimacy, romantic passion and commitment.[8] He says that the intimacy in loving relationships refers to close, connected and bonded feelings. Passion refers to the drives that lead to romance, physical attraction, and sexual consummation. Loving commitment consists of a decision that one loves someone and is committed to maintaining that love. Sternberg maintains there are two main forms of adult intimacy, *consummate* and *companionate*. Consummate love is experienced by couples who are romantically attracted to one another and who share deeply within the context of a committed sexual relationship, ideally marriage. Companionate love is experienced by people who love one another in a non-romantic way, but who communicate deeply within the context of a committed, non-eroticised friendship.

It is worth recalling that, according to St Augustine, 'there can be no true friendship unless those who cling to each other are welded together by you [God] in that love which is spread throughout our hearts by the Holy Spirit which is given to us.'[9] He described the delights of this kind of Christian love when he wrote in his *Confessions* that friends like 'to talk and laugh and do kindnesses to each other; to read pleasant books together; to make jokes together and then talk seriously together; ... to be sometimes teaching and sometimes learning ... These and other similar expressions of feeling, which proceed from the hearts of those who love and are loved in return, and are revealed in the face, the voice, the eyes, and in a thousand charming ways, were like a kindling fire to melt our souls together and out of many to make us one.'[10]

Despite its importance, apparently only one man in twenty experiences genuine intimacy whether in consummate or companionate love. This lack of interpersonal intimacy in the lives of men has many causes. Chodorow and Stoller have suggested that in early childhood boys develop their sense of male identity by suppressing their empathy for their female mothers. On the other hand, girls develop their sense of female identity by doing the opposite. As a result, in adult life, males find it harder either to tune in to their feelings, or to express them to other people, especially to other men. A sense of emotional closeness, i.e. feelings of affinity, affection, warmth, etc., is often substituted for intimacy, i.e. honest disclosure of feelings and experiences. Men are also competitive and hampered in relationships by macho stereotypes that imply that all sense of vulnerability has to be hidden. Besides, many older Catholics, especially priests, brothers and nuns, were taught to avoid so-called 'particular friendships'. This phrase was usually a euphemism for exclusive erotic type relationships, of a homosexual or a lesbian kind. As a result many of them ended up being friendly with all and friends with no one. This lack of interpersonal intimacy in the life of Christians, for whatever reason, can have many knock-on effects. For instance, I suspect that those who engage in abusive sexual behaviour have little or no real inimacy in their lives.

Firstly, they may identify almost entirely with a role, e.g. that of wife and mother. As a result their relationships will tend to be formal and dutiful rather than personal and spontaneous. This will be evident in their style of communication. It will tend to be objective and factual, rather than a sharing of personal experiences and feelings. Secondly, such people will tend to be immature. Research has indicated that many men and women have to cope with an unrecognised, but significant emotional block in their lives. So although they may be intellectually sophisticated and accomplished, they can at the same time, be emotionally underdeveloped and dysfunctional. As long as it is un-dealt with, this state of affairs can have serious knock-on effects. For example, many Christians will be inclined to displace their intimacy needs in the form of unhealthy attitudes and behaviours, many of them compulsive and addictive in nature e.g. overeating and drinking, working too much and the like. Thirdly, people who are emotionally underdeveloped in some way or other, will often fail to understand or to satisfy the legitimate needs of the men and women they live or work with. Fourthly, people who lack intimacy, and therefore adult maturity, will find it difficult to engage in meaningful collaboration with others. The latter involves an ability to become involved in such things as making decisions as a result of a group process, constructive conflict resolution, etc. This inability will often be due to the insecurity, self-absorption or unhealthy individualism which are often the characteristics of those who, through mistrust and fear, avoid the challenges of intimacy. Fifthly, such Christians will tend to substitute saying prayers, e.g. reciting the rosary, for spending regular periods of time in a more personal form of affective prayer and contemplation. In the light of these points alone, the recovery of interpersonal intimacy is essential if Christians are to mature as men and women.

Herterosexual Intimacy

Needless to say, intimacy with a same sex relative, colleague or friend is desirable. However, many people, especially men, will be more inclined to disclose that which is innermost to a trusted member of the opposite sex. Intimate relationships of this heterosexual kind have been viewed with considerable suspicion in the Western ascetical tradition. There were two main reasons for this. Friendship requires equality and, until relatively recently, women were considered to be inferior to men. As well as that, there was a cynical view that male-female friendships would inevitably end up in sexual intimacy. Of course, there are obvious dangers and difficulties in these kinds of relationships. But what is sometimes overlooked is the fact that there are even more difficulties and dangers associated with a life of isolation, devoid of intimacy. Unfortunately, in spite of having a sexual relationship, many married couples do not enjoy real emotional intimacy in their relationships. Frequently, though not always, the man finds it hard to share with his wife in any depth. As a result, she may seek that kind of intimacy outside her marriage. Usually it is with another woman, but not necessarily so. It can lead to an extramarital affair. Many conscientious people have already discovered that genuine non-romantic friendships with members of the opposite sex are possible. However, a number of conditions are necessary.

Firstly, and most important of all, the friends need to be whole heartedly committed to the Person and will of God. Secondly, if it is a matter of companionate love, they should focus their energies on mutual self-disclosure rather than on the physical expression of affection, especially of a sexual kind, such as mutual fondling. Thirdly, because the notion of Platonic non-sexual love[11] is probably a fanciful myth, the friends should be prepared to share honestly about their sexual feelings so that they can adjust to one another in a responsible way. After all, what might trouble one, might present no problem to the other. C. S. Lewis has pointed out in *The Four Loves*, that the so-called 'highest' loves cannot stand without the 'lowest'. Jungian psychologists would maintain that all relationships, especially heterosexual ones, including our friendships, have a bodily and sexual aspect to them, and that if there is no emotion or attraction between people, there will be no depth of intimacy either. Rosemary Haughton, among contemporary theologians, stresses how the incarnation makes holy all that is material and bodily, and how sexual attraction can lead us to greater maturity and self-giving. Fourthly, while privacy is necessary at times, the men or women should not be secretive about their friends. They should tell trusted relatives and colleagues about their hetero-sexual relationships. Because it is so easy to deceive oneself in this area, it is important to be receptive to any observations or misgivings they might want to express. Fifthly, they should avoid an exclusive or possessive type of relationship which would resent their friends getting close to other people of the opposite sex. Sixthly, if men or women are friends with a mar-ried person, they need to be sure that their relationships, no mat-ter how honorable they are in themselves, do not come between them and their spouses.

The Healing Power of Intimacy

Same-sex and heterosexual friendships have many good effects. In adult life most of us are aware of inner hurts. We lack integra-tion. As a result, we are debilitated by neurotic fears and com-pulsions. Psychologists argue that many of our adult problems can be traced back to childhood experiences. Some of these ex-perts maintain that healing can come only through psychotherapy or psychoanalysis. Both are expensive and time-consuming. Other experts, Erikson for example, believe that emotional and spiritual healing, of a retrospective kind, can come about as a re-sult of intimate relationships. When we are aware of the love of a friend, we begin to have the freedom to take off our masks. We sense a growing urge to give our friend the greatest gift we have, the gift of our true selves. As this desire strengthens, it begins to override our fear of rejection which echoes back to childhood. We begin to lower our defences and to tell our friend about the more vulnerable side of our nature. As we sense the understand-ing acceptance and love of a friend a wonderful healing begins to take place. In the light of this friendship love we begin to un-derstand, accept, and love ourselves as we are, and not as we have pretended to be. Conversely, as we focus our loving atten-tion on the inner life of our friend in an admiring, approving and sometimes a challenging way, we enable the potential which has been manifested in him or her to blossom and thrive. In doing this we learn what it is to love another person as a second self.

Not only that, two other benefits follow. Firstly, because of the complementarity of the sexes, male-female friends grow in psychosexual maturity. It is unlikely that such integration could take place without heterosexual intimacy. Secondly, in the course of commenting on the relationship of Dante and Beatrice, Joseph Pieper has said, 'If we look to well-documented experience of great loves, we learn that precisely this intensity of love turned toward a single partner seems to place the lover at the vantage point from which he realises for the first time the goodness and lovableness of all people.' Surely this was the experience of many saints such as Francis and Clare, Francis de Sales and Jane de Chantal, Vincent de Paul and Louise de Marillac, to name but a few. As they learned to love the beggar and the idiot in one another, they learned to love them, not only in themselves, but also in the wider community as well, especially in the poor.

Intimacy with God

Self-intimacy enables us to get in touch with our own experience. Interpersonal intimacy schools us in the arts of self-disclosure and loving attention to the inner life of another. Not only are these two forms of intimacy a prerequisite for prayerful intimacy with God, they find their fulfillment in this way. Indeed one could say that we are no closer to God than we are to our true self and our closest neighbour. As St Aelred of Rievaulx wrote: 'God is friendship ... I would not hesitate to attribute to friendship anything associated with charity, as for instance, he who abides in friendship abides in God and God abides in him.' As we relate to others, so we will pray. If our human relationships are formal, it is almost inevitable that our prayerful relationship to God will be much the same. But if some of our human relationships are intimate our prayerful relationship with God will tend to be more personal also. So, not surprisingly, St Vincent de Paul wrote, 'Prayer is a conversation of the soul with God, a mutual communication in which he interiorly tells the soul what he wishes it to do.' I would have little hesitation in saying that prayer as intimate relationship with the Lord is potentially the greatest single source of psycho-spiritual development and transformation in the life of a Christian (cf. 2 Cor 3:18).

When it comes to prayer, many Christians are like brains on stilts, all head and no heart. Of course rational reflection has its place, but it should normally give way to a more personal kind of self-disclosure. We do this when we tell the Lord about our feelings, e.g. anger about God's apparent failure to answer prayers on behalf of a sick parishioner, joy about the birth of a nephew, distress upon hearing of another atrocity on the news. Usually it is not too difficult to share our positive feelings with the Lord. The trouble arises when we have to come to the Lord, not in our Sunday best, but in the ragged clothes of our anger, fear, and guilt, associated as they often are with negative images of God. The extent to which we control our dialogue with the Lord by suppressing our true feelings and desires, or fail to disclose them, is the extent to which we will be unreceptive to God's self-revelation through scripture, nature, people, art, etc. Not only do Christians have to pay self-forgetful, empathic attention to one another, they have to pay the same kind of attention to the Lord, to the divine presence, word and will. In my experience only a minority of people are comfortable with this kind of affective prayer.[12] Even those who are, would be enabled to develop an even more intimate relationship with the Lord if they had the assistance of a skilled spiritual director.

Conclusion

If two people enjoy an intimate relationship either of the companionate or consumate kind, they are very fortunate from a human and a Christian point of view. In par 2347 of the *Catechism of the Catholic Church*, we read: 'The virtue of chastity blossoms in friendship. It shows the disciple how to follow and imitate him who has chosen us as his friends, who has given himself totally to us and allows us to participate in his divine estate. Chastity is a promise of imortality. Chastity is expressed notably in friendship with one's neighbour. Whether it develops between persons of the same or opposite sex, friendship represents a great good for all. It leads to spiritual communion.'[13] St Francis de Sales felt that genuine Christian intimacy, of whatever

kind, was a foretaste of heavenly delight. He said that when
Christians enjoy a genuine spiritual relationship: 'O God, how
precious this friendship will be! It will be excellent because it
comes from God, excellent because it leads to God, excellent because its bond shall eternally endure in God. How good it is to
love here on earth as they love in heaven and to learn to cherish
one another in this world as we shall do eternally in the next!'[14]

CHAPTER TWO

The Golden Rule and Empathy[1]

All of us need the Spirit-given ability to grasp 'how wide and long and high and deep is the love of Christ, and to know this love that surpasses knowledge – that you may be filled to the measure – of all the fullness of God' (Eph 3:18-19). Having experienced such a spiritual awakening, the same Spirit urges us to love one another as Christ has loved us (cf. Jn 13:34). In Gal 5:14, St Paul says: 'serve one another in love. The entire law is summed up in a single command: "Love your neighbor as yourself".' He endorsed and amplified these words when he said: 'The commandments, Do not commit adultery, Do not murder, Do not steal, Do not covet, and whatever other commandment there may be, are summed up in this one rule: Love your neighbor as yourself' (Rom 13:9). So love is central and vitally important in the Christian life, but what is it? The 'silver rule' of the Old Testament referred to one understanding of the word when it stated in rather negative terms: 'Do to no one what you would not have done to you' (Job 4:15). However, Jesus gave this ethical precept a more positive spin when he advocated the 'golden rule'. It states: 'In everything, do to others what you would have them do to you, for this sums up the Law and the Prophets' (Mt 7:12).

Some commentators argue that there is nothing particularly original about the golden rule. It is a guideline that is found in its negative form in many other religions. As a result, a scholar such as Pheme Perkins ignores it in her book *Love Commands In the New Testament*,[2] while others such as John Meier refer to it merely as 'a piece of common sense.'[3] He argues that we should concentrate on the more important saying of Jesus: 'You shall love the Lord your God with all your heart, and with all your soul, and with all your mind. This is the first and great com-

mandment. And a second is like it, you shall love your neighbour as yourself. On these two commandments hang all the law
and the prophets' (Mt 22:37-41). I'm more inclined to agree with
Scottish scripture scholar William Barclay's commentary on Mt
7:12. He observes: 'This is probably the most universally famous
thing that Jesus ever said. With this commandment the Sermon
on the Mount reaches its summit. This saying of Jesus has been
called the capstone of the whole discourse. It is the topmost peak
of social ethics, and the Everest of all ethical teaching.'

This precept takes on new meaning when we recall that Jesus
practised this rule in his own life. He wanted what was best for
people and had a deep insight into their innermost needs, sometimes because people told him about them, and on other occasions because he had either an intuitive or inspired awareness of
what was best for them. So, if in prayer we look at Jesus looking
at us with eyes filled with love, and ask, 'Lord what do you want
of me?' we may be surprised that, rather than insisting on what
he wants, he replies, 'Because I love you, I am at your service. I
want to know what it is, deep down, that you want.' You could
also imagine him adding: 'I really want what is best for you. For
example, I want you to look after your health, by taking exercise
and eating wisely because it is good for your sense of well-being.
I want you to make the most of your talents because, by doing
so, you will help others and thereby fulfill your potential. I want
you to avoid sin because it inhibits your spiritual development
and your relationship with me.' This awareness leads to the insight that when I look after my own deepest spiritual needs, I'm
doing the will of the Saviour who wants what is best for me in
every way. Surely, this insight Christianises the Golden Rule. It
is as if Jesus is saying, 'You know from experience how I express
my love in an empathic way to you. Now love one another, even
as I have loved you, that is, by observing the Golden Rule.'

Love as Empathy

To love in this Christian way, two things are needed, *goodwill*
and *insight*. A person with goodwill wants what's best for another.
But that is not enough. Benevolence needs to be accompanied by
an accurate awareness of the needs of the other person, which
may be quite different from one's own. For instance if a middle

aged man gave a girl of thirteen a birthday present of an electric razor he himself would like to receive, it would clearly be absurd. But because they love the other person, and wish him or her well, loving people, quite often, wrongly presume that they know what is best for the other person. I have a clear recollection of an incident that taught me the importance of this point.

Sometime ago an anxious mother asked me to visit her son who had tried to commit suicide by taking an overdose. Apparently he had become very depressed following the death of a friend in a car accident. Although some of his despondency was due to grief, a lot of it was due to the fact that he was suppressing anger against his widowed mother. As a child he had developed a heart murmur following a bout of rheumatic fever. Afterwards, his mum had become very protective. She wouldn't allow him to play football, go out in cold weather, or take any kind of physical risks. She was so aware of her love that she presumed that she knew what was best for her son. In reality she had very little awareness of what it was like to be a young man with an overly protective mother who, because of fear, wouldn't allow him to assert his independence. In spite of his repeated protests, she failed to sense the depth of his frustration or its causes. It was because he had to repress a lot of his resentment that he became dangerously demoralised. Arguably, in trying to protect her son's life, this loving but blinkered mother had contributed indirectly to his self-destructive desire to take his life. Good intentions are not enough. They need to be tempered by insight. What is needed is what Mother Teresa referred to us *understanding* love.

In recent years psychoanalysts, psychotherapists, counsellors, and spiritual directors have emphasised the importance of empathy in therapy, and in loving relationships such as marriage and friendship. The word 'empathy' comes from the Greek *en* in, and *pathos* feeling. In the nineteenth century it was used by art critics. By means of empathy a person would become aware of the inner experience of an artist that found expression in a work of art. Later the word's use was extended to cover human relationships. It referred to one person's ability to stand in another person's shoes. Gerard Egan defined it 'as the ability to enter and understand the world of another person and to com-

municate this understanding to him or her.'[4] Christian psychiatrist Frank Lake wrote: 'Empathy is an objective awareness and
understanding of the feelings, emotions and behaviour of another
person, without necessarily oneself sharing those feelings (as
sympathy does). This is primarily understanding. There is a
feeling for the other person, chiefly of acceptance of how they
feel, without participating in this feeling.'[5] Looked at more
closely, empathic relationships have at least five characteristics.

Firstly, by means of empathy one person becomes aware of
the inner life of other people. It involves moment by moment
sensitivity to the changing feelings which animate them, e.g.
fear, rage, tenderness, confusion, joy, sorrow, longings etc. It is
facilitated by an ability to interpret body language. Current
communications theory indicates that, contrary to the common
sense impression that interpersonal communication is predominately verbal, about 80% is conveyed by such things as subtle
movements of facial muscles, dilation of the eyes, tone and pace
of the voice, gestures, posture, mode of dress etc. These characteristics can mediate subjective states to observant people.

Secondly, empathy seeks to understand other people's lives,
by becoming aware of the unique perceptions, attitudes, values,
and beliefs that evoked their feelings, coloured as they are by
their past experiences and memories. Arguably, this kind of understanding is facilitated by intuition. Etymologically, the word
literally means to 'see within'. By means of imagination one can
also project oneself into another's inner life by making a construct of what it might be like. It is based upon one's general
psychological knowledge and personal experience of the ways
of the human heart.

Thirdly, empathy studiously avoids assessing other people's
experiences in the light of abstract norms of perfection. Many of
us were raised by parents who were idealistic and taught us to
measure what is, against what could be and should be. To illustrate the point, imagine a blue blob of ink is splattered on a large
sheet of white paper. When asked 'what do you see?' perfectionistic people tend to say 'a blue blob on white paper', whereas
accepting, non-judgemental people tend to say 'a white sheet of
paper with a blue blob on it'. They are the ones who are perceiv-
ing the situation in an accurate and accepting way. The fact is,

99% of the paper is still white! While empathetic people are aware of imperfections, they choose not focus on them. As St Paul once said: 'whatever is true, whatever is noble, whatever is right, whatever is pure, whatever is lovely, whatever is admirable – if anything is excellent or praiseworthy – think about such things' (Phil 4:8).

Fourthly, empathic men and women mirror back their awareness of other people's feelings. It gives them the opportunity to do two things. Firstly, it reassures the person who is speaking that the listener is aware of what he or she is trying to communicate. Secondly, it enables the listener to establish whether his or her sense of the speaker's inner life is accurate or not. For example, a man who has failed to get a promotion describes his feelings. An empathic respondent might say, 'You really felt you deserved to get the job. So now you feel humiliated, disheartened and angry that a younger colleague got it instead.' Subsequently, good listeners are guided by the responses they receive. For example, the man might reply, 'I didn't feel humiliated, but I did feel angry and disheartened.'

Fifthly, empathic people don't share the feelings of others, but they are not only aware of them, they spontaneously respond to them. For example, a woman is aware of the hurt and anger of a grieving colleague who has had a miscarriage. While she doesn't share those emotions, the awareness of the other woman's plight evokes heartfelt feelings of tenderness and sadness within her.

Whereas empathy identifies what others feel, without necessarily sharing their experiences, sympathy does participate in those feelings. Although etymologically the word literally means 'to suffer with', in modem English it has a wider connotation and implies a willingness to share any kind of feeling. Nowadays the caring professions advocate empathic rather than sympathetic relationships, because the latter often lead to debilitating levels of stress and even burnout. Empathy for a person who is enduring suffering, e.g. of a psychological or emotional kind, is compassion.

Levels of Empathy

At this point we will look at different levels and degrees of empathy. To illustrate them, let us take the example of a widow who is living on her own. She says, 'I'm growing old, my children have all left home and they no longer seem to need me the way they used to do.'

A level one response does not even correspond to the surface feelings of the one who is speaking. The insensitive listener might say, 'Aren't you lucky to have so much time on your hands. There is no point in complaining, why not seize your opportunity to read, to travel and to help others.' Not only does a response like this fail to sense the widow's feelings, it is mildly critical in tone, in so far as it seems to say, 'You shouldn't be complaining.'

A level two response only partly communicates an awareness of the widow's feelings. The listener might respond, 'There is nothing to regret, your children are doing well, and they will always need you in one way or another.' While this response does recognise that the widow feels un-needed, it doesn't take her threatening feeling, of not being needed, too seriously.

A level three response, what Gerard Egan refers to as basic empathy, conveys the impression that the person's feelings are appreciated. The listener might say, 'You are understandably disappointed over having less contact with your children, now that you are getting on in years.' The reply encapsulates in different words something of the essential content of the widow's statement. It echoes her surface feeling without adding or detracting from it. The listener thereby conveys the fact that he or she is tuned in to the widow's experience.

A level four response, what Egan refers to as advanced empathy, not only echoes the surface feelings, it enables the listener to explore deeper underlying feelings and their possible causes. The listener might say, 'It must be depressing and disconcerting to find that after so many years caring for your children, now they don't seem to need you in the way they used to do. You are worried about how useless and unwanted you may feel in your old age, especially when you have no companion.' This kind of understanding response gives the widow the opportunity to either confirm that that is how she feels, or to clarify what her deeper emotions really are, e.g. 'I'm not afraid of being alone, it's the feeling that I might end up being helpless and even a burden to my children that scares me.' As you can see from these examples, responses of the first and second kind are no help at all, but responses of the third and fourth kind are helpful.

Degrees of Empathy

Some psychologists have argued that there are three main degrees of empathy:

Apathetic responses where there is little or no identification with the feelings of others. So, strictly speaking apathy is the absence of empathy. The most common form is where a listener focuses on facts rather than feelings and offers advice rather than emotional rapport. Women often complain that men relate to them in this detached, objective way. They say that instead of offering emotional understanding, many men see the vulnerable experiences of the women in their lives as problems to be solved rather than inner states to be identified with. This kind of apathy is often rooted in emotional ineptitude and fear rather than illwill. However, there is a more callous form of apathy which is devoid of compassion. I know a woman who was badly injured when a stolen car which was being driven by two teenage boys crashed into hers. She spent a long time in hospital, endured a lot of pain and afterwards had to cope with a permanent limp. The police gave the woman the names of the two young men who had caused her injuries. When she was released from hospital she called to their homes and explained to them what she had suffered as a result of the accident. Besides confronting them with the effects of their irresponsible behaviour, she hoped that they would regret what they had done and offer her an apology. In the event they were unmoved, and said in a callous, apathetic way, 'It's your problem, lady, not ours.'

Research has indicated that if empathy levels are high, people won't cause others pain and suffering, because in doing so they would be inflicting a portion of that pain on themselves. A number of studies in the 1970s and afterwards have shown the link between high empathy and low delinquency. In his book *Emotional Intelligence*, Daniel Goleman has indicated that the outstanding characteristic of psychopaths, criminals and sexual molesters is the fact that they seem to be devoid of empathy for their victims.[6] The following chapter on violence deals with this point in greater depth.

Selective empathy is extended to members of the same family, group, nationality, religion, class, sex etc. In the film *Johnnie Brasco*, Al Pacino plays the part of an aging member of the Mafia. He becomes friendly with a younger man who, unbeknown to him, is an undercover cop. He explains to him that he has killed something like twenty six people over the years and seems unmoved by the prospect of having to assassinate another. However, when his drug-addicted son is dangerously ill he shows great feeling for him. Surely Albert Nolan was correct when he stated in his book, *Jesus Before Christianity*, that our Lord believed that the human propensity to divide people into 'us' and 'them' was one of the principal sources of evil. 'Satan's kingdom,' he says, 'is based upon the exclusive and selfish solidarity of groups, whereas God's kingdom is based upon the all-inclusive solidarity of the human race.'[7]

Universal Empathy is extended to anyone and everyone without exception. Jesus illustrates this kind of unrestricted empathy in the parable of the Good Samaritan. The priest and the Levite are apathetic in their response. They fail to respond to their fellow Jew who had been cruelly mugged and robbed. However, when a non Jewish Samaritan comes across the unfortunate victim he is unhesitatingly moved to compassion and offers practical help and aftercare (cf. Lk 10:25-37).

At this point we can look at a memorable modern day instance of this kind of universal empathy. It is estimated that up to twenty million citizens of the former Soviet Union died as a result of World War II. In his *A Precocious Autobiography*, poet Yevegeny Yevtushenko recalls a wartime incident which is redolent with the compassion of the New Testament.

In 1941 Mama took me back to Moscow. There I saw our enemies for the first time. If my memory serves me right, nearly twenty thousand German war prisoners were to be marched in a single column through the streets of Moscow. The pavement swarmed with onlookers, cordoned off by police and soldiers. The crowd were mostly women. Every one of them must have had a father or a husband, a brother or a son, killed by the Germans. They gazed with hatred in the direction from which the column was to appear. At last we saw it. The generals marched at the head, massive chins stuck out, lips pursed disdainfully, their whole demeanour meant to show superiority over their plebeian victors. The women were clenching their fists, the soldiers and policemen had all they could do to hold them back. All at once something happened to them. They saw the German soldiers, thin, unshaven, wearing dirty blood-stained bandages, hobbling on crutches or leaning on the shoulders of their comrades; the soldiers walked with their heads down. The street became dead silent – the only sound was the shuffling of boots and the thumping of crutches. Then I saw an elderly woman in broken down boots push herself forward and touch a policeman's shoulder saying: 'Let me through.' There must have been something about her that made him step aside. She went up the column, took from inside her coat something wrapped in a coloured handkerchief and unfolded it. It was a crust of black bread. She pushed it awkwardly into the pocket of a soldier, so exhausted that he was tottering on his feet. And now suddenly from every side women were running towards the soldiers, pushing into their hands bread, cigarettes, whatever they had. The soldiers were no longer enemies. They were people.

Female Empathy

Yevtushenko's quotation raises the question, are women more empathic than men? Common sense experience would point to the fact that they are. They are the main carers and nurturers in society. Although we know that women are responsible for nearly as many violent incidents as men in domestic situations, when one reads the papers, it becomes obvious that most though by no means all of the reported crimes, whether exploitative, sexual, violent or abusive, have been perpetrated by men.

Research tends to confirm the common sense impression that men are not as empathetic as women. Moir and Jessel write in *A Mind to Crime*: 'Women have a brain that feels – more than men's – much of what others feel, be it pain or joy, and the knowledge of the pain that can be inflicted on others militates against the commission of the deed – whether it is the defrauding of pensioners or the sabotage of a company and other people's jobs through embezzlement.'[8] Carol Gilligan has also pointed out that the more they develop from a psychological and a moral point of view, women become more and more opposed to violent behaviour because they feel for its victims.[9] It is probable that hormones also have a role to play. Because they have higher levels of testosterone, males are more easily aggravated than females. This form of arousal tends to provoke antagonistic feelings of anger and aggression that negate the likelihood of empathy.

As was mentioned in chapter one, some psychoanalysts have suggested that whereas boys have to suppress their empathy for their female mothers as they assert their male identities in early childhood, girls, on the other hand, affirm their emerging female identities by empathising with their female mothers. It is thought that ever afterwards women affirm their femaleness by identifying empathically with others, whereas men affirm their maleness by suppressing their empathy and disidentifying with others. Hence as a generalisation one could say that while women tend to stress the importance of cooperating with others, men tend to stress the importance of competing successfully with rivals.

Other authors have argued that men and women perceive the world slightly differently. The extent to which it is a matter of nature or nurture need not concern us here. One can understand the difference between male and female ways of looking at things in terms of two sets of polarities. Overall, while men tend to be general and abstract, women tend to be more concrete and personal in their approach to reality. They also tend to be more empathic. Gilligan points out that, whereas when men have to make a moral choice they tend to do so by looking at abstract principles of justice and deducing what should be done, women tend to look at a network of relationships in order to establish what would be the most caring thing to do in the circumstances.[10]

Without doubt, loving empathy of the universal kind is of central importance in the Christian life as we have suggested. Nevertheless, many writers have maintained that it is relatively rare. The philosopher, Simone Weil wrote: 'The love of our neighbour in all its fullness means being able to say: "What are you going through?" ... Nearly all those who think they have this capacity do not possess it.'[11] Even when they have understanding love for others, some men and women fail to communicate it effectively due to a lack of verbal and non-verbal skills.[12]

Typical Effects of Empathic Love
Empathy can have a number of beneficial effects. The relationship between love and feeling for others is reciprocal: the more empathy a person has for another, the better the chance of love resulting. On the other hand, the more love that there is, the higher the likelihood that empathy will be displayed.

a) Empathy facilitates intimacy. As was noted in chapter one, the word 'intimacy' literally means 'to publish, to make known that which is innermost.' In an intimate relationship, whether sexual or non-sexual, two things are required. Firstly there is a need for honest self-disclosure, whereby a person tells the truth, the whole truth, and nothing but the truth about him or herself. Secondly, there is need for empathic attention whereby the listener, whether a spouse, friend or counsellor, pays self-forgetful, and understanding attention to the speaker's innermost experiences.

b) Empathy overcomes isolation Personal suffering, such as coping with loss and bereavement, is hard in itself. But it is often made worse by a sense of loneliness that goes with it. There is a subjective impression that one is suffering alone because, for one reason or another, other people are either unable or unwilling to tune into what one is enduring. However, by reflecting back the main feelings and meanings they are aware of, empathic people help those who are suffering to feel understood and connected. This not only helps them to overcome painful feelings of isolation, it can also help them to identify and understand their own experience more effectively.

c) Empathy increases self-esteem. Empathic people also enable others to feel valued and appreciated. By paying sustained, self-forgetful attention to the experience of others, an empathic person says in a wordless way, 'I value you, I appreciate your dignity, that is why I'm giving you my undivided attention.' This sense of the other person's value may also be informed by a faith awareness that he or she is made in God's image, and that God's Spirit lives within him or her. This kind of affective attitude helps others to feel loved, because it approves of the perceived and potential inner worth of the people I am attending to in an empathic way. As Joseph Pieper has written: 'Love testifies to being in agreement, assenting, consenting, applauding, affirming, praising, glorifying and hailing ... All of them are expressions of the will and mean, I want you to exist.'[13] Not surprisingly, this kind of approval tends to increases self-acceptance and self-esteem.

d) Empathy enables people to grow. Empathic people sense the natural and supernatural potential that is present in the personalities of those they attend to, and they help them to acknowledge and develop it. More often than not, they say in non-verbal terms, 'become what you are.' As the German poet Von Goethe once said, 'if we take people as they are, we make them worse. But if we treat them as if they were what they could be, we help them to become what they are capable of becoming.' Although psychoanalysts, therapists and counsellors are guided by different, and often contradictory theories of personality, they all get good results. Research indicates that the common denominator in successful therapy is loving empathy. Because it acknowledges people's value it has the ability to release the potential of the personality. This is a central belief informing Rogerian and Jungian counselling techniques.

e) Empathy helps people to heal. People in the caring professions maintain 'unconditional positive regard' toward the other person, which is expressed in a sincere and gentle way, enables him or her to accept that he or she is accepted. This enables healing and integrating energies to be released in the depths of the personality in such a way that the civil war of the heart, the neurotic conflict between the acceptable and unacceptable self, comes to an end. As Carl Rogers once observed, a person who is loved appreciatively, not possessively, develops his or her own unique self while at the same time, the person who loves in a non-possessive way is himself enriched.

f) Empathy affirms people. The word 'affirmation' comes from the Latin, *affirmare*, 'to make strong.' Etymologically speaking it is virtually the same as the word 'comfort' which is derived from the Latin *con fortis*, which literally means 'with strength.' Empathy strengthens the personality. The Holy Spirit, the Comforter, is active in and through this form of Christian identification with others. As Eph 3:16 says, it makes the innermost self grow strong. It is worth noting that while empathy will usually comfort its recipients it won't necessarily console them by making them feel good. Research also points strongly to the conclusion that a high degree of empathy in a relationship is possibly the most important factor in bringing about transformative learning, and change.

g) Affective love leads to effective action. Love can be looked at as either empathic relationship or as service of a practical kind. Ideally, service of others in the form of appropriate action should be the expression of empathic relationship rather than a substitute for it, as it commonly is. Once empathic people know the real needs of others, they have both the desire and the graced ability to respond sensitively to them in emotional and practical ways. The following true story illustrates some of these points in a poignant way.

Although Tom worked in a psychiatric hospital he had no professional training. As a nurse's aid he cleaned the rooms and helped around the wards by bringing trays, lifting patients and so on. Mary was the sickest person in the hospital. She was a psychotic who had needed on-going care for the last eighteen years. Since her arrival she had never spoken to anyone or looked them in the eye. All day long she just sat in a rocking chair and moved back and forth, with her head down. The doctors had tried every type of therapy, but without success.

Tom noticed this woman. He found another rocking chair and pulled it over next to Mary's. By paying attention to her body language he began to sense the inner pain and profound mistrust that had imprisoned her. That evening he decided that during his meal break he would bring his dinner on a tray, sit in a chair and rock beside Mary as he ate. He returned the next evening, and the next and did the same. He even asked for permission to come in on his days off. In fact he came regularly every evening for six months, rocking beside Mary. She never responded. Finally one evening as Tom was getting up to leave, Mary looked him straight in the eye and said, 'Good night, Tom.' After that she began to get well. Tom still came each evening and rocked beside her. Eventually she recovered completely and was released from the hospital.

I find that story strangely moving. Tom had empathy for Mary. He was aware of the inner suffering that had cut her off from other people. Instinctively he knew that what she needed was consistent empathy of a committed. unconditional kind. As she sensed Tom's undemanding and accepting love, Mary began to trust, and to emerge like a latter day Lazarus, from the tomb of her inner hurts.

Blocks to Empathy
There are many typical blocks to empathy. From a moral point of view lack of understanding love it is rooted in willful egocentricity, a tendency to choose to be exclusively preoccupied with one's own needs and experiences, thoughts, feelings and desires. From a Christian point of view such a person has failed to die to self. D. H. Lawrence captured something of this mentality in one of his poems: 'How beastly the bourgeoisie is especially the male of the species ... Let him meet a new emotion, let him be faced with another man's need, let him come home to a bit of moral difficulty, let life face him with a new demand on his understanding and then watch him go soggy, like a wet meringue. Watch him turn into a mess, either a fool or a bully.'[14] Timidity, which is rooted in unacknowledged but willful egoism, seems to be the cause of such a lack of empathy. As Jesus said in Jn 12:24: 'Truly, truly I say to you, unless a grain of wheat falls into the earth and dies, *it remains alone.'*

From an emotional point of view many people suffer from what has been referred to as the toothache of the heart, i.e. the distracting ache of unacknowledged or unresolved emotional pain. It is usually rooted in the hurts, deprivations and traumas of the past. They commonly result in inner states such as separation anxiety, low self-esteem, chronic grief, phobic fears, angry resentment etc. These negative feelings can lead to either mistrustful isolation or clinging dependency.

As was mentioned already, those who are mistrustful tend to relate in an apathetic way. One cause of this is the fact that they find other people's feelings, especially negative ones, hard to cope with for two reasons. Firstly, they remind them of similar feelings in themselves, feelings they haven't come to terms with. Secondly, they often feel powerless in the face of other people's inner pain. They find it so hard to cope with the feeling of impotence that they switch off and listen in a rather detached, objective way.

Those who are dependant cling to others emotionally. They seek to be understood more than they seek to understand. They talk a lot about their own feelings, while being surprisingly disinterested in the feelings of the people they depend upon, unless of course, those feelings refer to themselves. As one joke puts it, 'Well that's enough about me, its over to you now, what do you think about me?'

When people with unresolved emotional problems listen to others, they often suffer from excessive self-reference. Their attention tends to boomerang back to themselves. Instead of entering into the unique experience of friends, colleagues and acquaintances, they tend to use the stories that others recount to remind them of the details of their own inner lives. As a result they will commonly say, 'I know exactly how you feel, I went through a similar experience,' while going on to recount the details at great length. So instead of listening to the other person, they end up getting him or her to listen to them.

Empathy can also be suppressed by adopting an evaluative attitude to life. Instead of accepting experiences in a non-critical, non-judgmental way, moralistic people are inclined to assess them in terms of perfectionistic ideals. This lack of unconditional regard, is conveyed in body language and phrases such as, 'what you ought ... must ... should ... have to do, is such and such.' This kind of response seems to be another way of saying in a discouraging way, 'If only you were different than the way you are now!'

Prejudice of any kind is another impediment to empathy. The word is derived from the Latin *praejudicium* i.e. a previous judgement. So instead of sensing the emotions of others, as they are, prejudiced listeners can unwittingly interpret those feelings and experiences in terms of preconceived ideas and stereotypes, e.g. of a sexual, racial, sectarian or religious kind. Most of these prejudices are largely unconscious and unrecognised. They lead people to filter and censor experience in accordance with their unexamined, and sometimes questionable, frameworks of understanding.

Unresolved anger, of the antagonistic, resentful kind, is also alien to empathy. A person with an unforgiving heart cannot identify with the feelings of the guilty person. Instead they tend to be judgmental, critical, and condemnatory. They are inclined to amplify and exaggerate the faults of the other person. As a result, their negative and aggressive feelings prevent them from sensing what the other person is experiencing. Deep down they suspect that if they allowed themselves to understand what the other person is going through, such an insight might move them to forgive, something they don't want to do.

A number of years ago I attended a conference in Wales. During one of the breaks I got into conversation with an older woman, who unbeknown to me happened to be a psychotherapist. I found myself telling her that I was saddened by the fact that the relationship between myself and my mother was not good. At one point Jane proposed that we do a role play, she would pretend to be my mother and she invited me to tell her how I felt. Following initial reluctance, I decided to give it a go. Soon I was freely pouring out my mixed feelings of love and admiration, on the one hand, and frustration and resentment on the other. When I finished, Jane suggested that we reverse the roles. 'By now I know what you feel,' she said, 'I'll act your part, you can pretend to be your mother.' I adamantly refused, maintaining that it was a senseless thing to do. As we parted Jane said, 'Promise me one thing: spend some time reflecting on why you refused to reverse the roles.' When I went back to my room I did think about Jane's question. All of a sudden the answer came to me: if for a moment I allowed myself to empathise with my mother, to see things from her point of view, I'd realise how painful it must have been to have sincere goodwill for such a demanding, articulate and critical son as myself. As soon as I half allowed myself to sense what my mother felt, in an understanding way, my resentments began to melt away. Subsequently our relationship improved a good deal, although it was never perfect.

There was an important addendum to the story. A few years later, sometime after my mother's death, I was at a conference in England. At the end of a long healing service, two lay people asked if I wanted some prayer myself. I didn't really, but to avoid hurting their feelings I reluctantly said 'OK.' They asked what I'd like to be prayed for. Without much conviction I said, 'My relationship with my mother wasn't always great, pray about that.' As soon as they started to pray I got more than I bargained for. I had a vivid imaginative sense of my late father standing in front of me. He looked disconcertingly real. I said nothing, but he spoke to me. 'Pat, I was delighted when you were born. But as you grew, I found you hard to understand, you were too imaginative and creative for me. But be assured that I was proud of you. But I didn't always know how to express my feelings. I know I let you down, I know that I failed to give you the encouragement and affirmation you needed as a young man. But don't for a moment feel that I didn't love you, because I did. Please forgive me for the ways in which I failed you.' At the end of this vivid visionary experience I found myself whispering, 'Daddy, of course I forgive you.' With that, the experience ended. Afterwards I realised that the Lord had indeed heard the prayer of the two lay people. I became consciously aware that although my father had always been physically present at home, like many other fathers, he wasn't always emotionally present. In some ways he had failed to affirm me as a male. As a result, I had unfairly switched my desire for affirmation on to my mother. When, not surprisingly, she failed to satisfy my need, I felt hurt and resentful. As a result of these two related experiences, I have come to see that if one desires to truly empathise with others one must cleanse the heart of resentment, especially against one's parents.

Growing in Empathy
There are a number of ways of growing in empathy. One of them, praying the scriptures in an empathic way, is dealt with in

chapter twelve. Before looking at other possible ways of developing empathy it is worth noting that the capacity to empathise is first developed in childhood. Parents and carers can help to nurture it in small boys and girls, especially by responding to them in an empathic way, what Daniel Stern of Cornell University has referred to as 'attunement'. It is made possible by a willingness to listen empathetically to children, becoming aware of their needs and emotions. This helps growing children to have a nascent ability to recognise what they feel and as a result to have a rudimentary sense of the feelings of others. Research indicates that if parents show that they are angry and upset when their children misbehave, by the age of six they experience these distressing emotions and sense that it is because they have offended against the rules, values and beliefs that are important to their parents. However, if children cannot feel the disapproval and upset of their parents they will experience little or no pain or distress, and the motivation to avoid wrongdoing will, as a consequence, be weaker. This is an important point which indicates that empathy plays a key role in children's emerging ethical sense. Children who feel secure in the love and approval of their parents and carers are more likely to grow in self-awareness, to empathise, and to act in a loving way. Conversely, those who are neglected, who experience emotional abuse rather than empathy, are more likely to grow up delinquent. That is why criticism and put-downs need to be avoided and praise and encouragement should be given as often as possible. Needless to say, this guideline continues to be relevant in adult life.

Empathy presupposes a good deal of emotional self-awareness. The extent to which a person is aware of his or her feelings, in an understanding way, will largely determine the extent to which he or she will be able to empathise with others. As was noted in chapter one, to grow in this kind of self-knowledge means spending regular quiet times alone. By empathising with the deeper as opposed to the surface self, people can become increasingly aware of neglected or repressed desires and memories, together with their associated feelings, especially those of a painful and negative nature such as worthlessness, loss, guilt, anger etc. Dream interpretation can be an important help in this regard. It enables one to become aware of unconscious feelings. Subsequently they can go on to own and understand them. As a result, they progressively grow in self-intimacy while making peace with their own pasts. As they do, they learn to trust their inner selves and their spontaneous capacity to tune into and react to the feelings of others.

Being empathic requires a number of relationship skills such as asking open-ended questions, reflecting back the principal feelings, noticing and bracketing one's own emotions, etc. Increasing awareness of the ways in which things such as body language intimates what people feel, can provide valuable clues about the subjectivity of others. As Freud wrote: 'He who has eyes to see and ears to hear becomes convinced that mortals can keep no secret. If their lips are silent they gossip with their fingertips; betrayal forces its way through every pore.'[15] However, skills such as these are only acquired with difficulty and with the help of others, e.g. by doing a counselling course. Even then, skills without genuine empathy are merely technique, while empathy without skill can be relatively ineffective.

Conclusion

Loving empathy is of central importance in the Christian life as we have suggested. German theologian Dietrich Bonhoeffer said that the first service that one owes to others in the community consists in listening to them. Just as love of God begins by listening to the Word, so the beginning of love for others is learning to listening empathetically to them. Many people are looking for an ear that will listen. All too often, they fail to find it among Christians, because they are too busy talking where they should be paying attention. But the person who can no longer listen to others will soon not be listening to God either, he or she will do nothing but prattle in the presence of God. This is the beginning of death as far as the spiritual life is concerned.

With these sentiments in mind, it is interesting to note that people who have had near death experiences testify that having passed through a dark tunnel, they were invited to evaluate their lives in the light of Divine Love and the Golden Rule. Dr Raymond Moody, well known author of *Life after Life*, said in an interview: 'Patients often report that during their life review they view the events of their lives not from the perspective that they had when they went through the event, but rather from the third person perspective. Their perspective is displaced, and as they watch themselves go through these life actions, they can also empathetically relate to the people with whom they have interacted. They take the perspective of the person they have been unkind to. And if they see an action where they have been loving to someone, then they can feel the warmth and good feelings that they produced in the life of that person.'[16] It would appear, therefore, that in the Autumn of our lives we will be judged largely – as Mt 25:31-46 suggests – on the basis of empathic love.

CHAPTER THREE

Religion and Violence

I have always had a strong aversion to violence, especially war. Something of its sheer horror was graphically depicted in the battle sequences in two popular films, *Saving Private Ryan* and *Gladiator*. As the Duke of Wellington observed in a dispatch he sent in 1815: 'Nothing except a battle lost can be half so melancholy as a battle won.'[1] To me the wanton killing and destruction involved in war is the antithesis of love, the epitome of evil, and has a clear demonic dimension. That said I am not an out and out pacifist. In certain limited circumstances, I believe that one can use violence, if absolutely necessary, as the lesser of two evils, e.g. to defend innocent women and children from an unwarranted and unjust attack. However, I do not think that aggressive violence can ever be justified as a way of pursuing one's aims, no matter how worthy they might otherwise be. As a result, I am against the death penalty for any crime, no matter how depraved. Happily the majority of Irish people share this point of view because they voted, in a referendum on 7 June 2001, to abolish the death penalty by a vote of 62% to 38%.

Because I conscientiously hold these views, I am scandalised, like so many others, by the way in which Christians have used aggressive violence, down the centuries, to pursue their questionable aims. The Crusaders (twelfth and thirteenth centuries) went to war in order to liberate and defend the holy places in Jerusalem. When he launched the first crusade against the Ottomans, Pope Urban II said to those who intended to kill the infidels: 'Let the army of the Lord, when it rushes upon its enemies, shout but one cry, God wants it!' The Inquisition in France (thirteenth century) attacked and slaughtered thousands of Cathar heretics with extreme cruelty. In 1209 the papal legate Arnaud Amaury led soldiers from the city of Lyon to the walls of Béziers. He is reported to have said: 'Kill them all, God will know His own.' Subsequently, Beziers was sacked and all its inhabitants slain. The Spanish Inquisition (fifteenth century) used torture in order to quell the influence of religious dissidents. In Seville alone, 4,000 people were burned at the stake over a forty year period.[2] Pope Julius II (fifteenth century) led his troops into battle in pursuit of his political and religious aims in Italy. A commentator called Guicciardini wrote at the time: 'It was certainly a sight, very uncommon, to behold the High Priest, the Vicar of Christ on earth ... employed in person in managing a war provoked by himself among Christians ... and retaining nothing of the Pontiff but the name and the robes.'[3] The Spanish conquistadors used terrible violence in South America (sixteenth century), not only to capture land and treasure but also to forcibly impose the Christian faith upon its pagan peoples. There were many massacres. For instance, the Governor of Cuba, Pamfilio de Narvaez ordered his men to kill 2,500 American Indians who had just distributed food to the invading Spanish. The Boers from Holland acted like the conquistadors in Southern Africa. Surely, the holocaust in twentieth-century Germany was made possible, at least in part, by Christian anti-Semitism.

In recent years two authors have written in an illuminating way about the problem of sacred violence. René Girard, a French intellectual, is currently a professor Emeritus of French language and literature at Stanford University. He is the author of a number of influential books, among them *Violence and the Sacred*,[4] *Things Hidden from the Foundation of the World*,[5] and *Scapegoat*.[6] In these volumes he deals with complex subjects such as victimisation, scapegoating, and what he calls order destroying and order restoring violence. Gil Bailie is clearly a disciple of Girard's. His prophetic book *Violence Unveiled: Humanity at the Crossroads*, uses aspects of his mentor's complex theory to explore the phenomenon of violence and its connection with religion. In these reflections I do not intend to give an overview of what these two important writers have proposed. Rather, we will narrow the focus by suggesting that Christian violence has at least some of its roots in aspects of biblical and church teaching and in the unredeemed shadow described by Jung.

Divinely Sanctioned Violence

It would appear that genocide and ethnic cleansing were divinely sanctioned in the Old Testament. For example, in Deut 7:1-2 Yahweh seemed to support genocide when the deity said: 'When the Lord your God brings you into the land you are entering to possess and drives out before you many nations – the Hittites, Girgashites, Amorites, Canaanites, Perizzites, Hivites and Jebusites, seven nations larger and stronger than you – and when the Lord your God has delivered them over to you and you have defeated them, then you must destroy them totally. Make no treaty with them, and show them no mercy.' Again in Deut 20:11-14 the Lord says: 'When you march up to attack a city, make its people an offer of peace. If they accept and open their gates, all the people in it shall be subject to forced labour and shall work for you. If they refuse to make peace and they engage you in battle, lay siege to that city. When the Lord your God delivers it into your hand, put to the sword all the men in it. As for the women, the children, the livestock and everything else in the city, you may take these as plunder for yourselves. And you may use the plunder the Lord your God gives you from your enemies.'

Ps 80:8-9 refers to ethnic cleansing when it says: 'You brought a vine out of Egypt; you drove out the nations and planted it. You cleared the ground for it, and it took root and filled the land.' This sentiment finds an echo in Deut 6:10-12, where we read: 'When the Lord your God brings you into the land he swore to your fathers, to Abraham, Isaac and Jacob, to give you – a land with large, flourishing cities you did not build, houses filled with all kinds of good things you did not provide, wells you did not dig, and vineyards and olive groves you did not plant – then when you eat and are satisfied, be careful that you do not forget the Lord, who brought you out of Egypt, out of the land of slavery.' The same kind of dubious thinking seemed to be accepted in an unquestioning way by Paul in the New Testament. For example, in the course of a sermon in Antioch, the apostle to the gentiles said: 'After God had destroyed seven nations in the land of Canaan, he gave them their land as an inheritance' (Acts 13:19). Incidentally, contemporary Zionists could quote biblical passages such as these in order to justify their arbitrary use of force and resettlement programmes in modern day Palestine.[7]

The Doctrine of Hell and Violence

Besides being influenced by biblical precedent, the violence of Christians may well have been influenced by the doctrine of hell. The *Catechism of the Catholic Church* says: 'The teaching of the church affirms the existence of hell and its eternity. Immediately after death the souls of those who die in a state of mortal sin descend into hell, where they suffer the punishments of hell, "eternal fire".'[8] While Catholics have to believe in such a possibility, however it is understood, they don't necessarily have to believe that there is anyone actually in hell. As Pope John Paul II has observed: 'Even when Jesus says of Judas, the traitor, "It would be better for that man if he had never been born" (Mt 26:24), his words do not allude for certain to eternal damnation.'[9]

I have long felt that, understood in a literal, uncritical way, the church's traditional, and largely mythological teaching on eternal punishment is appallingly cruel and violent. It seems to maintain that God is a vindictive tyrant who, in justice, condemns those who die unrepentant of even one mortal sin, e.g. an act of fornication between two loving people, to suffer endless torment. James Joyce gave archetypal expression to this horrifying notion in the famous hellfire sermon in *A Portrait Of The Artist As A Young Man*. It is a *tour de force* of Gothic terror. Among other things the Jesuit preacher, Fr Arnall, says to the hapless schoolboys assembled before him: 'A holy saint, one of our own fathers I believe it was, was once vouchsafed a vision of hell. It seemed to him that he stood in the midst of a great hall, dark and silent save for the ticking of a great clock. The ticking went on unceasingly; and it seemed to this saint that the sound of the ticking was the ceaseless repetition of the words – ever, never; ever, never. Ever to be in hell, never to be in heaven; ever to be shut off from the presence of God, never to enjoy the beatific vision; ever to be eaten with flames, gnawed by vermin, goaded with burning spikes, never to be free from those pains … never to behold the shining raiment of the blessed spirits; ever to cry out of the abyss of fire to God for an instant, a single instant, of respite from such awful agony, never to receive, even for an instant, God's pardon; ever to suffer, never to enjoy; ever to be damned, never to be saved; ever, never; ever, never.'[10]

In 1442, the Council of Florence stated that, besides being a punishment for unrepented mortal sin, hell fire could be a punishment for people, who through no fault of their own, were born as non-Catholics: 'The holy Roman Church ... firmly believes, professes and proclaims that none of those outside the Catholic Church, not Jews, nor heretics, nor schismatics, can participate in eternal life, but will go into the eternal fire prepared for the devil and his angels, unless they are brought into the Catholic Church before the end of life.'[11] While this teaching has never been formally rescinded, it has been modified by the notion of baptism by desire and the assertion that God's saving grace can and does operate outside the Catholic Church.[12] However, if mediaeval and post-Reformation Christians subscribed in an unquestioning way to the teachings of the Council of Florence, is it any wonder that they could commit the atrocities listed above. It is not really surprising that the conquistadors could give their victims a stark choice between baptism or death. If a just God could punish damned sinners and non-Catholics in this unimaginably terrible and unrelenting way, couldn't the servants of such a harsh God meet out equally merciless and savage violence on those who fell foul of their might and ostensibly Christian purposes? As we have already seen, some of the teaching of the Old Testament would also have supported the notion of ruthless violence.

The Unredeemed Shadow and Violence

As a psychologist Carl Jung believed that the violence perpetrated by Jews, Christians and others was only possible because groups and nations exercise selective empathy. Each side feels deeply for its fellow citizens, especially the women and children who are victims of the fighting. But they don't have the same feeling for those who are victims on the other side. As Jung suggested, 'the psychology of war is a matter of unconscious projection. Everything one's own nation does is good, while everything the other nation does is wicked. The centre of all that is mean and vile is always to be found several miles behind the enemy's lines.'[13] As a result, when enemy men, women and children are wounded and killed, instead of feeling any empathy for them, they either feel apathetic or rejoice to see them suffer.

I can remember attending the wake of a Catholic man in Northern Ireland. He had been murdered by paramilitaries on the day he retired from work. His death caused great grief among his family, friends and neighbours. Around the same time a Protestant politician called John Taylor was shot a number of times by the IRA. When Catholic nationalists heard the news on the police frequencies of the radio, women came out of their homes and banged dust bin lids in a customary sign of ritual celebration. The next day I visited the spot where the assassination attempt had occurred. There was a big pool of blood on the road. The police had used chalk to draw a silhouette around the place where the victim had fallen. Some nationalist person had drawn an arrow pointing towards the outline and callously written, 'pig's blood!' When I indignantly drew the attention of a passer by to the inscription, I was shocked when he replied, 'It is quite right, the man is a pig. He got what he deserved.' More recently we saw similar pictures of Palestinians rejoicing in the street when they heard that thousands of people had been murdered in the attack on the twin towers of the World Trade Centre, on 11 September 2001, in lower Manhattan.

To understand Jung's psychology of the values and attitudes that leave people devoid of empathy for enemy victims, one needs to have a grasp of his thinking on the shadow self. It is the darker, inferior, unconscious side of a person or a social group, whether racial, national, or religious, which is neither recognised or accepted. In Christian terms, the extent to which this is true, is the extent to which the person has failed to be fully justified by grace through faith in Christ's saving death and resurrection. God loves us unconditionally as we are, not as we could be, or may be, some day. But if we fail to grasp this truth in our deepest, darkest selves we will be unable to show unrestricted love to others, friends and foes alike. Instead, the unredeemed, hateful shadow will be projected onto other men, women and children. In many ways Jung was describing the psychological dynamics that may lie behind Jesus' words: 'Why do you see the speck that is in your brother's eye, but do not notice the log that is in your own eye?' (Mt 7:3). In Ireland Catholic nationalists see and reject the speck of injustice, sectarianism and selfishness in the eyes of 'black,' Protestant unionists, which they fail to see or accept in themselves and *vice versa.*[14]

Jung believed that the shadow was represented in mythological terms as the devil. It is interesting to note that the word 'devil' is derived from the Greek *diaballein*, 'to throw across, to slander'. It is also worth noting, in this context that the word Satan literally means in Hebrew, 'the adversary'. As always the etymology of these words is very revealing. Those who unconsciously project their shadow on others, feel antipathy for their sub-human victims whom they slander and accuse in a way that leads to alienation, ill treatment and even violence. I suspect that in describing the dynamics of the unacknowledged shadow, Jung was also describing the psychological basis of demonic oppression of a spiritual kind.

Some time ago there was a three hour dramatic reconstruction of the Nuremberg trials on TV. In many ways it illustrated Jung's point. One of the characters in the drama was a Jewish American officer who was a psychologist. He had access to the imprisoned Nazi leaders and had many conversations with them. He said that, among other things, his work was motivated by a desire to know the essence of evil. Having observed the responses of the defendants to the incontrovertible evidence of their monstrous crimes against the Jews, he noticed that they all had one thing in common, namely, a total lack of feeling for their victims. Therefore, he concluded 'evil is a lack of empathy'. I would be inclined to qualify this assertion by saying, 'when there is an absence of un-restricted empathy, any evil is possible'. Empathy dies when the unredeemed shadow is projected on to others.

The Non-violent Teaching of Jesus
Over the centuries the Israelites clearly grew in their knowledge of who God is and what God is like. They moved away from the crude excesses of their anthropomorphic thinking which tended to make God in their own tribal and violent image. For example, it is interesting to note that the Lord prevented King David from building the temple. Yahweh explained: 'You have shed too

much blood and have waged great wars; you shall not build a
house to my name, because you have shed so much blood before
me upon the earth' (1 Chron 22:8). Incidentally, David seemed to
be aware of his sins of aggression because he says in Ps 51:14:
'Deliver me from bloodguiltiness, O God.'[15]

Divine antipathy to the violence of the tribal war God depicted
in an anthropocentric way in the Old Testament came to a glorious climax in the life of Jesus. As God's Son, he had a unique
sense of the mind, heart and purposes of the Father God of unrestricted and unconditional mercy and love. As a result he was
opposed to all violence. He renounced the paramilitary ways of
the Zealots when he committed himself to be the suffering servant. Instead of endorsing the Old Testament teaching 'an eye
for an eye and a tooth for a tooth' (Ex 21:24), he said, 'do not resist
one who is evil' (Mt 5:39). He also said to his disciples: 'Love
your enemies, do good to those who hate you, bless those who
curse you, pray for those who abuse you. To him who strikes
you on the cheek, offer the other also ... And as you wish that
others would do to you, do so to them' (Lk 6:27-31).[16] On one occasion Samaritan villagers failed to welcome Jesus. The apostles
were incensed. We are told that: 'When the disciples James and
John saw this, they asked, "Lord, do you want us to call fire
down from heaven to destroy them?"' In response to this murderous reaction: 'Jesus turned and rebuked them' (Lk 9:54-55).
Evidently, he was adamantly opposed to the apostle's desire for
violent retribution. As I have said in the preceding chapter, to
carry out the Golden Rule, two things are needed, goodwill and
insight. The insight comes from empathy, the ability to sense
what others feel and desire, in an understanding way. What person, other that a deranged sadomasochist, would want to be attacked, wounded, despoiled and killed? St Paul echoed the
teaching of Jesus when he wrote: 'If your enemy is hungry, feed
him; if he is thirsty, give him something to drink. In doing this,
you will heap burning coals on his head. Do not be overcome by
evil, but overcome evil with good' (Rom 12:20-21).

The New Testament also pointed, unambiguously, at the demonic origins of the aggression that crucified Jesus, the God-
man, and, by extension, of all murderous aggression. For example,
we are told that Satan entered the heart of Judas who betrayed

Jesus (Lk 22:3). When Jesus was being arrested he said: 'This is your hour, and the power of darkness' (Lk 22:53), i.e. the power of the devil, who is 'ruler of this world' (Jn 16:11).

By acclaiming the victim as Lord, the gospels slowly began to awaken an empathy for victims everywhere, whether they belonged to one's own circle of relationships or not. Bailie believes that violence loses its legitimacy if and when this empathic perspective becomes widespread. 'The New Testament story of the crucifixion … invites those it confronts to see the scapegoating violence for what it is and to recognise their own complicity in it. By acclaiming the victim as Lord, the gospels slowly begin to awaken an empathy for victims everywhere.'[17] Bailie makes the highly significant observation that, in terms of its historical effects, 'empathy for victims is Christianity's cardinal virtue.'[18] He believes that this perspective is influencing more and more people. The media, especially TV, can help to end wars by showing the suffering of 'enemies' on our screens. No wonder army generals try to stop all such reporting during wars. If people felt empathy for victims on the other side, the prosecution of the war would become much more difficult. So, properly understood, Christianity undermines the whole ideology of violence. In the twentieth century Mahatma Ghandi, Martin Luther King and others showed how the teaching of Jesus could take the form of non-violent resistance to injustice of any kind.

Prophetic Christian Voices
Ghandi noticed how Christians often failed to live in accordance with the Golden Rule. He stated: 'It is a first class human tragedy that people of the earth who claim to believe in the message of Jesus, whom they describe as the Prince of Peace, show little of that belief in actual practice.' While there is a lot truth in what he says, it would only be fair to say that over the centuries a number of Christians have raised their voices in protest at the violence being inflicted by fellow Christians. Commenting on the Spanish conquest in South America one of them wrote: 'In four hundred years of captivity … the Hebrews increased in numbers and did not die. But our Indians in their own land, ever since the Spaniards entered in, have been wasted away in millions by the harassment and tyranny they suffer, and by the

severity of the personal services they have to carry out, which is greater and more terrible than that exacted by the Pharaohs of Egypt.'[19]

The most notable and controversial critic of Spanish colonial policy was a Dominican, Bartholome de Las Casas (1474-1566). He had the distinction of being the first ordained priest in the New World. He knew the Indians, empathised with them in their afflictions, and came to appreciate them very much. Over a period of time, this champion of civil and religious rights became convinced that the Spanish conquest was unjust. La Casas maintained that the main motive of the Spaniards was, 'Their insatiable greed and ambition, the greatest ever seen in the world. And also, these lands are so rich and blessed, the native peoples so meek and patient ... but our Spaniards have no more consideration for them than beasts ... But I should not say "than beasts" for thanks be to God, they have treated beasts with some respect; I should say instead like excrement on the public square.'[20] Las Casas argued that the Indians should not be coerced. Rather they should be won over to the saving power of the gospel by inspired preaching rather than the force of arms. He said in a text entitled *Tears of the Indians*: 'Now Christ wanted his gospel to be preached with enticements, gentleness, and all meekness, and pagans to be led to the truth not by armed forces but by holy examples, Christian conduct, and the word of God, so that no opportunity would be offered for blaspheming the sacred name or hating the true religion because of the conduct of the preachers. For this is nothing else than making the coming and passion of Christ useless, as long as the truth of the gospel is hated before it is either understood or heard, or as long as innumerable human beings are slaughtered in a war waged on the pretext of preaching the gospel and spreading religion.' Las Casas had quite an influence on official Spanish policy. It was modified in a more humane way in the light of his insistence on the human rights of the Indians.

Alvar Nunez Cabeza de Vaca was virtually unique among the conquistadors. He spent eight years travelling 8,000 miles from Florida to New Mexico (1528-1536). All the while he appreciated the beauty of the countryside, and admired the Indians, much as Las Casas had done. He thought that they were handsome, intelligent and humane. In the midst of his vicissitudes, he caught a sight of the bond that exists between all peoples. He wanted to bring Christian civilisation to the Indians. In chapter twenty three of his famous account of his adventures, he tells us that he and a companion found that they could cure their sicknesses. 'Our method,' he says, 'was to bless the sick, breathe upon them, recite an Our Father and Hail Mary, and pray earnestly to God our Lord, for their recovery. When we concluded with the sign of the cross, God willed that our patients should directly spread the news that they had been restored to health.'[21] He also communicated the Christian teachings to the Indians he met, and resolved tribal hostilities, thereby leaving the lands he passed through in peace.

How come de Vaca refused to use violence against the native peoples of North America? Reading his account of the epic journey, it is clear that the Indians empathised with him, and that he in turn empathised with the Indians. In chapter nineteen of his biographical narrative he recounts that on one occasion, 'the Indians, understanding our full plight, sat down and lamented for half an hour so loudly they could have been heard a long way off. It was amazing to see these wild, untaught savages howling like brutes in compassion for us.' As a result of incidents like this de Vaca, unlike the conquistadors in South America, respected and empathised with the Indians as human beings. He saw them as being equal in dignity to the Spaniards. As a result, he prohibited enslaving, raping, and looting of the Indians. Because he sought to live by the Golden Rule, he did not use violence against the native Americans. In the remainder of this chapter I will focus on the problem of sacred violence as we have experienced it in Ireland.

The Loyalist Religious Myth

Bailie is of the opinion that many modern political systems are founded on sacralised violence. They are commonly perceived in quasi religious terms as exodus events when the chosen people passed from foreign bondage to liberty by means of legitimate violence. For example, Protestant Ulster was founded on at least two bloody events. Firstly there was the fifteen-week-long siege of Derry in 1689, when about 30,000 planters took refuge in the city. On the day the siege was lifted Protestant forces, based at Enniskillen, massacred an Irish force at Newtownbutler. The second significant event, the battle of the Boyne took place the following year. The forces commanded by the Protestant, William of Orange, defeated the army of Catholic King James II. As Roy Foster, the author of *Modern Ireland 1600-1972*, observes, both events have given birth to a religious and political mythology that sometimes bears little relationship to reality.[22] Incidentally, I understand a myth to be a symbolic story, a meta-narrative, which encapsulates the shared meanings that animate a particular group of people.

In the late nineteenth and early twentieth centuries, the Protestants of the North were determined to resist Home Rule. To this end many of them signed the Ulster Covenant on 28 September 1912. Apparently some of them did so in their own blood. This quasi religious document read: 'Humbly relying on the God whom our fathers trusted ... to stand by one another in defending for ourselves and our children our cherished position of equal citizenship in the United Kingdom, and in using all means which may be found necessary to defeat the present conspiracy to set up a home rule parliament in Ireland.' In a speech given at the time, the Rev. J. W. Gibson indicated that the phrase 'all means' included the possibility of violence. He said: 'The Loyalists of Ireland would never submit to be ruled by a Parliament in Dublin ... The spirit of the men who fought at Derry, Enniskillen, Aughrim and the Boyne was with them still and, if need be, the men who subscribed their names to the Covenant would be ready, should the exigencies of the situation demand it, *to* shed their life's blood in defence of faith and fatherland.' Of course they were quite willing to shed Catholic blood also. Notice how Gibson is appealing to the foundational myth, to the sacral violence upon which the Loyalist political and religious identity was built.

In all, approximately 237,368 men signed the Covenant and 234,046 women signed a parallel document. On the night of 24 April, 35,000 rifles and 3,000,000 rounds of ammunition were successfully unloaded at Larne, Bangor and Donaghadee to back up Loyalist resistance to Dublin rule. Major F. H. Crawford helped to bring guns into Larne. He recalled what went through his mind when he was anchored offshore. 'I walked up and down the deck tormented by the thoughts of all those men waiting for me to bring them the weapons with which to fight for their religion, their liberty and all that was dear to them ... I went to my cabin and threw myself on my knees, and in simple language told God all about it: what this meant to Ulster.' The violence perpetrated by Loyalist paramilitaries during the thirty years of the troubles, and afterwards, has often been justified in terms of the sacred violence of the past. Murderous aggression was perpetrated 'for God and for Ulster!'[23]

The Republican Religious Myth

A similar notion of sacred violence was apparent in the twenty-six counties at around the same time as the Ulster Covenant was signed. In an essay entitled, *The Coming Revolution* (1913) Patrick Pearse wrote: 'We must accustom ourselves to the thought of arms, to the sight of arms, to the use of arms. We may make mistakes in the beginning and shoot the wrong people; but *bloodshed is a cleansing and a sanctifying thing*, and the nation which regards it as the final horror has lost its manhood.' Two years later, writing about the European war, Pearse said: 'The last sixteen months have been the most glorious in the history of Europe. Heroism has come back to the earth ... The old heart of the earth needed to be warmed with the red wine of the battlefields. *Such august homage was never before offered to God as this*, the homage of millions of lives given gladly for love of country.' Pearse echoed these perverse sentiments in an essay entitled, *Peace and the Gael*, in 1915: 'It is because peace is so precious a boon that *war is so sacred a duty*. Ireland will not find Christ's peace until she has taken Christ's sword. What peace she has known in these latter days has been the devil's peace, peace with sin, peace with dishonor. It is a foul thing ... Christ's peace is lovely in its coming, beautiful are its feet on the mountains. But it is heralded by terrific messengers; seraphim and cherubim blow trumpets of war before it.'

American historian, Thomas Coffey says in his *Agony at Easter: The 1916 Irish Uprising* that, in the General Post Office, leaders Patrick Pearse, Joseph Plunkett and Desmond FitzGerald repeatedly spoke about the theological justification for what they were doing.[24] The question was, how would it appear in the eyes of God? He says that there was no attempt to deny responsibility for the death and destruction caused by the rebellion. Pearse thought that the rebellion could be seen as a just war. It is worth recalling that St Thomas Aquinas said that for a war to be just three conditions are necessary – public authority, just cause, and right motive.[25] Assuming that Aquinas' criteria are correct and that the insurgent's cause was just and their motives right, the rebellion had no democratic mandate or public authority. In fact the majority of the people were against it.

Pearse felt that the sacrifice of Easter Week 1916 was reminiscent of the blood shed by Christ on the cross. Just as Christ's saving death was followed by the resurrection, so the blood of Ireland's modern martyrs would be followed by national rebirth. There was one fatal flaw in Pearse's questionable argument. Whereas Jesus was the hapless victim of state violence and other people's hate, Pearse and his followers were the instigators of such violence. Instead of loving their enemies in an empathic way, the rebels tried to murder them. As a result, hundreds of people, British soldiers and innocent citizens of Dublin were killed during the fighting. But as Bailie wryly comments: 'humanity's oldest and most tenacious illusion – is the one that makes victimisers proud of what they have done.'[26] For more on this point see the chapter on envy.

In more recent times, Irish Republicans, notably the Provisional IRA, have used Pearse's thinking to justify the dreadful violence that has led to the merciless killing and maiming of thousands of people in Northern Ireland. They could quote the following words of Pearse written in 1915: 'War is a terrible thing, but war is not an evil thing. It is the things that make war necessary that are evil. The tyrannies that wars break, the lying formulae that wars overthrow, the hypocrisies that wars strip naked, are evil.' Pearse's adage: 'Ireland will not find Christ's peace, until she has taken Christ's sword,' is a dangerous distortion of the Christian ethic, specifically of the Golden Rule which calls for empathic love of an un-restricted kind. When he spoke at Drogheda in 1979, Pope John Paul II confirmed the rightness of this point of view when he stated that politically motivated violence is evil, unacceptable as a solution to injustices and is unworthy of people. 'Violence is a lie,' he said, 'for it goes against the truth of our faith, the truth of our humanity. Violence destroys what it claims to defend: the dignity, the life, the freedom of human beings. Violence is a crime against humanity, for it destroys the very fabric of society.'[27]

When Peter used his sword to cut off the ear of a servant of one of the occupying Roman troops who arrested Jesus in the Garden of Gethsemane, Jesus said to him, 'put your sword back into its place; for all who take the sword will perish by the sword' (Mt 26:52). Having learned his lesson, Peter said some years later: 'Never pay back one wrong with another' (1 Pt 3:9). As these ideas and their implications sink into Christian consciousness, violence becomes ever more problematical. 'In our world a struggle is taking place,' says Bailie, 'between the power of the sacrificial and scapegoating myths, and the gospel's deconstruction of them.'[28] I believe that he is correct when he says that any notion of sacred violence has to be revealed for what it really is, the devil's work. As a result, like Desiderius Erasmus, he believes that 'the most disadvantageous peace is better than the most just war.'[29]

Rival Rights

The modern notion of civil liberties can be traced back to the Declaration of the Rights of Man during the French Revolution. It stated that all people are born free and that they are equal in dignity and rights. The Universal Declaration of Human Rights, which was promulgated in 1948, reiterated and amplified this fundamental point. The Good Friday Agreement of 1998 echoed both declarations when it affirmed its 'commitment to the mutual respect, the civil rights and religious liberties of everyone in the community.' For example, Orangemen can advert to the Good Friday Agreement when they insist that they have a civil and religious right to march on the queen's highway in any part of Northern Ireland. Nationalists argue that they have an equal right not to have provocative marches go through their areas because they trap them in their homes for long periods of time. Not only that, they consider them to be offensive, triumphalistic and sectarian in nature. By emphasising their rival rights and not their mutual duties, the two communities come into inevitable conflict.

Over the years I have been shocked and disappointed by the obvious lack of love that is evident in Northern Ireland disputes. Antipathy often spills over into violence. Orangemen are proud of their Protestant heritage. Many of them claim to accept Jesus as their personal Lord and Saviour and to be guided by biblical teaching. But it seems to me that they dishonor Christ in so far as they ignore the precepts of biblical ethics, especially the Golden Rule. Catholics can do much the same. They assert that they are committed Christians and members of the true church. But when provoked by Orange marches and protests, e.g. on the Garvaghy Road in Portadown and Ardoyne Road in Belfast, they often ignore biblical teaching, while trying to rationalise and excuse their reasons for doing so. Let us look at two examples.

In Phil 2:3-5 St Paul says: 'Do nothing out of selfish ambition or vain conceit, but in humility consider others better than yourselves. Each of you should look not only to your own interests, but also to the interests of others. Your attitude should be the same as that of Christ Jesus.' How many Orangemen consider the nationalists of the Garvaghy or Ardoyne Road to be better than themselves? How many are concerned with the interests of the residents? How many of the nationalists and republicans consider the Orangemen to be better than themselves. How many are really concerned with their interests? Sadly, the answer to both questions is very few, if any.

In 1 Cor 13:4-7 St Paul says in a well known passage: 'Love is patient, love is kind. It does not envy, it does not boast, it is not proud. It is not rude, it is not self-seeking, it is not easily angered, it keeps no record of wrongs. Love does not delight in evil but rejoices with the truth.' Isn't it true that members of both communities are often impatient, unkind, boastful, proud, rude, self-seeking, easily angered and keepers of long lists of wrongs committed by the other side? In other words they can display a surprising lack of Christian love. In terms of discernment of spirits, unloving actions are clearly not motivated by the Spirit of God. At best they are motivated by a self-centred human spirit, at worst by the evil spirit, the accuser and divider of the community.

I hope that, in future, the Orangemen who intend to march through nationalist areas, and the locals who don't want them to do so, will reflect on this divisive issue in the light of biblical teaching. It is clear that when Orangemen or nationalists deal with contentious issues in a proud, disdainful way, they usually evoke feelings of hostility. However, when they deal with those issues in a humble, understanding way, they often evoke feelings of surprise followed by a willingness to react in a generous and magnanimous way. For example, if the Parades Commission banned the Orangemen from marching down the Garvaghy Road, wouldn't it be great if the local nationalists freely invited them to do so? Conversely, if the Parades Commission gave the go-ahead for the march, wouldn't it be great if the Orangemen freely decided not to exercise their right to do so? Surely the extent to which these scenarios are unlikely is the extent to which the Golden Rule is being ignored by people who bear the name of Christ. While I have focused on a localised problem here, the principles involved apply to any conflict situation.

The Way of Peace

At an ecumenical prayer meeting a few years ago, a vivid image came spontaneously into my mind. I could see a number of tall flagpoles with their respective flags flapping in the wind. At the base of each flagpole were groups of people. They were shouting and gesticulating in an angry and hostile manner at the people gathered around the other flagpoles. Then in the middle, I saw the cross. At first the people didn't even notice it. Then, one by one, the irate protesters began to pay attention to the crucified One. As they beheld him, their antagonism turned to shame. Each group began to lower its flags, some slowly, others more rapidly. Soon the cross stood higher than all the flags. People began to drift away from their flagpoles and to gather around the foot of the cross. It seemed as if the Lord was saying: 'At the moment the flags of your denominational and nationalistic pride are raised higher than the cross. But when you look to me who was lifted up from the earth to draw all people to myself, you will lower the flags of your pride. Then and only then, will you find peace, for in the power of my cross the dividing wall of your divisions will crumble.' When we look at the crucified Lord we see the Suffering Servant dying at the hands of his enemies while loving them all the while (cf. Rom 5:6-8). He invites us to love our enemies, in the same empathic and loving way, especially when they are victims of violence. As Paul reminds us in Rom 12:14, 16-17, 'Bless those who persecute you; bless and do not curse them ... Live in harmony with one another; do not be haughty ... do not repay anyone evil for evil.'

In the *Ghost in the Machine*, the late Arthur Koestler observed: 'The crimes of violence committed for selfish, personal motives are historically insignificant compared to those committed *ad majorem gloriam Dei*, out of a self-sacrificing devotion to a flag, a leader, a religious faith or a political conviction.'[30] I believe that the time has come for Irish Christians, whether Catholic or Protestant, to deconstruct the myths upon which their respective political systems are founded. Ironically the governments that came into being as a result of bloody struggle, now inconsistently condemn the violence of modern day paramilitarism which derives a good deal of its inspiration from the sacral violence of the past. In the light of the cross and its non-violent message we, all of us, need to admit, governments and paramilitaries alike, that while our political regimes were born in a bloody manner, the devil was the invisible midwife. As Gil Bailie comments: 'The moral blindness a sacrificial crisis induces in those who get caught up in it is incredibly powerful. Speaking both etymologically and biblically, it is nothing less than the power of Satan (the accuser).'[31]

It is time for us to renounce all forms of violence. We need a moral equivalent to the Truth and Justice Commission in South Africa. Republicans and nationalists need to learn to weep for the loyalist and unionist dead and their dependants, and *vice versa*. Those who perpetrated violence over the years need to move away from the political and religious justification of murder and destruction to confess the wrongs they have done and to seek forgiveness from God, the victims who survived and the relatives of those who died or were maimed. All of us would do well to return to the Christian vision of Daniel O Connell who said in a speech delivered on 28 February 1843: 'Not for all the universe contains would I, in the struggle for what I conceive my country's cause, consent to the effusion of a single drop of human blood, except my own.'

CHAPTER FOUR

Envy: Cancer of the Soul

On one occasion when I was in the throes of writing a book on relationships I spent a lot of time trying to describe the nature of true love. Eventually I came up with the following definition: 'love is an act of will whereby one approves of the perceived and potential value of a person.'[1] It may not sound very romantic, but I feel confident that it describes something of the essence of all kinds of human love: the affection a mother has for her child, the fond feelings a son has for his father, the tenderness a girl experiences for her fiancée, the benevolence an aid worker extends to a disaster victim, etc. True love goes beyond appearances, to see the hidden qualities of a person. Once it is aware of them, it finds that it not only appreciates those qualities, it senses in an affirming and encouraging way that the person has a capacity for considerable growth in the future.

I was interested to see that a number of writers have defined love in a somewhat similar way. Psychologist, Rollo May says love is: 'A delight in the presence of the other person and an affirming of his value and development as much as one's own.'[2] Viktor Frankl, another psychologist says: 'By his love a person is enabled to see the essential traits and features in the beloved person; and even more, he sees that which is potential in him, which is not yet actualised but yet ought to be actualised. Furthermore by his love the loving person enables the beloved person to actualise these potentialities.'[3]

Envy
A question. What is the opposite of love? It would probably be true to say that most people would instinctively respond by saying that it was hate. While there is no love in hatred, I wonder whether it is love's true antithesis. Arguably, envy is the real

59

opposite of love. It is discontent with the good fortune of another. Envious people, like loving ones, perceive the worth and value of other people all right. But unlike loving people, instead of appreciating and approving their qualities or achievements, envious people feel antagonistic towards them. In the light of the apparently superior gifts of others, they feel inferior. Paradoxically, envy is a form of disguised admiration. Envious people are aware of other people's attributes such as good looks, intelligence, charm, sporting prowess, popularity, possessions, degrees, goodness, wisdom, etc. But instead of applauding these endowments they resent them. Willard Galin has suggested, rightly or wrongly, that the envious person begins to ascribe a causal relationship between his or her own deprivation and the abundance of others. 'It is not just that s/he does not have what they have; it is that s/he does not have it *because* they have it.'[4]

The etymology of the word envy would support this point of view. In English it is derived from the Latin *invidere,* meaning 'to look askance'. The dictionary describes it as: 'feeling displeasure and ill-will at the superiority of another person in happiness, success, reputation, or the possession of anything desirable.' Envy is more likely between equals, especially if they have to compete with one another, e.g. members of the same family, neighbourhood, profession, peer group or community. It has been suggested that because men and women in modern, competitive democracies assume that all people are born equal, envy is more likely. Austrian sociologist Helmut Schoeck has shown, in an influential book, how fear of envy, as well as envy itself, is a powerful motive force in social behaviour. This is especially true in Western, free market, economies.[5] Not surprisingly, ambitious people tend to be more envious than those who are not. For example, men and women in professions are keen to have good qualifications and status and can be envious of peers who do better from either point of view.

Although envy is common, it is rarely acknowledged. It is particularly characteristic of people who live in colonial or postcolonial countries. For example, it seems to me that, as such a people, the Irish are particularly prone to envy. While they may resent the British, they often focus their envy on fellow country men and women who seem to excel in one way or another. At first there will be praise. But before long the begrudgery will begin. As German poet Von Goethe once observed: 'The Irish seem to me like a pack of hounds, always dragging down some noble stag.'[6] I suspect that in the past envious resentment led to the persecution of exceptionally gifted and successful Irish people, who had to emigrate in order to receive the recognition they deserved.

Resentment

In the modern era Friedrich Nietzche and later Max Scheler, have examined the nature, dynamics and effects of another form of envy which they refer to as *ressentiment* in French. This kind of repressed resentment is a feeling of hostility, anger, and indignation that is neither acknowledged or even directly expressed. What it attacks is the perceived value of people it considers to be superior. Nietzsche says: 'The envious person is susceptible to every sign of individual superiority to the common herd, and wishes to depress everyone once more to that level – or to raise him or herself to the superior place.'[7] It leads them to have vengeful feelings. Scheler says that the resentful person 'is forever muttering: 'I could forgive you anything, except *that* you are, and *what* you are; except that I am not what you are; that 'I,' in fact, am not 'you'.' This 'envy,' from the start, denies the other person his very existence, which as such is most strongly experienced as 'oppression' of, as 'a reproach' to the person of the subject.[8]

Scheler goes on to say that this form of repressed hate begins by being critical of other people's qualities such as their way of walking or laughing, their taste in music or anything that expresses their personality. Finally, the impulse may break away altogether from the despised person and become a negative attitude towards those same qualities, no matter who has them. Thus the resentful person may come to hate a whole group, class or nation. So resentment which fails to approve of the genuine values it perceives, ends up by proposing substitute values. Nietzsche believed that the Jewish people in the Old Testament were resentful of their superior, more cultured neighbours. Instead of seeing and celebrating their higher qualities they learned to deny them in a spiteful, life denying way. In their place they proposed a new, but false set of values, such as poverty of spirit, meekness, gentleness, etc., which were rooted in their own unresolved sense of inferiority. As far as Nietzsche was concerned, Jesus and his teaching, especially in the Beatitudes, was the arch symbol of this resentful, life-denying, slave mentality. Scheler pointed out that while there was a good deal of truth in Nietzsche's description of the way in which resentment can lead to a corrupting transvaluation of values, he said that this dynamic was rooted, not in the authentic Judeo-Christian ethic but in the bourgeois morality of Nietzsche's day.[9] Psychiatrist Jack Dominian argues that rather than being motivated by an unacknowledged sense of deprivation and inferiority that could be traced back to childhood, Jesus was at ease with the marginalised people of his day precisely because he was at ease in himself as a result of his loving upbringing. As he says: 'Jesus had a solid, secure basis to his inner self, and was not afraid to be surrounded by the outcasts of his society, such as tax collectors and prostitutes.'[10]

That said, Christians can be secretly influenced by envy. Over the years I have become suspicious of the motivation of some of those who work for the poor and who campaign for justice. I suspect that some of them have unresolved feelings of inferiority and low self-esteem which are rooted in childhood feelings of deprivation. While their attacks on the injustices of the better-off, more successful segments of society, may have objective validity, a number of their criticisms can be rooted in an unacknowledged envy rather than a genuine and selfless concern for the rights and welfare of others. If envious people work for the poor, they may be secretly using their efforts on behalf of those they consider to be inferior to themselves, in order to boost their own self-esteem. As Melanie Klein has pointed out, because such individuals don't like competition they surround themselves with 'inferiors' so that they can feel a compensatory superiority.[11] It is not really surprising that people who are unconsciously motivated by negative attitudes and feelings are prone to burn-out. Needless to say, the last thing the poor need is this kind of patronising and condescending attitude. From a Christian point of view, only people who are free from envy can show genuine compassion to society's poorer more vulnerable members. If and when they take action for justice, such efforts will be motivated by genuine love rather than a hidden resentment.

Jealousy

Jealousy is closely related to envy and resentment. The *Shorter Oxford English Dictionary* describes it as being: 'Troubled by the fear, suspicion, or belief that one is being or might be displaced in someone's affections; disposed to be distrustful of the fidelity of a spouse or lover; overly possessive of a friend, lover, or spouse.' Whereas envy is antagonistic to a person's intrinsic value, jealousy is antagonistic to extrinsic rivals, so to speak, when competing for the affections of others. The jealous person fears that s/he will inevitably loose out because the rival will be more attractive to the loved one, for one reason or another. Needless, to say, a person might feel jealous because s/he is also envious of the fact that his or her rival is superior in intelligence, good looks, charm, etc. That said, jealousy is less malicious than envy.

When one thinks about this subject, it becomes evident that envy, resentment and jealousy are rooted in self-absorption and low self-esteem. When people make invidious comparisons between themselves and others, they conclude that they are inferior. Arguably, these negative feelings are rooted in a childhood sense of deprivation and sibling rivalry, when brothers and sisters may have had to compete with one another in order to win the affection and esteem of their parents or carers. Rightly, or wrongly, they may have got the impression that a more extrovert, successful, or intelligent brother or sister would be loved and appreciated more than they were. Hence, a feeling of self-pitying victimisation and a mean spirited inability to rejoice in the talents, gifts, and accomplishments of others. Rather, there is a hidden desire to see them brought down a peg or two. There is a perverse sense of satisfaction when they slip on the banana skin of weakness or misfortune and are humiliated in a public way. While it is true that hidden or overt hatred may be involved, it is the presenting emotional attitude. In reality it is rooted in the malevolent trinity of envy, resentment and jealousy.

Envy in the Old Testament

In the Old Testament *quana* and its derivatives are translated as envy, and in some cases as jealousy and zeal. A great deal of evil is attributed to envy in the bible. In fact it would be true to say that it is considered to be diabolical. In Hebrew the word *satan* literally means adversary or accuser. Envy is devilish because instead of approving people's giftedness and goodness it finds fault, criticises and seeks to diminish them in the eyes of others. In a significant text in Wis 2:24 we are told that the fall of our ancestors was due to the devil: 'God created us for incorruption, and made us in the image of his own eternity, but through the devil's envy death entered the world.'

In Genesis we are told about the first act of violence. It is a classic story of sibling rivalry. God finds the offering of Abel more acceptable than that of his bother Cain. 'So Cain was very angry, and his face was downcast.' Then the Lord said to Cain, 'sin is crouching at your door; it desires to have you, but you must master it' (Gen 4:4-5). Evidently, instead of mastering his envious anger, Cain succumbed to it and killed his bother.

Later in Genesis we are told how Israel had two sons, Esau his first born and Jacob. Strictly speaking, as the elder son, Esau was entitled to his father's blessing and all that went with it. However, at the instigation of his mother Rebekah, Jacob conned his blind father into thinking he was Esau. As a result, although he didn't deserve his father's irrevocable blessing, he received it nevertheless. Not surprisingly, Esau was sorely aggrieved when he heard what had happened. As the eldest son he felt he had a right to his father's favour. When he found that his father's benediction could be neither revoked or repeated, Esau became envious of Jacob. He resented the fact that he had been so richly graced, despite his clear lack of merit as the younger, dishonest son. Consequently, we are told: 'Now Esau hated Jacob because of the blessing which his father had blessed him, and Esau said to himself, the days of mourning for my father are approaching, then I will kill my brother Jacob' (Gen 27:41).

The story of the way in which Joseph's brothers sold him into slavery in Egypt is another classic example of sibling rivalry and envy. In Gen 37:4-5 we read: 'When his brothers saw that their father loved him more than any of them, they hated him and could not speak a kind word to him. Joseph had a dream, and when he told it to his brothers, they hated him all the more.' Acts 7:9 was later to observe: 'Because the patriarchs were envious of Joseph, they sold him as a slave into Egypt. But God was with him.' There are many other stories of envy and jealousy in the Old Testament, often to do with wives who had to compete with one another for their husband's affections, such as Abraham's spouses Sarah and Hagar (Gen 16:5,6; 21:9-10) and Elkanah's spouses Hannah and Peninnah (1 Sam 1;12-17).

Envy in the New Testament
In the New Testament the Greek word *phthonos* meaning 'envy,' is a feeling of displeasure produced by witnessing or hearing of the advantages and prosperity of others. This evil sense is always implied by this word. Surely, Jesus was aware that envy was alien to love. In Mark 7:21-23 he said: 'For from within, out of men's hearts, come evil thoughts, sexual immorality, theft, murder, adultery, greed, malice, deceit, lewdness, *envy*, slander, arrogance and folly. All these evils come from inside and make a man 'unclean'.'

I suspect that Jesus knew about the kind of envy he described because he himself was often the object of such a negative attitude. In Mt 13:54-58 an incident is recounted which seems to indicate that he was envied by his own neighbours. When Jesus spoke to the people in his local synagogue at Nazareth, he was addressing his equals. He was one of them, he had grown up in the midst of the local community and had shared in the same experiences as they had. But when he made his prophetic announcement, they sensed that, inexplicably, he was strangely different. As they exclaimed: 'Where did this man get this wisdom and these miraculous powers?' Clearly, they were consciously aware of his extraordinary gifts and spiritual authority. As the text attests, they were 'amazed' by them. But instead of approving of his endowments in a loving way, they began to take offence at them in an envious manner. It was if they were saying, who does he think he is? Does he think he is a cut above the rest of us?

I believe that Jesus really felt hurt and perplexed by the envy of his kith and kin. When he encountered their negative reaction he would have felt that they were antagonistic to his innermost self. It must have been a very painful, disconcerting experience. He may have asked himself, what did I do to deserve this? What is supposed to be wrong with me, or with what I have been saying and doing? Was he tempted to loose heart, as many envied people have done when they have encountered similar criticism and rejection? No wonder he uttered his well known observation, 'Only in his hometown and in his own house is a prophet without honour' (Mt 13:57). It was tantamount to saying: 'When God gifts a person in an unusual way s/he will not be accepted by relatives and neighbours because of envy.'

Although he was a lay man, the people regarded Jesus as a Rabbi. As such he was on a par with other eminent teachers of the law. Scripture scholars attest that, like Jesus, the Scribes and Pharisees were devout, learned and conscientious. Why, therefore, could they not accept him and his liberating message? Like them he was dedicated to the things of God. But in reality he outshone them in goodness, love, freedom, authority and spiritual power. Instead of approving of the goodness they could see, they denied it in a self-absorbed, irrational way. It would seem that, like the people in his home town, they envied him. Arguably, Jesus spoke indirectly about this kind of envy and its consequences in a number of his parables, such as the story of the Good Employer in Mt 20:1-16.

The story of the prodigal (Lk 15:11-32), like many others in the Old Testament, is about sibling rivalry. We are told about the father's acceptance of his wayward son, and the elder brother's envious reaction. In this story, the elder brother, the dutiful son, represented the Pharisees, Scribes and Sadducees. The younger brother, the wayward son, represented those who had seriously fallen short of what the Jewish authorities expected of them. Sinners of this kind included most of the rural poor, e.g. those who engaged in unclean professions such as prostitutes, tax collectors, robbers, herdsmen, usurers, gamblers, those who did not pay their tithes or neglected the Sabbath day rest and ritual cleanliness, and also those who through no fault of their own didn't know the law. There was no way out for them. They were the 'damned' (Jn 7:49). As a result they suffered from chronic guilt feelings which led them to fear divine retribution. But when the father in the parable welcomed his son home without recrimination, threw the cloak of honour around his shoulders, put the ring of authority on his finger, the shoes of freedom on his feet and killed the fatted calf in order to celebrate his home-coming, the elder brother envied his sibling. He resented the fact that he was being so well treated when, in terms of strict justice, he deserved to be turned away.

As I have reflected on this issue, it has occurred to me that it symbolises a fundamental clash between the notion of justific-ation by grace, represented by the prodigal son, and justification by good works, represented the elder brother. Those who live on the basis of justice expect to receive what they are due as a result of their personal merits, whereas those who trust completely in God's mercy expect to be richly blessed in spite of their lack of personal merits. The former attitude is rooted in a proud self-sufficiency, whereas the latter is rooted in a humble type of trust in the provision of a God who is unimaginably glorious, great, good, gracious, generous and giving. Surely, from a theological point of view, envy is ultimately an affective attitude that explic-itly resents the unmerited gifts of God in others, and in an im-plicit way, resents them in oneself. In other words, envy is ulti-mately a self-centred feeling of antagonism to the whole notion of grace. It is a share in the attitude of the fallen angels, who en-vied the greater glory of God and said: 'We will not serve.' The afflicted person does not want to depend of God for his or her blessings. S/he wants to deserve them. That is why invidious comparisons are made with others. Am I going to be outdone by his or her merits? No wonder a legalistic man or woman resents the blessings of others when s/he sees them being freely given in an unmerited way. In terms of strict justice they not only see it as being grossly unfair, they also find it profoundly threatening to their individualistic sense of significance as self-made men and women. It was the notion of unmerited gifts and graces, es-pecially the superior ones enjoyed by others, that the Scribes and Pharisees could not accept. It finally led them in an envious way to persecute Jesus for witnessing to such a different worldview. The extent to which envy and its concomitant feelings and atti-tudes remain in our hearts today is the extent to which we will continue to persecute Christ in our brothers and sisters, especially the more gifted ones.

I can remember a wonderful talk which was given by David Pawson, a Protestant preacher and writer from England. Having spoken about the parable of the Prodigal Son he commented that we didn't know how it ended. Did the elder brother join in the celebrations after a change of heart? Did he go off and sulk in solitude? I was quite shocked when Pawson suggested that sometime later the elder son went in to the house and killed his father. Perhaps. But surely his envy could equally have led him to kill his brother who had been so richly blessed. It is also conceivable that he would have killed both his father and his brother. In any case, Pawson said that he had good reason to say what he did. The elder brother was a symbol of the religious authorities of the day. They envied the fact that Jesus was welcoming the riff-raff of Palestine into the kingdom as if they had lived good lives like themselves. Their sense of indignation and resentment became so strong that they decided in a vengeful way to have Jesus killed. The New Testament confirms this opinion when it attributes only one motive to those who conspired to murder Jesus. In Mt 27:18 we are told that Pilate 'knew that it was out of *envy* that they had delivered him up.'

Ultimately, the envy that killed Jesus was rooted in pride. It had distorted the values and attitudes of the Scribes and Pharisees. Instead of being open, in an appreciative and approving way, to the goodness and message of Jesus, they perceived both in a spirit of suspicion and antagonism in so far as they threatened their self-importance or security in any way. As St Thomas Aquinas wrote: 'The proud are without pity, because they despise others, and think them wicked, so that they account them as suffering deservedly, whatever they suffer.'[12] There are two interesting passages which illustrate this point in a way that prophetically anticipate the passion and death of Jesus.

In his *Republic* Plato (427-347 BC) describes the attitude of the unjust who are motivated by pride. 'They will tell you that the just man who is thought unjust will be scourged, racked, bound, will have his eyes burnt out; and at last, after suffering every kind of evil, he will be impaled. Then he will understand that he ought to seem only, and not to be, just.' A passage in Wis 2: 14-21 mirrors this point in a more religious way, when it vividly encapsulates the malice involved in envious resentment: 'Let us lie in wait for the righteous ... He professes to have knowledge of God, and calls himself a child of the Lord. He became to us a reproof of our thoughts; the very sight of him is a burden to us, because his manner of life is unlike that of others, and his ways are strange ... he calls the last end of the righteous happy, and boasts that God is his father. Let us see if his words are true, and let us test what will happen at the end of his life; for if the righteous man is God's son, he will help him, and will deliver him from the hand of his adversaries. Let us test him with insult and torture, that we may find out how gentle he is, and make trial of his forbearance. Let us condemn him to a shameful death, for, according to what he says, he will be protected.' Is it any wonder that St Paul associated envy with life without the Spirit (cf. Gal 5:21) and the apostle James said that envy 'is earthly, unspiritual, of the devil' (Jas 3:15). St Cyprian echoed the New Testament attitude when he described envy as 'the worm of the soul'. St Vincent de Paul referred to it, in an equally vivid image, as 'a serpent of the heart'.

An Incidence of Murderous Envy

In his book entitled, *The Passions: The Myth and Nature of Human Emotion*, philosopher Robert Solomon says: 'Envy is an essentially vicious emotion, bitter and vindictive. Yet it is usually a harmless passion, except to oneself, for again unlike anger, it is an emotion of marked impotence and inferiority.'[13] While there is some truth in what he says, envy can and does motivate people to inflict mental and physical suffering on others.

A few years ago two boys murdered a teacher and a number of their fellow pupils in Columbine school in Denver, Colorado. Eric Harris and Dylan Klebold enjoyed many advantages. Their parents were not divorced. By all accounts they gave their sons a good deal of support. Both families were prosperous. For example, the Harris household had seven registered cars and Eric owned his own BMW. Both teenagers were well above average in intelligence. But in a country that constantly preaches equality, Harris and Klebold, didn't seem to feel equal. The members of two school gangs called the 'jocks' and the 'preps' often taunted them. One girl said: 'You know kids can be really mean to each other, really cruel.' Another stated that everywhere members of the Blackcoat Mafia went, they were treated as outsiders. They were 'teased about the way they dressed and were accused of being gay'. It was obvious that they were very upset by the bullying tactics employed by the other students.

Deprived of the emotional oxygen of approval and inclusion, it would seem that the hurt and inferiority felt by these shy young men turned to envious and resentful anger. Writing about envy, a criminologist called Glueck observed: 'Persons in whom this attitude is strong are not so much concerned with the positive attempt or hope of bettering their own situation as with the desire that others should be denied the satisfactions and enjoyments which they feel are being withheld from themselves. Resentment, in other words, is different from mere envy or the wish to have what somebody else has got.'[14] Harris and Klebold's sense of indignation was both mirrored and nurtured by the violent videos that they often watched. One such movie depicted Leonardo Di Caprio gunning down pupils in a school. As part of a class project the disaffected youths made a video of their own. It showed people in trench coats shooting athletes in the school corridors. Apparently they were upset when they were not allowed to show it to their classmates. Sin was clearly crouching at the door of their hearts, and instead of mastering it, they allowed it to master them. It would appear that over a period of time the youths planned to attack their school with guns and bombs. On an internet site, Harris said that he couldn't wait to start killing people. He added that he would do so without remorse. These were the sentiments of a resentful psychopath.

As we know, the two young men did engage in the vengeful violence they had threatened. They killed the people they envied most, athletes, and devout Christians. In the library one of them singled out Cassie Bernall. 'Do you believe in God?' he asked. As soon as she said: 'Yes, I do believe in God,' he shot her. Some time later Harris and Klebold shot themselves. The anger and loathing that they had projected outwards was finally redirected inwards and they did to themselves what they had already done to their victims.

Acknowledging Envy
How does one overcome envy? I think that step one is diagnostic.

It involves two points. Firstly, try to recall, have you been the object of envy by a member of your family, by colleagues at work or by a rival in the world of business or sport? How was the envy expressed, e.g. by ignoring your achievements, telling critical stories about you behind your back, using barbed, sarcastic humour to embarrass and belittle you in public? Were you treated unfairly? How did you react? Were you confused and deeply hurt? Did you begin to hide or even deny your gifts and achievements in order not to evoke the envy of others? Did you loose self-belief and confidence as a result of the resentment of others?

Secondly, are you inclined to be envious yourself? By and large those who are prone to this attitude suffer from tell-tale attitudes. Ask yourself the following questions: Do you often suffer from a lack of self-acceptance and low self-esteem? Are you overly ambitious to get on well in life, in sport, relationships, work, academic pursuits, etc.? Does your self-image depend upon your achievements? Are you very competitive, seeing other people, family members, peers, and fellow workers as rivals rather than collaborators? Do you suffer from excessive self-reference. Instead of admiring the gifts and successes of others in their own right, do you tend to compare yourself unfavourably with them?

Overcoming Envy

All of us need to consciously acknowledge the envy which may have been secretly informing our relationships with people we regard as superior to ourselves, in one way or another. I have discovered that there are a number of ways of overcoming such envy.

Notice the first intimations of this attitude. St Thomas Aquinas commented: 'The first stirrings of envy are non-fatal sins, and may be found in holy men and women.'[15] If we fail to tackle incipient envy it can spawn such things as proud, self-centred, critical, judgmental, resentful and vengeful attitudes.

By the grace of God some people avoid ever committing serious sins. However, this fortunate fact can lead them to share in the self-righteous attitudes of the Scribes and Pharisees by saying: 'God I thank you that I am not like other people' (Lk 18:11). Sometimes the Lord allows us to commit more serious sins so that we have to surrender the illusion of self-sufficiency, and have to rely solely on the divine mercy (cf. Rom 11:32). It is only when one is deeply convinced that grace is unmerited, as a result of firm trust in the efficacy of Christ's death and resurrection, that one will be truly freed from envy.

We have to recognise our call to be our true selves with our own special gifts of nature and grace. If we have a sense of divine providence, not only will we believe that God has a unique plan for each of our lives, we will also be convinced that he has blessed us with whatever we need to carry it out (cf. Phil 2:13).

If we have feelings of inferiority, we need to have a growing sense that God lives within us by the Spirit, and that God the Father sees and loves in us what he sees and loves in Jesus (cf. Mt 3:17). For more on this point see chapter eleven.

Instead of seeing others in an individualistic way as rivals with whom we must compete, we can see them as people we co-operate with in the Body of Christ. If one member of the community is blessed with a special talent or gift of grace, all are blessed in and through that person (cf. 1 Cor 12:12, 27).

We need to have a grateful sense that all gifts, our own and those of others, are unmerited. We need to focus on this truth in whatever way it manifests itself. As St John Chrysostom once wisely wrote: 'Would you like to see God glorified by you? Then rejoice in your brother or sister's progress and you will immediately give glory to God. Because his servant could conquer envy by rejoicing in the merits of others.'[16] St Teresa of Avila wrote: 'If you hear someone being highly praised, do not be envious, but rather be more pleased than if they were praising you. This will become easy if you are humble ... To be glad when your neighbour's virtues are praised is a wonderful thing.'[17]

Often Christians learn to do what John Chrysostom and Teresa of Avila advocate, in their intimate friendships. Because a friend is a second self, I rejoice to know that s/he is blessed with gifts and success. In a self-forgetful way friends say, 'I'm delighted that you are realising your potential and becoming what you are.' There is a great example of the way in which friends delight in each other's gifts and achievements in the writings of St Gregory Nazianzen. St Basil the Great was his intimate friend. Speaking about their Christian friendship he says: 'We were driven on by equal hopes in the pursuit of learning, a thing especially open to envy. But there was no envy between us and competition intensified our zeal. For there was indeed a contest between us. But it was not as to who should have first place for himself but how he could yield it to the other. For each of us regarded the achievement of the other as his own.'[18] It would appear that by loving friends in a selfless way, we learn to love all other people in the same way.

We can pray for repeated outpourings of the Spirit of love (cf. Eph 5:18). As the poet Goethe once rightly observed: 'Against another's great merit, there is no remedy but love.'[19]

Conclusion

This reflection began by suggesting that envy, not hatred, was the true antithesis to love. Instead of carrying out the Golden Rule of treating others the way we would like to be treated ourselves (Lk 6:31), it does the opposite. Envious, resentful and jealous people are solely concerned with their self-image. They strongly desire to have a positive one and to have other people see and appreciate their good points. But instead of approving of the good points of others, they disapprove of them. They do to others what they would not want done to them (cf. Job 4:15). While it is true that pride is the root of all sin, surely envy is one of its most insidious and unloving manifestations. Ironically, while envious people begin by attacking others, they end up wounding themselves most of all. As a Russian poet has wisely observed: 'A show of envy is an insult to oneself.'[20] So by definition envious people cannot love their neighbours as themselves (cf. Mt 19:19; Rom 13:11).

CHAPTER FIVE

Boundary Violations in Ministry[1]

Pastoral ministry is more demanding than ever. The pace and pressure of life is causing increasing strain for many people. As a result a growing number of men and women are suffering from psycho-spiritual problems such as anxiety, depression, grief, anger, loss of meaning, etc. Understandably, many of them are turning to carers of one kind or another, including priests and religious, for assistance. Some are disappointed because their local pastors are either unwilling or unable to help. There are a number of possible reasons for this. Some say that, because of the current shortage of priests, they don't have the time to counsel individual parishioners. Others feel threatened by people with emotional problems because they are struggling with unresolved difficulties of their own. Others feel that they are not trained to get involved in this kind of demanding pastoral care, so they tend to refer parishioners to doctors, social workers, counsellors, etc.

I'm convinced that one of the most important ways that priests and others can 'shepherd' modern day Christians, is by spending quality time with those who have been afflicted in one way or another. Sometimes all that is needed is an hour's chat, concluding perhaps with a prayer. At other times, a number of face to face meetings may be needed. The parishioner may want to talk about emotionally charged personal issues such as bereavement, marriage breakdown, depression, addiction, sexual problems, etc. This kind of pastoral contact can be draining. It has led some priests and pastoral carers to experience unhealthy levels of stress and even burn-out. In this chapter I want to focus on a specific but related issue, namely, the dangers that can arise in pastoral relationships between priests and female parishioners. They can lead, not only to emotional problems of different kinds but also to inappropriate behaviour, infidelity and scandal. Obviously what I say about the dynamics of priestly ministry to females could be adapted to fit many other caring relationships. For instance, it could equally apply to females, whether lay or religious, offering counselling or spiritual direction to men. I wrote this chapter this specific way, mainly because many priests have been in the news because they have failed to observe boundaries in relationships with women and children.

In the caring professions many of these problems are attributed to the phenomenon of projection, which was briefly discussed in the chapter on religion and violence. Nowadays it is common for people such as psychiatrists, therapists, counsellors and spiritual directors[2] to talk about two interrelated forms of emotional projection. In Freudian terms, there is the problem of transference and counter transference. In Jungian terms there is the propensity to project the *animus* or *anima* on to a member of the opposite sex. Either of these dynamics can occur in interpersonal relationships of a pastoral kind.

Transference and counter transference

The notion of transference and counter transference has been widely used in recent years in the caring professions to explain romantic and erotic attachments in particular. We will propose a brief definition of each term. Incidentally, instead of talking about helping relationships in general, the focus centres on the relationship between a priest and his female parishioners. Remember that the word priest could be applied to any carer. We will use the word parishioner in a generic way to refer to clients, counsellees, or directees whether they are from the parish or not. We will refer rather loosely to the purpose of such relationships as psycho-spiritual counselling.

Transference is the unconscious projection of hopes, desires, and fears, from one person on to another. It occurs when feelings and attitudes to do with significant people in the parishioner's past life, especially parents or siblings, are transferred on to the priest. Freud described this unconscious dynamic in these words: 'By *transference* is meant a striking peculiarity of neurotics. They develop toward their physician emotional relations, both of an affectionate and hostile character, which are not based upon the actual situation but are derived from their relations toward their parents.'[3] Freud was of the opinion that, by and large, transference was a form of resistance. Instead of acknowledging, owning and dealing with her feelings, the parishioner disowns them by projecting them on to the priest.

Counter transference is a reversal of transference. It occurs when the priest projects his feelings on to the parishioner because she unconsciously reminds him of a significant person in his past. The priest's counter transference can often be evoked by the parishioner's transference. It is most likely to occur when the parishioner's transference corresponds to the contents of the priest's own unconscious, for example, a need to belong because of poor bonding with his mother in early life. The counter transference may be so intense as to interfere with a realistic understanding of the parishioner. Not surprisingly, therefore, people in the caring professions believe that those involved in helping others, need to come to terms with the contents of their unconscious minds. Otherwise they might surface in the form of counter transference. Nowadays most pastoral training programmes put considerable emphasis on the importance of in depth self-knowledge for would-be carers.

There are three characteristic kinds of transference and counter transference: negative, erotic and sensible.

Negative transference occurs when the parishioner projects negative feelings, such as anger, distrust and fear, on to the priest. Jung drew attention to the fact that a parishioner can project her shadow, i.e. her inferior, neglected, unacknowledged self, on to the priest. He, in turn, may project unacknowledged negative feelings from his past, or his unconscious shadow, on to the parishioner whose transference may have evoked his counter transference. S/he will see and reject in the other what s/he fails to acknowledge or accept in him or herself.

Sensible transference is more realistic and positive. The parishioner may see the priest as a father figure, a benevolent and supportive ally in her struggle against dysfunctional feelings and attitudes.

Erotic transference turns the priest into the object of romantic love and sexual desire. Freud noticed, as a result of his own personal experience, that a helper, such as a priest, can experience the counter transference of feelings such as admiration, tenderness and sexual attraction. They may be rooted in repressed sexual longings and unresolved emotional issues from his own past.

Physical contact between the priest and parishioner would tend to reinforce transference and counter transference of a romantic and erotic kind.[4] As a result, while a priest might shake hands with a parishioner who comes to him for spiritual counselling, he would be wise not to put his arm around her shoulder, to pat her on the back, to hold her hand or to hug, embrace, or kiss her during their time together. Even though such gestures might be intended to express sympathy in a reassuring and innocent way, they could be misinterpreted either as sexual harassment or as a sign of romantic love. By and large, they are imprudent and inappropriate. In any case, for personal reasons, some parishoners will be quite uncomfortable about bodily contact. It is interesting to note that Freud insisted that the analysts he trained should always observe this rule.

We can take a brief look at an example of romantic/erotic transference and counter transference. A single woman of thirty five asks a local priest for spiritual counselling because she trusts him. She regards him as a reliable and dedicated celibate who will not make a pass at her. She also believes that he is both knowledgeable and understanding. When she confides in him she senses an empathy and sensitivity that she hasn't experienced for some time. This helps her to consciously appreciate something of the goodness and tenderness of God. At the level of unconscious awareness she feels like a child who is being held in the arms of a nurturing parent. In reality, the parishioner has fallen in love with the remembered feeling of being loved and cherished as a baby, and consequently may think that she has fallen in love with the priest. The woman's positive attitude to the priest may evoke an answering counter transference in him. At a conscious level he may find the young woman attractive and fascinating. But at an unconscious level something else could be happening. He has always yearned for a closer connection with his mother. The bonding between them was never good because she was prone to intermittent bouts of depression when he was growing up. As a result he has often been troubled by nagging feelings of separation anxiety. Now, as a priest in his early forties, he often feels lonely and longs for a sense of belonging. As he senses the woman's increasing devotion and dependence he mistakes it for true love and finds himself falling in love with her.

If he is unprofessional, he may arrange to meet the woman more frequently and for longer than the one hour he would normally devote to spiritual counselling. Instead of seeing her as a 'client' he begins to see her as a 'friend', and to meet her socially. He may even show her physical affection in an intimate and inappropriate way. While the priest and the parishioner may rationalise their behaviour, believing that their relationship is a sacred gift, from a psychological point of view it is an instance of transference and counter transference. In reality it has led the priest to violate professional boundaries in such a way that it is likely that the relationship will end in grief for the woman he is supposed to be helping. Although one could give many other examples of this dynamic, e.g. drawn from the priest's relationships with female co-workers, social acquaintances or friends, they would be similar. The only important difference would be the fact that, in a helping relationship especially, the priest is in a responsible position of authority. As a result, transference and counter transference are more likely.

Projection of the animus and anima

The English word 'sex' is derived from the Latin *secare* which means to cut or to divide. The sexes are divided, one from the other, in two interrelated ways. Firstly, they are divided from one another by physical and psychological differences. Some of the latter can be attributed to nature, others to nurture, i.e. the influence of cultural prejudices and stereotypes. Secondly, men and women are divided within themselves. Carl Jung suggested that all of us are bisexual from a psychological point of view.[5]

At a conscious level a man is predominately male. But at an unconscious level of awareness he has a feminine dimension or *anima*. The man's, largely unconscious, image of the feminine is a synthesis of impressions created by the women in his life, especially his mother. Conversely, at a conscious level, a woman is predominately female, but at an unconscious level of awareness there is a masculine dimension or *animus*. The woman's image of the masculine is a composite, made up of impressions of the men in her life, especially her father. As far as Jung was concerned, the *animus* and *anima* were archetypes of the unconscious mind, i.e. structured patterns of a psychological kind which are similar to biological instincts.

He believed that the *animus* and *anima* often expressed themselves in the form of mythological images drawn from the collective unconscious, i.e. the collective memory of the human race. For example, a woman might idealise the masculine side of her nature in images such as the hero, shaman, king, wise man, etc. A man might idealise the feminine side of his nature in images such as the princess, huntress, priestess, earth-mother, etc. He believed that by means of heterosexual intimacy of a realistic kind, men and women could be reconciled not only to one another but also to the male and female sides of their own inner selves.

However, Jung believed that when a priest and a female parishioner relate in a one-to-one ministry situation, an unrealistic projection of the *animus* and *anima* can occur. This is especially likely if the priest or the female parishioner have failed to consciously come to terms with the female or male aspects of their unconscious minds. Incidentally, Jung didn't think that marriage, as many Protestant clergy have discovered, necessarily puts a person in touch with either his or her *anima* or *animus*. As a result the priest may project his unconscious ideal of femininity on to a female parishioner who has come to see him for spiritual counselling. She becomes the carrier of this magical image of womanly perfection. The woman, for her part, may project her *animus*, i.e. her unconscious image of male perfection, on to the priest. In Jungian terms this is the deceptive experience of falling in love. While it is a powerful, hypnotic and even a numinous experience, it isn't entirely realistic. Until the projections are withdrawn, the priest and the woman are actually loving projected aspects of themselves in one another. This kind of romantic self-absorption is dangerous because it can lead to different kinds of blindness and boundary violation. To adapt a phrase: 'O romantic love, what follies are committed in your name!'

Predictable effects of counter transference and projection
When romantic or erotic feelings and desires are stirred up in a priest, it is important that he deal with them. He is faced with three options.

Firstly, he may recognise that as a result of counter transference, or projection of his *anima*, he needs to end the ministerial relationship by referring the woman to someone else. Obviously this is the responsible and prudent thing to do. However, if he fell in love with a female friend the situation would be different. In those circumstances one could argue that instead of ending the relationship, the priest should try to recognise his projected *anima*, to withdraw it from his friend, and to consciously acknowledge it as part of his inner self. If the woman was in love with him, she could try, with the help of others perhaps, to recognise, withdraw and integrate her projected *animus*.

Secondly, the priest may decide to leave the ministry in order to marry the woman. He might do this without being laicised, thereby scandalising some people.

Thirdly, he might try to rationalise the situation by thinking it is all right to have a sexualised relationship while continuing the spiritual counselling. His pastoral meetings with his woman 'friend', who may be married, separated or divorced, would then be used as a smokescreen for more intimate purposes. Sooner or later such a man would have to end the relationship. Research indicates that, when a priest ignores professional and vocational boundaries in this way, the woman is usually badly affected. She is likely to feel rejected, betrayed, angry, ashamed, depressed, and guilty for having engaged in a clandestine and abusive relationship. As a result, she may reject everything to do with the institutional church, feel angry with God, distrust all authority figures, become confused about her sexuality, and need expensive therapy to deal with the knock-on psycho-spiritual effects.

A Case Study
At this point we will illustrate the points made so far by looking at a case study. See what you make of it.

I am a secretary in a parish which is run by a religious order. I had an affair with the parish priest. At that time, I was experiencing a tremendous amount of stress and stress-related illness in my life. It was due to problems in both my personal life and my work. My emotional needs were being ignored. I needed help and, unfortunately, I turned to the wrong person. Instead of my problems being lessened, they were added to. It has now been almost a year since the affair ended and I'm still suffering, suffering alone. At times I feel like telling my story to others. At other times I am burdened with feelings of guilt and depression. I refuse to take the chance of ruining the priest's career and reputation as a result of my sharing my problems.

Seduction is easy for priests because very often they are involved in counselling women who are overstressed and hurting, women who are vulnerable, women like me who need help, not hugs; women who need someone who cares enough to listen, advise and encourage. They do not need physical closeness. Because of their pain, they may want it, but they do not need it.

My problem arose when the priest, who was also my employer, responded to my cry for help by hugging me. At first I interpreted this hugging as a caring act. But before long the hugging turned into long, passionate embraces. We quickly recognised that we were both in trouble. We felt a strong emotional and physical need to be together. For some time our feelings grew stronger and we seemed powerless to escape. I have struggled with the question, 'How could I have let this happen?' In the beginning I felt I had no control. I was being held closely by a man I trusted and who had control over me. As my boss and my parish priest, he held the power position in our relationship and he used it. At that particular time, I was unable to push him away. I was defenseless. I was hurting and I wanted to be held and comforted. I was too weak to stop the progression of his advances. I was afraid that if I said no to him, he wouldn't talk to me anymore and, at the time, I truly thought I desperately needed his emotional support.

The priest I was involved with is extremely dedicated and committed to his ministry and to Christ. He is well known both within and beyond the diocese. He seems to have friends and colleagues throughout the country. So now I know from bitter experience that a man is not exempt from sexual immorality simply because he is a priest.

In my case, the recovery process is taking an extremely long period of time. I am angry, ashamed, and full of guilt. I rang up the *Faoiseamh* line, which was established by the Irish religious orders to offer free counselling to the victims of abuse by their members.[6] Currently, I am in therapy, at their expense, and am trying to understand how and why I could have let this happen. I'm trying to free myself from the bondage of depression. I am also attending a doctor and am taking antidepressants and sleeping pills. In spite of all my efforts, I'm still adversely affected by what has happened. I have to admit that there have been times when I felt so low that I have been tempted to commit suicide.

My priest friend did not seek counselling. He has chosen to keep the whole sorry experience locked up inside. Perhaps he feels the episode is now in the past. Perhaps he has mentioned it in confession and thinks that it has all been taken care of and over. But, as far as I'm concerned it is not over. I still have inner pain and until I am healthy and happy again, it will not be over.

I left the parish, both as secretary and as a parishioner, not because I wanted to, but because I had to. I felt driven to protect this man with whom I had been intimate. The church tells us to flee from temptation and that is what I chose to do. I followed my head, not my heart. I miss my friends, I miss the church, but most of all, I miss my work.

Nowadays when I listen to a sermon, I often find my mind wandering. I wonder about the personal life of the priest who is speaking instead of his message. I often wonder, 'Are these empty words, does this man practice what he preaches, or are his teachings just for others?' My trust is in the Lord; I cannot yet bring myself to trust in any priests. But, although I am not involved in any particular parish at present, I visit a different church most Sundays for Mass. I cannot yet permit myself to get involved in any particular community. I'm afraid of getting hurt again. Memories are powerful, they creep into your mind when you're not looking, sometimes even when you're sleeping. Sometimes they are prompted by something you're reading, or by something on radio or TV. You can push them aside and go on. But you can never be free of them.

Before reading any further, you might like to reflect on the following questions.

- What did you feel as you read this account?
- Is the woman abdicating responsibility for her part in the affair?
- What kind of relationship existed between the woman and the priest?
- Does the priest need counselling as the woman suggests?
- If you were to pick out the single most important point the woman made, what would it be?

A constructive way forward

A priest who wants to be conscientious about interpersonal relationships could ask himself the following interrelated questions. Firstly, 'I know that I give out lots of emotional energy to other people, but where do I get my energy from?' Secondly, he could ask, 'I know that I care for many people, but who cares for me?' While many priests, like many lay people, find it easy to describe how they expend their energy and who they care for, they often find it difficult to name the sources of their energy or the people who care for them. Men like this are at risk. They are likely to try, albeit in an unconscious way, to find both energy and emotional caring by means of improper dependency relationships with women who come to them for help.

A priest needs to be consciously aware of the different kinds of roles and relationships he has with women, such as those of employer, colleague, spiritual counsellor, social acquaintance, brother, son, relative, and friend. While it is good to express Christian love in all of these roles and relationships, he needs to appreciate that different codes of behaviour are appropriate in each. For example, if he is meeting a woman for spiritual counselling he should make it clear how often they will meet, e.g. once every three weeks, and for how long, e.g. for no more than an hour. It is best to stick to such an understanding and to avoid both physical and social contact, e.g. having meals together.

If possible a priest would be well advised to do a counselling course, such as a ten week unit of Clinical Pastoral Education (CPE). As I know from personal experience, it could help him to grow in listening skills and self-knowledge. It would alert him to the need for a regular self-awareness exercise, such as the one described in the first chapter. That would give him an opportunity to recognise, name, own, and understand what he feels about the events of the day, especially his encounters with females.

Needless to say, the priest needs to develop a real as opposed to a notional understanding of his sexual needs and vulnerabilities, e.g. his sensitivity to the seductive vibes of some female parishioners, as well as a knowledge of the ways in which his own affective attitude is perceived by them. For example, some of his female friends might have noticed that he can be flirtatious in subtle ways. To grow in such self-awareness it can also be helpful to take one's dreams seriously, because they are, as Freud said, 'the royal road to the unconscious'.

It is also wise to talk to a confidant, such as a confessor or spiritual director, about a problematic relationship with a female parishioner. Supervision groups serve much the same purpose. They are made up of people in the caring professions, e.g. counsellors and directors, who talk about their contact with parishioners with a view to helping one another to recognise things like transference and counter transference. At a typical meeting a participant reads a verbatim, i.e. a segment of a recent conversation with some client. The group then assist the one who has made the presentation to look more closely at his or her neglected emotions and attitudes. Often this kind of friendly probing can uncover incipient but unrecognised feelings, e.g. of a romantic or sexual kind.

I'm convinced, that the best protection against improper relationships in ministry are good, healthy friendships of a same sex or a heterosexual kind. One can talk openly and frankly to a friend about anything and everything including relationships with members of the opposite sex. Friends can often throw a sympathetic but objective light on what one has said. They may be aware of unacknowledged feelings of a romantic kind. As Shakespeare wrote: 'And since you know you cannot see yourself so well as by reflection, I your glass, will modestly discover to yourself that of yourself which you yet know not of' (*Julius Caesar* Act 1, Sc II). Furthermore, if his intimacy needs are being met in this way, in a genuine friendship, not only will a priest grow in psycho-sexual maturity, he will be less likely to use parishioners, albeit in an unconscious way, to satisfy unacknowledged personal needs.

Conclusion
Although the contemporary church is administered by male clergy, the majority of the people they minister to are female. Priests need to avoid two extremes, not engaging in one-to-one contact with women on the one hand, and violating professional and vocational boundaries through improper conduct on the other. In these days of heightened expectations, when women are aware of issues such as sexual harassment and psycho-sexual abuse, priests need to grow out of a culpable naïvete in these matters so that they can show the compassion of Christ in a responsible and knowing way. The on-going formation committees in the different dioceses would do well to arrange workshops which deal with all these issues in an insightful and practical way. They could point out that while it is true that there are some dangers implicit in helping relationships, the fruits they can bear, far outweigh them. Not only can a priest mediate the healing and strengthening love of God to women through one-to-one spiritual counselling, he himself will be blessed in many ways as a result. One has only to think of Jesus' encounter with the Samaritan woman at the well of Sychar to see how this is true.

CHAPTER SIX

Is Prayer Good For Your Health?[1]

A growing percentage of people seem to be motivated by a personal search for wholeness. That might explain why self-help books are so popular. They inform their readers about such things as how to get in touch with the inner child, heal hurting memories, develop creative potential and increase self-esteem. They also explain how to foster physical wellbeing by means of such things as diet, exercise, imaginative visualisation, biofeedback and relaxation exercises. It is arguable, however, that the holistic self-fulfilment so many people desire will elude them, to a greater or lesser extent, until they become consciously aware of the mystery of God in their lives.

Prayer and Mental Health
Twentieth-century psychology conducted an important debate about the relationship between religious experience and mental health. Sigmund Freud believed that religion was a form of obsessional neurosis. He maintained that God was nothing other than an exalted father, a projection of the need for otherworldly care and protection. So if people wanted to become psychologically healthy, they had to abandon their childish religious belief, take responsibility for their lives and learn to live in a realistic way, in a world that is often harsh, without the aid of this emotional crutch.

In marked contrast Carl Jung argued forcefully that the human psyche could only be fulfilled when the individual enjoyed a conscious awareness of the numinous, i.e. the divine. For example, in *Psychology and Western Religion* he wrote: 'In thirty years I have treated many patients in the second half of life. Every one of them became ill because he or she had lost that which the living religions in every age have given their followers, (i.e. religious experience) and none of them was fully healed who did not regain his religious outlook.' Jung went on to add: 'This of course has nothing whatever to do with a particular creed or membership of a church.'[2] It is interesting to note that among Jung's neurotic patients were a number of clergymen. He believed that although they were devoted to their religious duties in a conscientious way, they were lacking integration because of an inner famine of the experience of God.

In general terms Viktor Frankl agreed with Jung. He felt that in modern culture a lack of prayerful religious experience left people with a vacuum at the centre of their lives. In *Man's Search for Meaning,* he said that this emptiness caused existential frustration, which he described elsewhere as 'the unrewarded longing and groping of men and women for ... an ultimate meaning to their lives.'[3] He maintained that when people's underdeveloped and restricted spirits were deprived of the oxygen of meaning, their psyches became disorientated. Consequently they suffered from predictable neurotic problems such as addiction, obsession and violent tendencies, together with an unhealthy and sometimes idolatrous preoccupation with things like money, power, status, and pleasure especially of a sexual kind.[4]

Abraham Maslow's research also indicated that rather than being a sign of neurosis, as Freud had maintained, religious experience was a sign of psycho-spiritual health. Instead of forming a picture of the psyche as a result of studying dysfunctional people, Maslow formed his views as a result of studying people who were highly integrated. He found that self-actualised men and women tend to have more peak-experiences than others do. He also found that many of the ecstatic episodes of heightened consciousness they reported were religious in nature. They were clearly an indication of psycho-spiritual health and served to strengthen a sense of well-being and harmony. In *Religions, Values and Peak Experiences* he stated his belief that the power of prayerful peak-experiences 'could permanently affect one's attitude to life ... It is my strong suspicion that one such experience might be able to prevent suicide and perhaps many varieties of low self-destruction such as alcoholism, drug addiction, and addiction to violence.'[5]

In an article entitled, 'Religious Orientation and Psycho-logical Well-being: The Role of the Frequency of Personal Prayer,' three researchers examined the effects of what Gordon Allport referred to as intrinsic religion, on mental health.[6] People who have intrinsic, as opposed to extrinsic religion, are those who have internalised their faith in such a way that it influences every aspect of their everyday lives. Instead of engaging in infrequent prayer of a ritualistic kind, they spend time in regular prayer of a personal, God-centred variety. Consequently, they are more inclined to have conscious awareness of the divine, and are more likely to have higher than average levels of self-esteem together with lower than average levels of anxiety and depression. These conclusions have been confirmed by a number of other studies.

Prayer and freedom from addiction

Those who advocate the use of twelve step programmes in order to overcome process and substance addictions, accept that prayerful religious experience seems to be the only really effective antidote to the obsessional, frustrated self. For example, in a letter to one of the founders of Alcoholics Anonymous, Carl Jung suggested that the alcoholic's thirst for drink, i.e. spirits, was a misdirected thirst for the Spirit, i.e. the divine. This kind of thirst can only be satisfied as a result of a spiritual awakening, whether sudden or gradual. There are many graphic accounts of how addicted people had such liberating experiences. For example, Dr Bill Wilson, one of the founders of AA, described how he was delivered from his destructive addiction at the age of thirty-nine. He said: 'I became acutely conscious of a Presence which seemed like a veritable sea of living Spirit … For the first time I felt I really belonged. I knew that I was loved and could love in return.'[7]

Sometime afterwards, Dr Wilson wrote: 'Salvation in Alcoholics Anonymous consisted in emerging from isolation to the feeling of being at one with God and man, to the sense of belonging that comes to us.' While an addicted person's healing begins with the spiritual awakening envisioned in step three, it is deepened by following the subsequent steps. For example, number eleven states: 'Sought by prayer and meditation to improve our conscious contact with God as we understood him, praying only for a knowledge of his will for us and the power to carry that out.'[8]

Prayer and Physical Health

The scriptures encourage believers to pray with expectancy for healing of our own bodies and the bodies of others. In Sir 38:9 we read: 'My child, when you are ill, delay not, but pray to God, who will heal you.' Later the same chapter says: 'There are times when good health depends on doctors, for they in their turn, will pray the Lord to grant them the grace to relieve and to heal, and so prolong your life' (Sir 38:13). In the New Testament Jas 5:14-15 advocates anointing sick people, in a prayerful way, with oil: 'Is any one of you sick? He should call the elders of the church to pray over him and anoint him with oil in the name of the Lord. And the prayer offered in faith will make the sick person well; the Lord will raise him up.' Healing can also be experienced as a result of the prayerful laying on of hands. In Mk 16: 17-18 we read: 'And these signs will accompany those who believe ... they will place their hands on sick people, and they will get well.'

Early in the twentieth century Alexis Carrel, who won the Nobel Prize for medicine in 1912, maintained in *Man the Unknown* that prayer could bring about positive changes in the body. Speaking about such improvements he wrote: 'These organic phenomena are observed in various circumstances, among them being the state of prayer ... Prayer should be understood not as a mere mechanical recitation of formulas, but as a mystical elevation, an absorption of consciousness in the contemplation of a principle both permeating and transcending our world.'[9] Carrel said that such prayer could, in some instances, bring about miraculous cures. Some time later he investigated the miracles at Lourdes. He was so convinced that they could only be explained by the power of prayer and the influence of the Holy Spirit that he became a Christian.

There is a growing body of evidence to support his overall point of view.[10] For example, by using the electroencephalograph, or EEG, Maxwell Cade of the Psychobiology Institute in London discovered in the 1970s that when reputable healers are praying, they have strong alpha and theta rhythms, of 7 to 13 cycles a second, in both halves of their brains.[11] Although they are wide awake, these are the rhythms characteristic of the sleeping state. After about 15 minutes or so their client's beta rhythms of 14 to 20 cycles per second begin to mirror those of the healer, thereby bringing about the kind of deep relaxation that seems to be conducive to recovery.

Dr Randolph Byrd conducted another interesting study in 1988. He got born-again Christians to pray for 393 patients in a coronary care unit.[12] They were divided into an experimental and a control group as is normal in scientific studies of this kind. The patients, hospital staff and Byrd himself were unaware, throughout the research, of which of the patients were receiving daily prayer for their recovery. At the end of the experiment, statistical analysis suggested that the group who were prayed for suffered fewer instances of congestive heart failure, cardiopulmonary arrest and pneumonia than the control group. Furthermore, fewer of them required diuretics, antibiotics or ventilatory support.

In 1998, Dr Elisabeth Targ and her colleagues at California Pacific Medical Center in San Francisco, conducted a controlled, double-blind study of the effects of 'distant healing,' by means of prayer, on patients with advanced AIDS. Those patients receiving prayer survived in greater numbers, got sick less often, and recovered faster than those not receiving prayer. Prayer, in this study, looked like a medical breakthrough.

Around the year 2000, Dr Mitchell Krucoff at Duke University Medical Center in Durham, North Carolina, studied the effects of prayer on patients undergoing cardiac procedures such as catheterisation and angioplasty. Apparently, patients receiving prayer had up to 100% fewer side effects from these procedures than people not prayed for.

These are impressive double-blind studies, meaning that no one knows who is receiving prayer and who isn't. This eliminates or at least reduces the placebo effect, which is the power of suggestion or positive thinking. However, other impressive studies have been done on non human life. For example, when bacteria are prayed for, they tend to grow faster; when seeds are prayed for, they tend to germinate quicker; when wounded mice are prayed for, they tend to heal faster. These studies are convincing because they can be done with great precision, and they eliminate the influence of suggestion and positive thinking, since we can be sure the results aren't due to the placebo effect. Mice, seeds, and microbes, presumably, don't think positively!

Michael Argyle has shown in his *Psychology and Religion*, that research has tended to confirm the fact that prayerful religious experience does indeed help people to enjoy better physical health.[13] For example, he cites the fact that Hummer studied 21,000 responses to the American National Health Interview Survey. He concluded that on average, churchgoers of twenty years of age had a life expectancy which was seven years longer than the average. Apparently it was due to the fact that these believers enjoyed better community support and were less likely to engage in risky activities such as smoking, drinking to excess, or promiscuous sex.

Implications

Dr Larry Dossey, author of the best selling, *Prayer is Good Medicine*[14] was asked what were the implications of research results like these. He responded by saying that he and his wife were invited to consult with a large hospital in a major city. The Chief Executive Officers (CEOs) and a few doctors on the staff had become aware of the evidence supporting the health effects of religious devotion and prayer. How, they asked, should they respond to this evidence? Should they relegate responsibility to the clergy or to hospital chaplains? Should the doctors and nurses play an active role? A meeting was held that involved prominent leaders of the community. One woman stated, 'If I were sick and came to this hospital, and you didn't offer me some form of spiritual support, I would be very angry!'

This illustrates the situation hospitals face. The American public, by and large, wants spiritual support to be available. A survey on the East Coast of the United States found that 75% of hospitalised patients believed their doctor should be concerned about their spiritual welfare; and 50% wanted their doctor to pray not only for them, but with them. In response to the evidence which shows a positive role of prayer and spirituality on health, 61 of America's 126 medical schools were offering courses on spirituality and health in 1999. Duke University has established a Centre for the study of Religion/Spirituality and health. The fact that young doctors are now learning about these issues is an important indicator of future developments. Indeed, it has even been suggested that, in the future, disappointed patients might take legal action against those doctors who overlook the spiritual dimension of healing. I suspect that the same trends could develop here in Ireland as well.

Conclusion

Western medicine readily accepts that there is a psycho-somatic dimension to many illnesses. Nowadays there is a growing body of evidence which suggests that we could talk of pneuma-psycho-somatic disorders, i.e. illnesses that have a spiritual dimension. It is both interesting and encouraging to find that in many instances the research findings of psychiatrists and medical experts tend to confirm the fact that prayerful religious experience can have a positively healing effect upon mind and body. It would appear that, all things being equal, those who pray in a personal way are healthier on average that those who don't. Of course, prayerful people can suffer from serious illnesses. But overall, the available evidence indicates that prayer is good for your health.

CHAPTER SEVEN

Mass Means of Communication and Religious Experience[1]

When I was a child, a number of things could evoke a sort of religious wonder in me. For example, at one time a favourite book of mine was about Rupert the bear. One chapter recounted, in words and enchanting images, how Rupert and his parents flew on white winged horses to a cave under the sea. It glowed and twinkled with a greenish mystical light and was peopled by elf like creatures with diaphanous wings. To me it was a magical place, one that evoked feelings of awe and wonder. I have always thought that there was something numinous about that story. It intimated that beneath the appearances of every day life there exists another more mysterious reality.

In adult life I have often felt that radio has some of the same magical qualities that I once associated with Rupert's cave. I first became interested in broadcasting as a young boy. In the late 1950s I read an article which described how to construct a simple crystal set. I proceeded to buy a diode, capacitor, earphones, and some insulated antenna wire in a city centre shop. When I got home I wrapped some wire around a toilet roll to form a coil and attached it to the capacitor and crystal diode. Then I placed the lot inside an Oxo tin. I attached the antenna wire to the radio, fed it out my bedroom window and tied it to the clothes line at the end of the back garden. When I was snugly wrapped up in bed I would don the earphones, tune in, and wonder of wonders, I could hear different stations, principally Radios Éireann, Luxembourg, and Moscow. Invisible radio waves from all over the world were picked up by the antenna, and translated into intelligible sounds I could listen to. What added to the sense of magic was the fact that the set needed no electricity.

Ever since then I have not been rational, as far as radio is concerned. Over the years I must have bought dozens of receivers. My particular fascination is with short wave sets, the kind that can pick up all kinds of distant stations. If I purchase a good receiver, inevitably I'll see an even better one soon afterwards. As a result I become disenchanted with the one I currently own and dream of buying a more refined and up to date model which is capable of picking up weaker, more remote signals. Currently, I'm fascinated by the potential of Digital Audio Broadcasting (DAB) and WorldSpace radio which bounces digital signals off geo-stationary satellites which are orbiting about 24,000 miles above the earth. When I travel away from home, as I often do, packing my radio is a priority. When I arrive at my destination the first thing I do is to tune in my transistor to local stations and to the BBC world service. As soon as I have done this I feel as if I have truly arrived and that I am temporarily at home in the new location.

Transitional Objects

A few years ago it occurred to me that my fascination with radio amounted to a relatively harmless addiction. I began to ask myself the question, why do you suffer from this strange obsession? A possible answer occurred to me some time ago when I was teaching a psychology course. It was about the way in which object relations theory can throw light on the understanding of conscious awareness of God. William Meissner describes it in his book *Psychoanalysis and Religious Experience*.[2]

When we are babies we enjoy a sense symbiotic union with our mothers. It is sometimes referred to as 'oceanic feeling'. We feel as if we are at one with them, especially while being nourished at the breast. As Tennyson wrote in his poem *In Memoriam*:

The baby new to earth and sky
What time his tender palm is prest
Against the circle of the breast
Has never thought that 'This is I.'

Of course the time comes when we have to separate from our mothers in order to establish a separate sense of personal identity. Speaking of the growing baby, Tennyson went on to say:

But as he grows and gathers much
And learns the use of 'I' and 'me'
And finds 'I am not what I see
And other than the things I touch'

So rounds he to a separate mind
From where clear memory can begin.

This process can cause a good deal of anxiety in the child. Simply put, object relations theory suggests that, in order to facilitate the psychological separation from the mother, the growing child will invest some external object such as a blanket, doll, or teddy bear with the feelings it has for the mother and her nourishing breasts. This explains why the child will sometimes hold the transitional object to its mouth. In a sense it becomes a mother substitute which, like her breasts, is constantly available and apparently under its control. I can clearly remember two of my transitional objects in childhood. When I was very young I used to make a sort of matchstick person out of strips of cardboard and placed it in the bed beside me at night. As long as it was there I felt secure. Sometime later an aunt, who was visiting from Australia, gave me a small, cuddly koala bear. It took the place of the cardboard figure. For years it was my constant companion, especially at night.

Psychologically, transitional objects serve important purposes. On the horizontal level of human relationships, a material transitional object acts as a symbol of the *unio oppositorum*, i.e. the union of the now separate infant with the surrounding world and its mother. No wonder the child can feel as strongly about the object as it does about its mother. It invests it with great emotional significance. It represents primordial connection. As such the transitional object has a quasi-religious function. Etymologically speaking, the word religion is derived from the Latin *religio*, which literally means, 'to bind together, to unite'. On a more vertical level of relationship with God, the child's relationships with its parents, especially the mother, can give rise to a pre-conceptual awareness of a divine presence. Psychoanalyst Ana Maria Rizzuto states in her *The Birth of the Living God*[3] that the child's emerging God image is inextricably tied in with its experience of the nurturance and protection of its parents. In that sense, it's images of God are transitional objects of an inner, mental kind. They enable the child to escape the pain of separation anxiety by simultaneously relating it to a dependable and caring God in and through relationship with its dependable and caring parents, who are represented by its material transitional object. So the blanket, doll or teddy bear can be the simultaneous focal point of horizontal and vertical, worldly and other-worldly connection and belonging.

Separation Anxiety

It is worth noting, however, that for one reason or another, small children can suffer from separation anxiety. Psychiatrist Frank Lake wrote in his *Clinical Theology*: 'So long as the mother is present, and satisfactorily so, the baby experiences its being and well-being in identification with her. It cannot conceive of life going on without her, except for short times when her coming is delayed.'[4] The infant becomes so dependant on the mother's presence that, if for some reason or other she fails to return, the power of being-by-relatedness-to-her is depleted to dangerous levels of hopelessness. A lively expectation of receiving love gives way to despair because the child's emerging sense of identity and worth are at risk. The feeling of unlovability causes a feeling of anxiety and acute distress. Lake adds the sobering words: 'even though at this point of maximal tolerable panic the mother returns and the experience is split off and repressed, it remains as an indelible aspect of personal identity.'[5] Not surprisingly such memories are buried in the unconscious. But they continue to influence the person's feelings and attitudes in adult life.

I can recall two such experiences in my early life. The first harks back to the time when I was in my dark red pram. One summer's day I was in the back garden facing in towards the house. At one point my mother came out through the dining room door. She looked into the pram, said something, tucked in my blanket, and then turned to go back indoors. I didn't want her to leave me. I couldn't speak. I probably cried. But she took no notice and went back into the house. I felt abandoned and alone. A year or more later, when I was about two and a half, I had a similar experience. I woke up during a thunder storm. I repeatedly cried out for my parents, but there was no response. In panic I got up from my bed, came out of my bedroom on to the dark landing at the top of the stairs. Suddenly, the door opened and to my immense relief my mother and father entered the house. I felt secure again. Despite the fact that we had a live-in maid, I had briefly felt a strong fear and acute separation anxiety. This experience was the opposite to the secure sense of belonging that I usually enjoyed and which was symbolised by my koala bear.

The Joy of Ultimate Belonging

In his *Playing and Reality*[6] Donald Winnicott maintained that transitional objects, whether material or mental, belong to the realm of illusion. Rather than using the word in a pejorative sense as a synonym for delusion, i.e. an illusion that does not accord with objective reality, he used the term to describe a subjective psychological dynamic. The word illusion is derived from the Latin *ludere*, which means 'to play'. As such our illusions are playful inventions which enable us to relate to the world in an imaginative way which may or may not be delusional. Winnicott argued that none of us ever completely leaves this kind of illusory activity behind. In childhood and later in adult life a person can invest objects with a significance that is carried over from childhood. He writes: 'The task of reality-acceptance is never completed … No human being is free from the strain of relating inner and outer reality, and … relief from this strain is provided by an intermediate area of experience which is not challenged, such as the arts or *religion*.'[7]

As I was reflecting on these experiences, I realised that my adult sense of anxious separation, on the one hand, and my joyful sense of belonging on the other, can be traced back to early childhood. As I see it, one way I try to escape from the former and to strengthen the latter is by investing my radios with a kind of religious significance. They take their place among my transitional objects. They help to create the realistic 'illusion' of connection. The radio is like the hub of a wheel whose spokes radiate outwards to the very circumference of the planet. It puts me in touch with mother earth and all of humanity. For me, it also mediates a more vertical sense of belonging to the God whose presence I first intuited in my childhood. In that sense, radios have an almost mystical aura, an ability to connect me to the surrounding world and to the One who is Emmanuel, God with us.

Since becoming aware of the symbolic significance of radio in my life I have been trying to overcome the distinctly obsessional aspects of my attachment. I feel I should try to let go of an almost idolatrous dependency in order to rely on more specifically religious symbols to mediate a sense of union with God. I suspect that eventually I will even feel called to let go of imaginative and conceptual transitional objects in order to enter the cloud of unknowing where a person is at one, in a pre-conceptual way, with the incomprehensibility of the divine.

Postmodern Yearning for Transcendence

As an itinerant evangelist I spend a good deal of time in airports. I have noticed that many people on the move seem to have a strong attachment to their mobile phones as if they were childhood dolls or teddy bears. In the terminal they produce them from briefcases, handbags and pockets. Soon their owners are either receiving calls or, more commonly, calling people near and far. Some discuss business matters others tell a family member, colleague or friend where they are and when they expect to arrive. It has occurred to me that, at a deeper level, their phones seem to represent what radio signifies for me. After all, times of travel are usually times of parting. Not surprisingly, many people rely on their mobiles not just for their practical uses, but also to escape from feelings of alienation and loneliness. They try to move from feelings of separation anxiety to the joy of belonging, by connecting with people they know.

It has occurred to me that implicit in that desire for human contact there may be an unconscious desire for relationship with a more ultimate, abiding Reality which was first intimated in childhood. It is both symbolised and mediated by the mobile phone. If that is true, and I think it often is, the same principle could also apply to other forms of communication such as TV, fax machines, e-mail and the internet. They are technological aids that help us to create and also to relate to, what Teilhard de Chardin referred to as the noosphere, i.e. an interconnected envelope of human thought and consciousness. While the noosphere is a secular reality, it has mystical potential in so far as it enables people to become more united with one another and with their true selves. But this increased unity and inwardness can only find its ultimate fulfilment in and through a sense of transcendent connection with the Reality that is mediated by our transitional objects, whether they are specifically religious or more secular in nature. Perhaps we need a renewed appreciation of the significance of the mass media in facilitating the spiritual aspirations of humankind. Despite the fact that they may contain unsavoury content or be used to escape from reality, they can also be the sacraments of a widespread but often unconscious desire for union with the Beyond who is in our midst.

CHAPTER EIGHT

St Patrick's Nightmare[1]

In her excellent book, *Patrick The Pilgrim and Apostle of Ireland,* Máire de Paor suggests that the mysterious temptation recounted by St Patrick, in his *Confessio,* was the sixth of his twelve perils.[2] The saintly bishop tells us that in the course of his escape from Ireland he experienced a mysterious inner trial. It probably occurred in war torn Britain in the aftermath of the Roman withdrawal. 'That night when I was asleep Satan tempted me with a violence which I will remember as long as I am in the body. There fell on me as it were a great rock and I could not stir a limb. How did it occur to me in my ignorance to call on Elijah? Meanwhile I saw the sun rising in the sky, and while I was shouting 'Elijah, Elijah!' at the top of my voice the brilliance of the sun fell suddenly on me and lifted my depression.' An obvious question arises. How should this passage be interpreted?

Like many before him, Patrick received guidance in dreams. As Job 33:14-18 explains: 'For God does speak – now one way, now another – though man may not perceive it. In a dream, in a vision of the night, when deep sleep falls on men as they slumber in their beds … to preserve his soul from the pit.' We know from his *Confessio* that Patrick was led to escape from Ireland, and later to return to the country, as a result of a succession of such inspired dreams.

In recent years a great deal of research has been done on sleeping and dreaming. Put briefly, the results indicate that our sleep is divided into ninety minute segments. For some of that time our brain waves are relatively inactive. We sleep very deeply and have no dreams. During the alternating periods, of shallow sleep, our brain waves are nearly as active as they would be during the day. We experience REM or rapid eye movement, and simultaneously have our dreams. Researchers have discovered that during this phase of sleep the brain paralyses the body so that only the chest and the eyes can move.

Old Hag Nightmares

In recent years David Hufford, Professor of Behavioural Science at Pennsylvania State University, has investigated a particular kind of nightmare where subjects suffer a paralysis attack. They feel that there is an alien presence threatening them, in a terrifying way, and that a heavy weight is pressing down on their chests. Professor Hufford makes a number of assertions about these kind of dreams. Firstly, about one in five of the population seems to experience them, at one time or another. I know that I did when I was a young man. Secondly, this type of dream is reported in the literature of all cultures, places and times. For example, in Greenland they are referred to as 'old hag' dreams where accounts still figure prominently in contemporary folklore.

The words 'nightmare' and 'hag' are related. The word 'nightmare' refers to a female spirit or monster who is supposed to settle on a sleeping person thereby causing a feeling of suffocation. It is derived from the Old English *mara* which literally means 'night crusher'. St Patrick reports that he literally felt that he was being crushed by something like a great rock. The word 'hag' comes from Anglo Saxon and means 'a witch'. It could refer to an evil spirit, a demon, or an infernal being in female form. In Jungian terms this could be the negative *anima,* in the form of a mother complex. In an analysis of archetypal imagery in Celtic legends, John Layard has suggested that the natural mother who nurtures the physical side of the hero's early life, can later be psychologically metamorphosed into an old hag, who, from the unconscious, opposes his spiritual quest.[3] Some scholars believe that the hag is a remnant of belief in primitive nature goddesses. Understood in this way, one would be led to believe that Patrick the Christian was tempted to adopt pagan beliefs either of a Roman or Celtic kind.

Psycho-Spiritual Oppression

Whatever interpretation might have been involved, Patrick says that he felt that he was being tempted by Satan. The Hebrew word *satan* appears twenty four times in the Old Testament and is used to describe the cosmic struggle between God and the opposing forces of darkness. In the New Testament Satan is seen as the opponent of God's kingdom and the adversary and accuser of the people of God. He is variously referred to as 'ruler of this world' (Jn 12:31) and as a 'liar' (Jn 8:44). 1 Jn 5:19 reminds us of the chilling fact that: 'We know … the whole world is in the power of the evil one.'

Professor Hufford has discovered that for many people the old hag nightmare, however it is understood, is so vivid that, paradoxically, they believe that they are fully conscious when they are having it. Apparently, there is scientific evidence to suggest that this could be virtually true. When the brain waves of subjects were investigated, it was discovered that they were characteristic of someone who was conscious, while at the same time they were in a REM, lucid dreaming, state. That would explain why they were aware of being paralysed. Significantly, Patrick says that when he felt oppressed by Satan: 'I could not stir a limb.'

It seems to me that Patrick's sleeping patterns would have been seriously disrupted because of having to travel so far, firstly by sea, and later by land. But that was not all. From a physical point of view he was hungry during his sojourn in the wilderness. Psychologically it was, in all likelihood, a time of emotional turmoil and strain. As a result his unconscious mind would have tried to process his negative feelings such as apprehension, hopelessness and anger. They were quite likely to express themselves in a nightmare similar to the one he described. The symbolism suggests that the ominous adversities he had to endure, threatened to overwhelm him.

The dream has spiritual significance also. We know that as a teenager Patrick would have had strong sensual desires. He hints at the fact that he had committed a serious sin 'in my boyhood in one day'. Although it may have been a sexual sin, such as adultery, I suspect that Maire de Paor is quite correct in thinking that it is more likely that it was a sin against religion, such as participating in pagan sun worship.[4] One way or the other, Patrick had experienced a spiritual awakening while he was in Ireland, an outpouring of the Holy Spirit through which he received a new and significant commitment to the Lordship of Jesus and an openness to the power and gifts of the Holy Spirit. As a result, he had become a man of fervent prayer. However, he probably continued to experience a strong conflict between his old self and his newfound dedication to life in the Spirit. The nightmare suggests that the power of his shadow self aggressively reasserted itself while he was in the wilderness. Like Jesus and Paul before him he experienced desolation of spirit and an intense spiritual struggle. Fearing he would be overwhelmed he called out on Elijah, the greatest of the Old Testament prophets who, as a result of his unshakeable trust in God, had triumphed over the pagan prophets of Baal (cf. 1 Kgs 18). He tells us that the crisis ended when 'I saw the sun rise into the heavens ... lo, the splendor of his sun fell on me, and immediately freed me of all oppressiveness.'

Consequences

A few comments are in order here. Firstly, if Patrick was semiconscious when he experienced the old hag nightmare, he would have seen the sun rise at dawn. Secondly, awareness of the rising sun would probably have ended the REM aspect of his experience with its associated sense of oppressive paralysis. Thirdly, the light of the sun would have transformed a pagan image into a powerful symbol of an in-breaking of the light of God's comforting and liberating Spirit. From that time forward Patrick was experientially aware that he could do all things in him who strengthened him, for God's power was made perfect in his weakness (cf. Phil 4:13; 2 Cor 12:9). While Patrick may have been tempted to adopt pagan practices, any suggestion that he engaged in pagan devotion to a sun God are unwarranted. Later in the *Confessio* he says quite explicitly: 'For this sun which we behold, rises daily at God's command for us; but it will never reign, nor will its splendour endure; all wretched people who adore it will, moreover, come to a wretched punishment. We however ... believe and adore the true sun, Christ.'

Conclusion

Surely, Patrick's struggle is an instructive metaphor for modern Christians, especially those in Ireland. Like our father in faith, we face a stark choice. It was expressed in a prophetic manner by Pope John Paul II when he spoke at Limerick in 1979. 'Your country,' he said, 'seems in a sense to be living again the temptations of Christ: Ireland is being asked to prefer the "kingdoms of the world and their splendour" to the kingdom of God (cf. Mt 4:8). Satan the tempter, the adversary of Christ, will use all his might and all his deceptions to win Ireland for the way of the world. What a victory he would gain, what a blow he would inflict on the Body of Christ in the world, if he could seduce Irish men and women away from Christ. Now is the time of testing for Ireland. This generation is once more a generation of decision.' Like Patrick, we will be sustained in our crucifixion points of powerlessness by the power of God. Commenting on his own successful struggle, Patrick wrote: 'I believe that I was sustained by Christ my Lord and that his Spirit was even then calling out on my behalf.' Hopefully it will be same for us. In times of temptation we too can discover that 'God is faithful, and will not let us be tempted beyond our strength' (1 Cor 10:13).

CHAPTER NINE

Popular Devotion and Primal Piety

The poet Tennyson wrote: 'The old order changeth, yielding place to the new; And God fulfills himself in many ways.'[1] That has never been truer than today. Like the rest of Western society, Ireland is experiencing an accelerating rate of change. For example, in the three years 1998-2000 the gross national product grew by around 27%. This kind of rapid development is putting pressure on all our institutions, values and beliefs. For many years now, the Catholic Church in Ireland, to which 95% of the people belong, has been seeking, like the Protestant minority, to respond to that testing challenge.

Secular, Postmodern Culture

Firstly, there is the problem of *secularisation*. It does not specifically mean a loss of faith, but the isolation of faith and religion from the rest of life. This process seems to be well under way in Ireland. There has been a drop from 80% to 60% in the practice rate of Irish Catholics in recent years.[2] The percentage drop among adolescents is significantly higher. In some urban parishes fewer than 10% attend church. Some time ago *The Irish Times* published the results of an MRBI poll on religion. When asked what the Catholic Church in Ireland would be like in twenty years time, 69% of the respondents said that it would be Catholic in name only.[3]

Two observations about the fall in church attendance. I suspect that many of the people who lapse are those who have been sacramentalised but not truly evangelised. In all likelihood many of those who lapse espouse what psychologist Gordon Allport referred to as extrinsic as opposed to intrinsic religion. In other words they fail to internalise their faith, and it often fails to effect the way in which they live their everyday lives. I also

suspect that it is these people with extrinsic faith who are lapsing in large numbers at the moment. In terms of Batson's Quest
Dimension scale[4] we don't know what percentage of Irish people are religious/spiritual seekers, but many of them are. That is
one of the reasons why our theological colleges are full to capacity with lay people.

Secondly there is the phenomenon of *Post-modernism*.[5] It is a
characteristic of Western societies, including Ireland. It maintains that, rather than being an objective fact, our knowledge of
truth is subjective and at best probable, partial and provisional.
Nothing is absolutely certain. There is only an endless sequence
of contexts and interpretations. Generally speaking, post-modernism is anti-authoritarian in outlook. It does not believe in all
embracing explanations of life such as those offered by
Christianity. As a result, traditional Christian spirituality has become increasingly problematical.

Incidentally, I believe that we are living at the interface between two periods of history. Instead of being the beginning of a
new cultural era, I suspect that postmodernism is probably the
dying gasp of the modernist movement which has its roots in
the Enlightenment. In so far as believers like Descartes, Kant,
Hegel and Schleiermacher subordinated ontological problems
to epistemological ones they unwittingly made the infinite God
a function of finite human subjectivity. In doing so they implicitly
laid the foundations of the relativism, subjectivism and agnosticism which are so characteristic of the postmodern era.
Although Pope John Paul II says that postmodern developments
in hermeneutics and the analysis of language can be very helpful for an understanding of the faith,[6] I believe that he is correct
when he observes: 'It should never be forgotten that the neglect
of being inevitably leads to losing touch with objective truth and
therefore with the very ground of human dignity. This in turn
makes it possible to erase from the countenance of man and
woman the marks of their likeness to God and thus lead them
little by little either to a destructive will to power or to a solitude
without hope'[7]

Secular-postmodern culture has a number of characteristic
effects on religious attitudes.

Experience is trusted more than authority.[8] The accelerating rate of change in modern society tends to undermine the claims of traditional authority. In Ireland, as in the rest of Europe, the centre of gravity is shifting from the experience of religious authority to the authority of religious experience. In many instances such experiences are pre-rational and expressed in feeling-laden images rather than in abstract religious truths. Pope John Paul II adverted to this trend – though not necessarily with approval – when he observed: 'People today put more trust in ... experience than in dogma.'[9]

Conscience is trusted more than the moral teaching of the church. As a result of these rapid changes, a growing number of people disagree with the church's teachings, especially those to do with sexual morality.[10] There are a number of reasons for this. Firstly, there is evidence of increasing subjectivism and relativism in the realm of ethics. Secondly, many lay people, especially women, are in a state of dissent when it comes to Paul VI's ban on artificial means of birth control and John Paul II's ban on the ordination of women. Thirdly, church scandals to do with sex and money have also undermined the church's authority. So, for these and other reasons, an increasing number of Catholics tend to rely solely on their consciences when making decisions. An MRBI poll in the *Irish Times* in December 1996 confirmed that 78% of Irish people did so.

There is a movement from institutional commitment to spiritual seeking. While increasing numbers of people in Western countries have become alienated from the institutional churches there are some hopeful developments. Researchers David Hay and Kate Hunt have indicated that over the past 25 years in the United Kingdom there has been a startling 110% rise in the number of people reporting a sense of a mysterious Power or Presence, beyond their everyday selves. Hay and Hunt remark: 'we are in the midst of an explosive spiritual upsurge.'[11] They go on to say: 'We know, from the research we have done, that most people's spirituality is a long way away from institutional religion. This spirituality has little doctrinal content, and few people have more than the vaguest remnants of religious language to express their experience of God. The phrase we commonly hear is 'I definitely believe in Something; there's Something there.' Their spirituality is based upon a longing for meaning.'

While that kind of research hasn't been done in Ireland, there is reason to believe that a similar, if less pronounced, trend would be discernible.

Religious Reactions

When I was a student in the 1960s I read an influential book by Harvey Cox entitled, *The Secular City*[12] in which the author tried to work out a theology for the 'post religious' age that many sociologists were confidently expecting. Thirty years later in a book on Pentecostalism, entitled *Fire from Heaven*,[13] Cox says that while it is clear that, in the twentieth century, increasing numbers of people became disillusioned with conventional religion and its institutional expressions, they were also becoming disillusioned with its more secular alternatives. Now they are looking for new options. Cox argues that Pentecostalism with its trances, healing, speaking in tongues and other archetypal forms of religious expression has come to the fore as the most significant one.

Pentecostalism's primal ways of experiencing the numinous are reminiscent of what Otto referred to as the mysterious, awesome and fascinating awareness of the Holy. While it can be partially explained in cultural and psychological ways, ultimately many people believe that Pentecostalism is a sovereign work of God's Spirit. It is a form of religious revival which had its roots in British Methodism and the great awakening in New England in the eighteenth century. Wild devotion was a characteristic of both of these religious movements.[14] It is also arguable that Pentecostal piety is a rejection of post-Enlightenment rationalism whether of the Protestant or Catholic variety and a return to the supernatural perspective of the pre-modern era. I suspect that it is an instance of what Paul Ricoeur referred to as a second naïvete, one that can transcend the simplistic assumptions of pre-modernism, by means of a sophisticated differentiation of separate realms of meaning on the one hand, and a synthesis of those realms on the other. Implicit in this form of piety is a new worldview and a new theory of religious knowing, one that rejects Kantian agnosticism on the one hand and Hegelian panentheism on the other. It would not be appropriate to explore those complex themes here. Suffice it to say that others have begun to do so.

It is estimated that there are more than 400 million Pentecostals in the world today.[15] As such, surely, Pentecostalism must be one of the fastest growing religious movements in Christian history. It is a striking fact that, while many of the mainline churches seem moribund and in a state of terminal decline in Western countries, Pentecostal churches are growing by as many as 20 million new members every year. What should we make of all this?

In his many books, Morton Kelsey has argued that there is a crisis of religion in post-Enlightenment culture because people don't believe in the possibility of a direct relationship with a supernatural reality or with God. He says that we need to return to the worldview of the bible and Plato. For instance, the latter wrote: 'There is also a madness which is a divine gift, and the source of the chief blessings granted to mankind.'[16] Surely this is an historically important reference to the possibility of primal experience in the Western cultural tradition, a move from Apollonian rationality to the wild devotion of Dionysus, the Greek god whose cult was frequently marked by ecstatic rites which were inspired by instinct and emotion. Nearly two thousand years later Plato's words found an echo in the writings of William Shakespeare. He proffered a wonderful description of the creative process which has experiential affinities with wild devotion:

> The lunatic, the lover, and the poet,
> Are of imagination all compact ...
> The poet's eye, in a fine frenzy rolling,
> Doth glance from heaven to earth, from earth to heaven;
> And as imagination bodies forth,
> The forms of things unknown, the poet's pen
> Turns them to shapes and gives to airy nothing
> A local habitation and a name.[17]

Surely, the contemporary notion of wild or primal devotion refers not so much to forms of awareness which are untamed by the institutional church as to the spontaneous and instinctive experiences and behaviours which would have been associated with Nietzsche's will to power, understood as 'the dynamic self-affirmation of life.'[18] In Christian terms, it is arguable that ultimately the Spirit of God is the indispensable source of such self-affirmation in and through self-transcendence.

Kelsey says that Plato believed that 'through divine inspiration, possession, or madness, people can be given access directly to the realm of the non-physical in: a) *prophecy;* b) *healing* actions; c) *artistic inspiration;* and d) most particularly, *love.* Through all of these people come to *know.* They are all ways of knowing *in addition* to sense experience.'[19] Kelsey points out that New Testament abounds in such experiences.[20] In the context of these reflections we can say that this way of knowing can lead to a primal, pre-rational awareness of divine revelation which is reminiscent of the ecstatic experiences of the *nabi,* or pre-classical prophets in ancient Israel (cf. 1 Sam 19:20).[21] For example, in the Acts of the Apostles, 1007 verses refer to various spiritual experiences such as dreams 3, visions 63, prophecy 77, and tongues 16 which can include prophetic utterances which require interpretation.

Kelsey goes on to observe that nowadays the Pentecostals are the only large group of Christians who take the idea of such a direct, divine encounter seriously. However, they have come in for harsh criticism, both from within and without the churches, ever since their inception in the early 1900s. He says that Pentecostal leaders realised that they couldn't stand against the powerful rationalistic and naturalistic thinking of modern society and so they withdrew into their own structured sub-culture.[22] Kelsey also argues that Carl Jung was the only major twentieth-century psychologist who described the dynamics of such primal piety in a credible way. He outlined the psycho-spiritual manner in which God could be intuitively revealed to the inner self, by means of such things as symbols, myths, dreams and visions which are rooted in the pre-rational, archetypal activity of the collective unconscious.

Popular Piety
In this reflection I want to focus on some characteristics of the popular devotion movement in Ireland because I believe that in some respects it is similar to Pentecostal/Charismatic piety. It has a large following of tens of thousands of people. Many of them are disillusioned with the church. As traditional certainties

are questioned and many Christian practices are changed, an increasing number of Catholic men and women feel anxious and uneasy. Post Vatican II liturgy is too wordy, conceptual and abstract to meet their needs. It has left their imaginations and hearts unnourished and unmoved. Meanwhile, they are troubled by a disturbing decline in faith and morals in many of their co-religionists and a corresponding growth of violent crime and selfish greed in society. What the members of the popular devotion movement seem to be looking for is a restoration of traditional values and beliefs and the development of new forms of devotion that will move them emotionally while giving them a sense of the nearness of a mysterious God who answers prayer in accordance with the divine promises, comforts the afflicted and transforms lives. Instead of lapsing or leaving the church, the followers of popular devotion espouse a do-it-yourself kind of piety which is an implicit protest against current church spirituality.

Before looking at some of its characteristics, an introductory comment. The followers of the popular devotion movement are sometimes described as the church's lunatic fringe. I believe that this is a condescending attitude that shows very little respect for conscientious Catholics from all walks of life. We need to listen to what its members have to say in an empathic, understanding way. The following account is intended to be an impressionistic representation of popular devotion rather than a detailed and systematic one.

a) Devotees of popular devotion are influenced by:
- Seers such as Christine Gallagher of Achill Island.[23]
- Stigmatists such as Sister Natalie in Hungary, Mother Elena Leonardi in Italy and Christine Gallagher in Ireland.
- Prophets such as the two Patricks of Cookstown who receive private revelations.
- Healers such as Fr Peter Rookie, Sr Briege Mc Kenna, Mary Malone and a number of other lay men and women.

b) The devotees of popular devotion are impressed by supernatural phenomena such as:
- Moving statues, e.g. at Ballinspittle and Mount Mellary.

- Weeping statues of Our Lady where her tears are in the form of blood.
- Rosaries that turn to gold.
- Apparitions mostly of Our Lady, e.g. those of the two O Mahony women at Ballinspittle (1985); Four girls at Carns Grotto (1985); Beulah Lynch & Mark Trenor at Bessbrook (1987); Sally Ann & Judy Considine at Inchigeela (1987); Christina Gallagher at Achill (1988).
- Natural phenomena such as the dancing of the sun, e.g. at Medjugorje where many Irish followers of popular devotion go on pilgrimage.
- Healings at Knock shrine, and also as a result of being blessed by relics such as the mittens worn by Pade Pio.

c) Devotees of this spirituality have a particular devotion to:
- Padre Pio who is associated with the smell of perfume, answered prayer and apparitions.
- Our Lady of Medjugorje and they are guided by the messages which she allegedly gives to the visionaries.
- The Divine Mercy devotion of Blessed Faustina Kolowska.
- The *Rosa Mystica* which is based on the fact that Mary is alleged to have appeared to Pierina Gilli, a nurse, in 1947 (7/13; 10/28; 11/22; and 12/8).[24] She called herself the mystical rose and asked people to repent for sins against faith and morals. She called the noon hour of 8 December 1947 an 'hour of grace.' Today Irish people bring a statue of the *Rosa Mystica* to people's homes for prayer and veneration.
- Messages given in other countries to people such as William Kaam, 'The little Pebble' of Wollongong, Australia, and Vassula Ryden, a Greek Orthodox woman who lives in Switzerland and who claims to have heavenly revelations.

d) They communicate in various ways:
- By word of mouth and informal networking.
- At well known meeting places such as shrines and grottos.
- By means of publications which are often privately produced.
- By means of the internet.

The followers of popular devotion tend to be conservative as far as faith and morals are concerned. They commonly exhort people to repentance, and devotion to the sacraments, especially the Eucharist and reconciliation, otherwise a great chastisement will befall mankind. Many of them are opposed to things such as divorce and are strong and even aggressive supporters of the pro-life movement, e.g. Youth Defence. They are also adamantly opposed to anything that they associate with New Age spirituality such as The Enneagram, aromatherapy, yoga, or reflexology.

Prophecy in Symbols?
Within this context, the phenomenon of weeping and moving statues, which has been reported around Ireland, e.g. at Ballinspittle and Mount Mellary, is instructive. I am inclined to interpret such experiences in a Jungian way as daydreams. Therefore I believe that they should be understood in a symbolical manner as expressions of wishful thinking. For example, if one looks up the entry on 'religious statues' in Tom Chetwynd's insightful and well researched *Dictionary for Dreamers*, it says that when inanimate figures are seen to move in a lifelike way it is a sign that 'what was a dead theoretical concept suddenly has new inner meaning for the dreamer' and that 'new potentialities are awakening in the dreamer.'[25] As we know, a dry doctrinal approach to religion does very little for people. Evidently, what the supporters of popular piety are looking for are doctrines that come alive with experiential meaning. In this context it is interesting to recall something Jung wrote: 'Today Christianity is devitalised ... God has in fact become unconscious to us. This is what always happens when things are interpreted, explained, and dogmatised until they become so encrusted with man-made images and words that they can no longer be seen.'[26]

I also believe that claims that rosaries turn to gold should not be summarily dismissed. This phenomenon is reminiscent of the Alchemist's dream of turning base metal into gold and inanimate matter into spirit. Jung believed that this was a symbol of an unconscious desire for inner transformation.[27] As for the sun dancing in the heavens, it is harder to ascribe symbolic meaning to it. In Jungian terms the sun could refer to the light of consciousness, and dancing as a preliminary to love making. So the dancing sun might be an intimation of a movement from left brain activity, which is typically rational, objective and detached, to right brained activity, which is typically intuitive, subjective and relational. This movement from a characteristically male sort of awareness to a more female one can lead to an ecstatic form of unitive consciousness.

The repeated emphasis on apparitions of Mary has also a similar symbolic and prophetic importance. In Jungian terms this could be a manifestation of the need for the *anima*, i.e. the feminine archetype and all it represents, in an overly male and patriarchal church and culture. I was interested to see that at the end of his magisterial study *The Passion of the Western Mind* Richard Tarnas says: 'The Western mind, has been founded on the repression of the feminine – on the repression of undifferentiated unitary consciousness, of the participation mystique with nature: a progressive denial of the *anima mundi*, of the soul of the world ... The crisis of modern man is an essentially masculine crisis.'[28] Having diagnosed the key problem he goes on to prescribe a cure. The Western mind, he says, must be willing to open itself to a reality the nature of which could challenge and overturn its most established beliefs about itself and the world. This is the great challenge of our time. It is the evolutionary imperative for the masculine principle. The left brained approach to reality has to overcome its male one-sidedness by choosing to enter into a fundamentally new relationship of mutuality with the feminine in all its forms. 'The feminine then becomes not that which must be controlled, denied, and exploited, but rather fully acknowledged, respected, and responded to for itself. It is recognised, not as the objectified 'other' but rather as source, goal, and immanent presence.'[29] Although Tarnas writes about the rehabilitation of the feminine from a secular point of view, his point has profound Christian implications. It may well be the key that could open postmodern people to the possibility of the kind of revivifying religious experience already enjoyed by the devotees of popular devotion..

Common Characteristics of Pentecostalism and Popular Devotion
Although many followers of the popular devotion movement would adamantly deny the fact, I suspect that it has many affinities

with the primal piety of Pentecostalism and especially the Charismatic Movement within the Catholic Church. It seems to me that broadly speaking they have a number of characteristics in common such as:

- They focus primarily on experiential awarenesses of a quasi-mystical kind rather than on authoritative doctrinal teachings.
- In a secular age they are re-sacralising nature in the sense that they believe that God is active in every aspect of everyday living, and can be revealed in and through the twin bibles of scripture and created reality.
- They have loose organisational structures of their own. As a movement the members work together mostly in informal, spontaneous ways to further their religious aspirations.
- They believe in private revelations that are granted to seers, visionaries and prophets, both at home and abroad.
- They believe in the importance of supernatural phenomena such as healings, miracles, speaking in tongues (Pentecostals/ Charismatics) and weeping statues, signs in the heavens, etc. (popular devotion).
- They emphasise intuition more than reason, and emotionally laden myths and images more than concepts.
- The feminine aspect of religion is honoured in so far as there is a great emphasis on the role of women in ministry (Pentecostals/Charismatics) and of Mary the mother of God and female seers (popular devotion).
- There is an emphasis on the future, e.g. the second coming (Pentecostals/Charismatics) and on a purifying time of chastisement to come (popular devotion).[30]
- While the popular devotion movement professes loyalty to ecclesiastical authority, it is an ironic fact that, when members of the hierarchy question any of its cherished beliefs, the misgivings of bishops are not likely to be well received. Followers of the movement believe that, after a time of misunderstanding and opposition, God will vindicate their cause.

Conclusion

I think that the church authorities would do well to listen to what the followers of the charismatic and popular devotion movements are saying about an overly rational and masculine approach to spirituality. That point was particularly obvious during the visit of Thérèse of Lisieux's relics to Ireland between 15 April and 28 June 2001. Huge crowds went to venerate them, young and old, active and inactive Catholics alike. As Fr Joseph O Leary said in his typically perceptive way, in a letter to the *Irish Times*, 'The enthusiasm about St Thérèse scotches the myth of a post-Catholic Ireland. It may be the values of faith and love are better appreciated than before, for we have glimpsed the ugly face of a faithless and loveless society. What is evidently not appreciated however, is the paralysis of the ecclesiastical establishment. Routine liturgies and theologically destitute sermons are not meeting people's spiritual hunger.'[31] By and large, those in academic life tend to ignore the importance of popular devotion and the groups that promote it. As a result, very little in-depth research has been done on the significance of the beliefs and practices of these forms of primal piety. This would be particularly true of popular devotion. That research is needed in order to critique some of the less desirable elements of both movements, and to incorporate the best of their primal piety within the framework of the church's mainline spirituality.

I believe that, just as New Age Spirituality is a non-Christian response to secular postmodernism, so popular devotion and Pentecostal/Charismatic spirituality are interesting Christian responses to the same phenomenon. It is worth remembering that before it was ever a doctrine, Christianity was an experience. Perhaps it would be true to say that in many instances Pentecostals and followers of popular devotion have recovered something of the primal experience that gave birth to Christianity but are not good at expressing it in a sophisticated theological way. On the other hand, for many contemporary Christians, especially well educated ones, the order has been reversed, 'they have the meaning, but miss the experience'. Although they are theologically erudite they can loose touch with the primal religious experience that ought to animate Christian life. Pentecostals and followers of popular devotion could help them to recover not only the wild devotion which is so evident in the Acts of the Apostles, but also the worldview that is implicit in it.

As Karl Rahner perceptively observed before his death: 'Our present situation is one of transition from a church sustained by a homogeneously Christian society and almost identical with it, from a people's church, to a church made up of those who have struggled against the environment in order to reach a clear, explicit, and responsible personal decision of faith.'[32] He added: 'The Christian of the future will be a mystic or he or she will not exist at all, if by mysticism we mean ... a genuine experience of God emerging at the very heart of our existence.'[33] Amen to that.

CHAPTER TEN

Experience and Belief
in Theological Reflection[1]

Job the Archetypal Sufferer

Job is the archetypal example of an afflicted person. His story can teach pastoral ministers important lessons. As you may recall, he was a virtuous man, but he lost everything, his wife, family, livestock and possessions. As a result, he was not only afflicted in physical and emotional ways, he had to endure a spiritual crisis. The Jewish theology of his time maintained that misfortune was the result of personal sin. But Job knew that he had led a good life. So why was he suffering such adversity? He had no answer to this age-old question. As a result he felt bereft and even betrayed by God.

Then three friends came to visit Job. They sat silently observing him for a long time. They were aware of his suffering. But they failed to pay attention in an empathic way. Theirs was a more detached and objective form of relationship. The three men sensed that if they attended, in an open-minded manner, to Job's sufferings and their implications, they would have to face a religious dilemma. They might have to let go of their current understanding of good and evil, without necessarily being able to replace it with a new one. In the event they were more concerned with theological orthodoxy, and the sense of personal security it gave them, than they were with the disquieting challenge posed by Job's situation. Clearly they trusted more in the religion of God than they did in the God of religion. They argued, in an *a priori* manner that, although he seemed to be a good man, Job *must* have offended God is some secret way. How else could his plight be explained? So in the name of a religious truth, they denied the truth of Job's lived experience.

The Lord responded to the three men by telling them that instead of being displeased with the weeping, mourning and complaints of Job, he was displeased with them. They were like the priests in the parable of the Good Samaritan. Although they were aware of Job's suffering, they avoided any real involvement with him. Lacking in genuine compassion they focused, in an apathetic way, on theological niceties rather than on Job's problematic feelings. They kept him, and the thorny issues raised by his sufferings, at arms length, by resorting to pious cliches and religious claptrap.

Instead of comforting Job, the trio's lack of empathic understanding increased his sense of anguish and isolation. Job responded to his friends by saying: 'I have understanding as well as you' (Job 12:3). And again: 'I have heard many such things ... I also could speak as you do, if you were in my place; I could join words together against you, and shake my head at you. I could strengthen you with my mouth, and the solace of my lips would assuage your pain' (Job 16:2, 4-5). And again, echoing the sentiments of many suffering people down the centuries, Job said: 'Oh that you would keep silent, and it would be your wisdom!' (Job 13:5).

Pastoral Empathy
There are many forms of pastoral ministry. For the sake of clarity, I will focus on chaplaincy work in hospitals in this chapter. However, the principles that apply to this form of caring apply, in large part, to other forms of ministry. Hospitals are places where everyone, especially staff members, patients, their relatives and friends, are constantly confronted with challenging human and religious realities, reminiscent of those faced by Job. At the human level they have to face life-and-death issues. At a religious level, people in hospital often have to acknowledge the gap that can exist between what they believe at a notional level, and what they actually believe at an experiential level. For example, in the light of human suffering they might have to ask whether they really believe in such things as the existence of divine providence, the power of petitionary prayer and life after death. Typically, the chaplain ministers at the point of intersection between these human and religious realities. It is not an easy place to be.

I think we would all agree that pastoral ministers should try to relate to people they serve in a loving way. Jesus offered a clear, succinct, description of such love when he advocated the 'golden rule.' He said, 'Do to others as you would have them do to you' (Lk 6:31). As I suggested earlier in the book, to carry out this injunction two things are needed, *goodwill* and *insight*. A person with goodwill wants what's best for another. His or her insight is the fruit of empathic attention. Empathy, as was noted in a previous chapter, is the ability to sense what other people feel in an understanding way. Dr Frank Lake described this gift as 'the ability to relate situations to the feelings that arise out of them, and accept them as matters of fact ... Christian empathy, by which a person makes him or herself available to the Holy Spirit to feel for others far beyond his or her own experience or capacities, is as desirable as it is rare.'[2]

It is hard to empathise with people's painful experiences, not only because they are upsetting in themselves, but also because they can impinge on pastoral carers in an intimidating way. As they identify with the problems of others, they may have to face personal issues, such as their own mortality, together with disconcerting theological issues raised by those experiences, such as the immortality of the soul. It is important that those who engage in pastoral care should reflect on such experiences. As T. S. Eliot once wrote: 'We had the experience but missed the meaning.'[3] We can discover the meaning by means of theological reflection. By doing so, *perception*, i.e. being aware with the senses and emotions, changes to *comprehension*, i.e. intellectual understanding. The human and religious meanings, which were formerly implicit, become explicit at a new level of cognitive awareness. As Eliot rightly observed, 'Approach to the meaning restores the experience.'[4] However it does so in a new, more intelligible way.

Forms of Theological Reflection
In pastoral formation circles, theological reflection refers to those occasions when ministerial experience and theology, personal faith and church tradition, dialogue with one another. In *The Art of Theological Reflection*, Killen and de Beer define this activity as 'the discipline of exploring individual and corporate experience in conversation with the wisdom of a religious heritage. The conversation is a genuine dialogue that seeks to hear

from our own beliefs, actions, and perspectives as well as those of the tradition. It respects the integrity of both. Theological reflection may confirm, challenge, clarify, and expand how we understand our own experience and how we understand the religious tradition. The outcome is new truth and meaning for living.'[5] According to the Whiteheads' influential book, *Method in Ministry: Theological Reflection and Christian Ministry*[6] this activity, which is sometimes referred to as contextual, experiential, or praxis theology, usually involves these four stages:

1. It begins with the pastoral experience, such as counselling a couple whose son of nineteen has just committed suicide in prison.

2. It continues with an analysis of the experience. This could involve such perspectives as the human sciences, politics, economics, civil law, local government or social analysis. The latter often requires that relevant empirical research be done, e.g. why so many of the young men in prison come from the same deprived area of the city, and why they suffer from a lot of depression.

3. Then it proceeds to theological reflection. What theological issues are relevant to the experience? What does the Christian tradition have to say about these issues? This could involve such perspectives as scripture study, ecclesiastical history, spirituality, and the teachings of the church. Then the question is reversed, what do these human issues have to say to the church's tradition?

4. Finally, theological reflection concludes by trying to see what the practical implications of the reflection might be. What new insights, sensitivities, convictions, behaviours and the like could inform one's pastoral caring in the future?[7]

James and Evelyn Whitehead suggest that mature forms of theological reflection need to embrace the following three points of reference:

a) Christian tradition, e.g. scripture, church history, spirituality, official church teaching, ethics, etc.

b) Secular wisdom/culture, e.g. philosophy, social sciences, psychology, politics, economics, law, aesthetics, etc.

c) Personal experience, e.g. what the individual minister and possibly the group bring to the reflection.[8]

Their relationship can be illustrated in a triangulated way as follows:

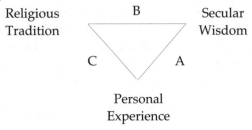

Religious   B   Secular
Tradition   Wisdom

              C   A

              Personal
              Experience

- If you are only working along the A axis, and relating personal experience to secular culture, while ignoring the religious tradition, you are operating as a *secular humanist*.
- If you are operating along the B axis, and relating religious tradition to secular wisdom, while ignoring personal experience, the danger is that you will be *intellectualising*.
- If you are working along the C axis, and relating personal experience to the religious tradition, while ignoring secular wisdom, you are in danger of being a *fundamentalist*.

Ideally, in theological reflection, the three axes, A, B, and C, are brought into dialogue with one another.

Reflection on the Interrelationship of Experience and Belief

At this point I want to propose a simple three point methodology which chaplains and other pastoral carers might find helpful. It focuses mainly, though not exclusively, on the C axis mentioned above.

Firstly, it is obvious that when chaplains listen in an empathic way to patients and others in hospital, their faith should inform those relationships. For example, they should listen to people with loving reverence in the belief that, as children of God, there is something sacred about those who confide in them. But they need to be careful not to interpret the experiences that are shared in terms of their own preconceived religious ideas, whether liberal or fundamentalist. It is a matter of accepting people's experiences without prejudice, no matter how disconcerting they might be from a theological point of view.

Secondly, chaplains need to reflect upon their pastoral encounters, especially the more notable and disturbing ones.

Ideally, they would do this with the help of a peer group, or a trained supervisor, or spiritual director. They can try to consciously acknowledge the feelings and issues their pastoral experiences have evoked. They may recognise that they had two kinds of feelings, some that were evoked by the person and his or her story, and others that were evoked by a sense of the Holy One whose presence can be mediated by relationship with the patient, relative, staff member, etc.

Thirdly, chaplains need to meditate on how their pastoral experiences might be inviting them to repent, by changing their thinking. This is the literal meaning of the New Testament word, *metanoia*.[9] Such changes lead to a more comprehensive, subtle and nuanced understanding of religious faith. Furthermore, when pastoral carers reflect in this way, they will have an opportunity of sharing all their feelings with the Lord in prayer.

Case Study
Rather than dealing with the subject of experience and belief in theological reflection in a rather abstract way, I'd like to illustrate how to do so by looking at a case study. It occurred when I was doing a Clinical Pastoral Education course in an Irish hospital. I will begin by recounting the experience. I have changed some of the details in order to ensure that confidentiality is not breached. Then I want to reflect on the experience, using the three point methodology already mentioned. Not surprisingly, there will be a certain amount of overlap between the three points. A word of caution. The focus is not on the issue of evil spirits and the appropriateness of deliverance prayer – interesting and important as it is in itself – but rather on the way in which theological reflection can be conducted.

> One evening I gave holy communion to a girl of twelve, who sometime before had a tumour removed from her brain. The next day, I met her again and she told me she was under the influence of an evil spirit. She said that it all started when she began reading people's palms and found that she could tell them about their past and future. Some time later she was disturbed by apparitions of her dead grandmother. My first reaction was one of instinctive belief. It was quickly followed

by a more rational type of incredulity. It was hard to believe that such a young girl could be oppressed by an evil spirit. I presumed that there was some psychological or physical explanation for her state of mind.

I had many conversations with Mary and discovered that although she was only twelve, she was endowed with a maturity and intelligence way beyond her years. I also talked with people who knew her and discussed her case with a neurologist, a psychiatrist, a number of priests, two experienced exorcists, and a theologian who was familiar with this kind of problem. After a two month discernment process, a consensus emerged. The facts were pointing toward the probability of oppression by an evil spirit. The theologian encouraged me to anoint Mary. I told him that she had already been anointed prior to an operation some time before. However, her problem had persisted. He said it wasn't surprising, because the priest who performed the anointing hadn't known anything about her spiritual oppression. So he encouraged me to anoint her again and to perform a simple exorcism by praying silently for deliverance during the laying-on of hands.

I told Mary of my intention. Meantime I prepared by prayer and fasting and enlisted the supportive prayers of a couple of other people. Finally, the time of the anointing arrived. When I reached the ward, I was delighted when this strange and remarkable girl informed me of her own accord that she was willing to give up the occult for good. I promised her that when I put my hands on her head the evil would go away and that she would be filled with the Holy Spirit. He would protect her from evil in the future. She replied with startling clarity, 'I have trusted my mother for her love, my doctor for my life; now I trust you for my soul.' I assured her that Jesus wouldn't let her down, with more confidence than I actually felt. Then I proceeded by celebrating the sacrament of reconciliation. After giving her absolution I moved on to the sacrament of anointing. During the laying-on of hands, I prayed silently, 'In the name of Jesus, I commanded the spirit of the occult, and any other spirit that may be disturbing you, to yield to the power and the will of God.'

Because I was morally certain that I was praying within the will of God, I had a growing conviction that what I was asking was already being granted. I concluded the prayer by requesting the Lord to fill Mary's soul with the light, peace and protection of the Holy Spirit.

When I went home that night, I asked the Lord to confirm whether the deliverance had been successful or not. The next day, when I returned to the ward around noon, I discovered that, unexpectedly, my young friend had been released earlier that morning. I was grateful to divine providence that I had managed to anoint her in the nick of time, just before her departure. As I stood there, a middle aged woman beckoned to me. When I got to her bedside she said, 'You know Mary who was in the bed opposite; she went home at nine this morning. Father, I want to tell you something. I have seen a lot of life, and I wouldn't say this lightly. I know that Mary was young, but there was something peculiar, even sinister about her.' 'Why would you say that?' I asked. 'Well, Father,' she replied, 'Just take one example. Some time ago, about four of us were due for surgery. We had a bottle of Lourdes water and we all blessed ourselves with it. But when we offered it to her, she recoiled in horror. You should have seen the look on her face. It wasn't normal. But something must have happened recently, because this morning she asked me for the Lourdes water. When I gave it to her, she went over to her own bed and blessed herself from head to toe. Not only that, she was changed somehow. The sense of evil was gone. And, by the way, she left a letter for you.' I said goodbye to the woman and went off thanking God for this indication that the prayer for deliverance had been answered. This impression was confirmed when I read Mary's memorable words. She said that all her occult powers had left her as a result of the anointing. They had been replaced by an inward sense of God's presence and peace.

The Method Applied
1.) Reverencing the Patient's Experience
When Mary told me that she was oppressed by evil, I accepted what she said at first. But then the hermeneutic of suspicion

kicked in. A few years ago I read an article on spiritual direction by Jesuit William Barry. In it he said that when we listen to people's stories we should do so with a contemplative attitude that respects what they say, in an unquestioning way. Questions should only arise when there is very good reason to suspect that their sharing is either unrealistic or insincere. I agree with Barry's point in principle. However, in Mary's case I found it hard to put into practice. Was her claim realistic? I thought that she was too young to have been oppressed by evil. In any case did the devil really exist? There must have been some psychological explanation for her state of mind. I can also recall feeling very uneasy, threatened and resentful. Some time before I had experienced a spiritual awakening. Subsequently, I had become increasingly aware of the supernatural realm of good and evil spirits, and non-rational forms of religious experience, such as visions, dreams, praying in tongues and healing. I had mixed feelings about these things. Part of me found them to be very real and fascinating and another part of me resented them as threatening phenomena. They didn't fit in with the post-Enlightenment, reductionist paradigm I was familiar with. I felt that if I embraced the supernatural worldview I'd be a cultural outsider, I'd loose the respect of my peers, especially my academic colleagues.

Furthermore, I recognised that I would have to accept responsibility for the new awareness. For example, if Mary was really oppressed by evil spirits, as she believed, I'd have to pray for her deliverance. But I wasn't at all sure I could do so authoritatively or effectively. I was aware of at least two impediments. Firstly, at that time I had unresolved feelings of unworthiness and felt, therefore, that God wouldn't or couldn't act through me. Secondly, although I believed in the promises of God, in theory, especially the one in Mk 16:17 which says: 'using my name you will cast out demons,' in practice I was full of doubts and hesitation. Nevertheless, I thought that if I couldn't minister effectively to Mary I'd feel like a fraud, for as St Paul once said, 'the kingdom of God does not consist in talk but in power' (1 Cor 4:20).

2.) Reflective Discernment

Pastoral ministers can reflect upon their pastoral encounters in a number of ways.

a) Reflection can be facilitated by using a self-awareness exercise. The pastoral carer focuses primarily on his or her feelings, rather than those of patients, because they are revelatory and the fingerprints of his or her subjectivity. As we noted in the opening chapter, while his or her feelings are similar to those experienced by other people, they are, nevertheless, unique. They put him or her in touch with two realities, the perceived world of external values[10] and his or her our own inner world which is conditioned by familial, cultural and ecclesial influences.

- What were the main feelings that were stirred up in me as I related to the patient?
- What values, beliefs or personal memories evoked those feelings? It is worth remembering that we don't have feelings about external values, but about our *perception* of them, coloured as it is by so many subjective factors.
- Were some of my feelings, e.g. joy and peace, evoked by a sense of the Lord's presence as it was mediated by means of my relationship with the patient?
- If I experienced negative feelings was it because the patient's experience threatened me at a personal level, e.g. because I'm very uncomfortable when I feel powerless to do anything practical to alleviate distress. Or perhaps I felt threatened at a theological level? I was standing in the no-man's land between notional and heartfelt belief.

b) To submit a verbatim or case study to a group of peers who, with the assistance of a competent facilitator, would help the chaplain to reflect on the relevant personal and theological implications of his or her ministry to a particular patient. I may say in passing that it is good for Christian pastoral carers to establish such reflection groups, e.g. within a hospital, or if needs be, within a region. It could serve the members of chaplaincy and pastoral care teams in a number of hospitals or by extension in any kind of pastoral work. Ideally, the members could organise three or more reflection sessions a year.

c) To talk to a trained supervisor or spiritual director. The latter would help the chaplain to look at those feelings and experiences which either tended to lessen or to increase his or her conscious relationship with God.

Following my first encounter with Mary, I thought a lot about the issues raised by her case. I didn't submit a verbatim or case study to my peer group, mainly because there were confidentiality issues involved and also because, for personal reasons, I felt too fragile and vulnerable at the time. Neither did I speak to a spiritual director, because I didn't have one. But I did discuss the case at length with my supervisor. I expected him to be very unsympathetic. But to my surprise, he said that that it was likely that I was dealing with a genuine case of spiritual oppression. He also said, in an encouraging way, that he was confident that I could deal with it effectively. As I mentioned already, I also discussed the issue with many medical and religious experts. As I did so, I began to reaffirm my first instinctive impression, that Mary was indeed in need of deliverance ministry.

When I reflected on the feelings I experienced as I talked to Mary, I had to acknowledge that I liked the girl herself. She was charming, intelligent and strangely different from other girls of her age. She evoked a fatherly sentiment within me, a desire to be a mentor who would protect and nurture her as a vulnerable, young person. That was a new feeling for me. However, instead of sensing God's presence in our meetings, I was sometimes aware of feelings of disquiet. They seemed to be evoked by a sense of something negative, a spirit that was not from God. They convinced me that there was certainly something out of kilter in Mary's life. But when, sometime later, I came to administer the sacraments of reconciliation and anointing, I did have a strong sense of the presence of the all Powerful One who desires to liberate us from all oppression.

3.) Prayer and Transformation

Chaplains also need to reflect on how their pastoral experiences, which are the fruit of empathic attention, might be inviting them to modify and deepen their religious beliefs. It is worth noting that the Greek word *epistrophe* for 'attention' can also mean 'conversion'. So ministry as loving attention to the experience of others, can involve a cognitive crucifixion, one that disrupts familiar systems of meaning that, up till then, afforded a sense of security to the ego. In Job's day the danger was that people would impose their black-and-white, fundamentalist religious ideas on the reality of people's lives. In the modern world, which is so influenced by secular postmodernism, there is a danger that Christian pastoral care workers, who espouse liberal and arguably reductionist religious views, would arbitrarily interpret experiences that people share with them in a rather watered-down, rationalist way. There are two levels of awareness involved in such a process of transformation.

Firstly, one's sense of *self* can change as a result of growing self-awareness. As I mentioned already, when I was ministering to Mary, I became aware of my capacity for strong paternal feelings and of my reluctance to step out from the crowd in order to embrace a worldview that would be considered anachronistic and naïve by others. By the way, I subsequently found that my fears were well founded. I also felt totally inadequate in the face of the spiritual challenge that faced me.

Secondly, we have to come to terms with the gap between our *professed* and *operative* theologies, i.e. the difference between what we say we believe at a conscious level of experience (professed theology), and what we actually believe, largely at an unconscious level of experience (operative theology). This often involves our images of God and ourselves. At a conscious level of awareness they can be positive and consoling. At an unconscious level of awareness, however, they can be negative and associated with feelings of desolation.

For example, if anyone had asked me, before I did the Clinical Pastoral Education course, whether I believed in the devil's existence, I would have said I wasn't sure. But my encounter with Mary forced me to clarify what I really believed. Was the devil simply a metaphor for the sum total of human evil; the unjust and oppressive structures of society; or the dark and destructive potential of the human unconscious, as so many people maintain, or was the devil an angelic being opposed to God's purposes, who is perverted and perverting, as the teaching of the church seems to assert? As I reflected deeply, I came to believe in the devil's existence and malign activity more firmly that heretofore.

Finally, chaplains, should pray about their relationships with patients. While it is good to ask God to help them and their relatives and friends, it is also necessary that pastoral carers should honestly share their feelings about them with the Lord in prayer. Martin Luther once said that 'prayer is not telling lies to God'. In other words, it is a matter of acknowledging how they really feel as a result of ministry to others. Chaplains need to talk to the Lord about those feelings. The people who pray in this way have to let go of inner control in two senses. Firstly, they have to allow all of their true feelings to surface without censorship. Secondly, they have to tell the Lord the truth, the whole truth and nothing but the truth about those feelings. Otherwise, they will not be open in the depths of their personalities to the inspirations of the Lord.

For example, I had a lot to say to God about my relationship with Mary. I was sad and perplexed to see such a young girl suffering from a brain tumour which would begin by causing blindness and eventually bring about her death. I had also to talk to the Lord about my reluctance to leave the familiar world of the material, the empirical and the rational, in order to enter the more unfamiliar world of the supernatural. I told Jesus that I didn't particularly want to be marginalised because of my beliefs, especially among my peers and relatives. As I prayed I realised that this was precisely what happened to the Lord. Following his spiritual awakening, his family 'went out to seize him, for people were saying, he is out of his mind' (Mk 3:21). I had a real sense of being drawn into spiritual combat (cf. Eph 6:1-17).[11] The prospect of having to confront the evil one really scared me. I realised that I was lacking firm trust in the power of God at work both in the sacraments and in myself. Over a period of time I was led in prayer to affirm the truths, 'For God is at work *in you*, both to will and to work for his good pleasure' (Phil 2:13), and 'For he who is within you (God) is greater than he who is in the world (Satan)' (1 Jn 4:4).

Conclusion

These reflections are only intended to be a brief introduction to one aspect of the practice of theological reflection. They don't pretend to be comprehensive. For example, I have said very little about social analysis.[12] Admittedly, it is more relevant in some other forms of pastoral caring than it might be in hospital chaplaincy work. It is difficult to engage in, because it often requires a good deal of fact finding and empirical research. Presumably, that is why this dimension is often neglected in theological reflection. It strikes me that pastoral care workers who are doing post graduate degrees in the future, could be encouraged to gather and interpret relevant empirical data that would be useful to their colleagues.

Apart from helping chaplains to grow in self-awareness, intimacy with God, religious maturity, and pastoral skills, theological reflection, as we have tried to describe it, can also enable pastoral ministers to plan their work in a more sensitive and effective way. Needless to say, any Christian could adapt, the method of theological and spiritual reflection described here, for use in his or her life. It is my belief that this kind of theologising not only inculturates the faith, it can have a prophetic dimension, by discerning the presence and the *elan* of God's activity in the postmodern world.

CHAPTER ELEVEN

Christ Within and Among Us[1]

A number of years ago some Travellers in north Dublin asked me to say an inaugural Mass in a hut they had built on their halting site. Most of the people who attended were women and children. The following day I returned to the site and visited the families who were living there. When I knocked on one caravan door, it was opened by a good looking young woman with blonde hair. She gave me a warm welcome, invited me in, and said, 'I'm glad you called, father, because there is something I want to tell you.' When I asked her what it was, she replied: 'I was at the Mass last night. When you gave out holy communion you said that we should close our eyes and imagine that Jesus was standing in front of us looking at us with eyes full of love and humility.' 'Yes, I can remember saying that,' I responded. 'Well, father,' said the travelling woman, 'I did see Jesus standing in front of me. He was as real to me as you are at the moment.' 'So you saw Jesus, after receiving holy communion,' I said, 'that must have been deeply moving.' 'It was, father, but that wasn't all. Jesus walked into me.' 'What do you mean?' I asked. 'Father, Jesus walked over to me and then walked into me.' I was still confused. 'What do you mean exactly, when you say that Jesus walked into you?' 'Father Jesus walked through my skin into my body. I knew he was living inside me.' I was struck with awe when the woman said this in a quiet way, so much so that my strong emotional reaction caused shivers to go up and down my spine. 'That is wonderful,' I whispered, 'what did you feel when you knew that Jesus was living within you?' The young woman paused. Then she replied, 'Joyful, I never felt so happy in my life, in fact I still feel the same happiness today.' One had only to look at her lovely, radiant face to know that what she said was true.

Afterwards I reflected, more than once, on that conversation.

Clearly, like many other Christians before and since, this young woman had experienced a spiritual awakening at the Eucharist. Up to then she had known the Jesus who is *with* us in an external way by means of such things as Christian doctrines, rituals and iconography. But following her vivid religious experience, she knew Jesus in a more intimate and personal way as the One who lived *within* her. Of course this is a very biblical notion.

Jesus often spoke about the way in which God the Father dwelt in him. For example in Jn 10:18, he said: 'Believe in the work I do; then you will know for sure that the Father is in me and I am in the Father.' Again in Jn 12:45 he said: 'Whoever sees me, sees the one who sent me.' But what is surprising is the fact that he promised that he would dwell in the believers in much the same way that the Father dwelt in him. For example, referring to the Holy Spirit, he said: 'He lives *with* you and will be *in* you' (John 14:17). Later Jesus described the effect of the promised in-filling. He declared: 'I am the true vine … Remain in me, and I will remain in you. No branch can bear fruit by itself; it must remain in the vine. Neither can you bear fruit unless you remain in me. I am the vine; you are the branches. If a man remains in me and I in him, he will bear much fruit; apart from me you can do nothing' (Jn 15:5-6).

Writing some years after the death and resurrection of Jesus, St John returned to this notion of the divine indwelling. He said that there were three ways of knowing that Christ lived within. Firstly, 'By this we know that we abide in him and he in us because he has given us his Spirit' (1 Jn 3:24; 4:13). Secondly, he stated: 'God abides in those who confess that Jesus is the Son of God and they abide in God' (1 Jn 4:15). Thirdly, he added, 'Those who abide in love, abide in God.' St Paul mirrored this teaching on numerous occasions when he used phrases such as 'in Christ' or 'Christ within.' For example, in Eph 3:16-17 he says: 'I pray that out of his glorious riches God may strengthen you with power through his Spirit in your inner being, so that Christ may dwell in your hearts through faith.' In 2 Cor 13:5 Paul asks rhetorically: 'Do you not realise that Jesus Christ is within you?'

One only grows to have a sense of the immanence of Christ as a result of a gradual or sudden spiritual awakening, an in-filling of the Holy Spirit that enables one to have a new and vibrant relationship with the God who is at once the God beyond and the God within. The in-filling of the Spirit can be described as a religious experience that inaugurates a new and decisive awareness of the presence, love and power of God in one's life. This awareness is often associated with one or more of the gifts of the Spirit. The American bishops described such an experience when they said in a 1997 document entitled *Grace for a New Springtime,* 'The in-filling of the Spirit makes Jesus Christ known and loved as Lord and Saviour, establishes or re-establishes an immediacy of relationship with all those persons of the Trinity, and through inner transformation affects the whole of the Christian life. There is new life and a new conscious awareness of God's power and *presence.*'

I had such an awakening many years ago. After my ordination I knew a lot *about* Christ, but I didn't know him in a *personal* way. To me he often seemed distant and a bit unreal. I found it hard to pray or to read the scriptures with spiritual insight. I wasn't happy with the situation. I began to have a great desire for an outpouring of the Holy Spirit and a spiritual awakening in my life. For nearly two years I prayed for this grace.

In February 1974, I was invited to attend a Charismatic Conference in Benburb Priory in Co Tyrone. On Saturday 4 February, Cecil Kerr, a Church of Ireland minister from the Christian Renewal Centre in Rostrevor, Co Down, gave an inspiring talk about Jesus as our way of peace. Quite frankly, his anointed words moved me to tears. I wanted to know the Lord in the way that Cecil did. Afterwards a nun introduced me to him. We had a brief chat and arranged to meet privately some time later. When we did, I told Cecil that I was looking for a new awareness of God in my life. Then he read the memorable passage from Ephesians 3:16-20 which says among other things: 'I pray that you, being rooted and established in love, may have power, together with all the saints, to grasp how wide and long and high and deep is the love of Christ, and to know this love that surpasses knowledge – that you may be filled to the measure of all the fullness of God.' Then he began to pray for me, firstly in English, then in tongues. Suddenly and effortlessly I too began to pray fluently in an unknown language. I had been filled with the Spirit.

For the next six months or so I was on a spiritual high. Inwardly I was flooded with a feeling of wellbeing. In the words of the travelling woman already quoted, it was as if Jesus Christ had walked through the walls of my body to live within me by his Spirit. I could identify with the experience of St Paul who said: 'It is no longer I who live, but Christ who lives in me' (Gal 2:20). There are some lines in a poem by Tadhg Gaelach Ó Súilleabháin, which were translated from Irish into English. They express something of what I felt:

> The light in my heart, O Saviour, is thy heart,
> The wealth of my heart, Thy heart poured out for me
> Seeing that Thy heart, Love, filled with love for me
> Leave Thy heart in keeping, hooded in mine.[2]

A Jungian perspective

Since having that Pentecostal experience I have found that the writings of Carl Jung have helped me to understand what such a spiritual awakening might involve from a psychological point of view. This is a legitimate perspective because Catholic theology maintains that the grace of God builds upon the dynamics of our human nature. It does not bypass them. On one occasion Jung wrote in his rather distinctive manner: 'Christian education has done all that is humanly possible, but it has not been enough. Too few people have experienced the divine image as the innermost possession of their own souls. Christ only meets them from without, never from within the soul.'[3] I don't believe that the Lord can be known directly within the human spirit. However, that presence can be indirectly experienced in and through its activity in the psyche. Jung maintained that the psyche has a certain affinity for relationship with God. What makes it possible is what he referred to as the God-archetype. It is the most important capacity of the self. It is the psychological equivalent of what Karl Rahner referred to as the supernatural existential or an obediential potency of the human person for supernatural grace.[4]

Archetypes are like the scaffolding and frameworks that builders construct which are filled with concrete. In other words, the God archetype represents a capacity rather than a content of the unconscious mind. It is open to the possibility of an experience of the divine. All people everywhere have this potential. Jung said: 'When I say as a psychologist that God is an archetype, I mean by that the 'type' in the psyche. The word 'type' is, as we know, derived from *typos*, 'blow' or 'imprint'; thus an archetype pre-supposes an imprinter ... The religious point of view, understandably enough, puts the accent on the imprinter, whereas scientific psychology emphasises the *typos*, the imprint – the only thing it can understand. The religious point of view understands the imprint as the working of an imprinter; the scientific point of view understands it as the symbol of an unknown and incomprehensible content.'[5]

Jung believed that the mystery of the incomprehensible God was mediated to the self by means of what he called God images, myths and symbols. While he would acknowledge that many symbols could act as God images, Christ was the God image *par excellance*, especially for Western culture. He mediates the mysterious presence of God to the self. In one of his writings, 'Christ as a Symbol of the Self', he wrote: 'In the world of Christian ideas Christ undoubtedly represents the self.'[6] Jung was accused of regarding the words *self* and *God* as interchangeable. He himself denied this. He wrote: 'The self can never take the place of God, although it may perhaps be a receptacle for divine grace. Such regrettable misunderstandings are due to the assumption that I am an irreligious man who does not believe in God ... How could any sane man suppose he could displace God, or do anything whatever to him? I am not so mad that I could be suspected of intending to create a substitute for God. How could any man replace God?'[7]

Jung believed that by coming to know Christ, a person could experience his presence within his or her deepest self. He wrote: 'He is in us and we are in him. His kingdom is the pearl of great price, the treasure buried in the field, the grain of mustard seed which will become a great tree, and the heavenly city. As Christ is in us, so also is his heavenly kingdom. These few, familiar references should be sufficient to make the psychological position of the Christ symbol quite clear. Christ exemplifies the archetype of the self.'[8] Jung believed that as one related in faith to Christ, one experienced his presence within. Speaking about himself he said: 'Christ is in us, and we are in him! Why should the activity of God and the presence of the Son of Man within us not be real and observable? Every day I am thankful to God that I have been allowed to experience the reality of the Divine Image within me. Had this not been granted me, I should indeed have been a bitter enemy of Christianity, and of the church especially. But thanks to this act of grace, my life has meaning, and my inward eye has been opened to the beauty and greatness of dogma.'9 When one reads Jung's religious writings carefully it becomes apparent that although he was a great advocate of the immanence of the divine, because of his psychological empiricism and philosophical Kantianism, he had little or no apparent appreciation of the simultaneous transcendence of God.

Awareness of God's Love

As I have become progressively aware of the divine indwelling I have become consciously aware of the fact that Jesus loves me in the way that the Father loved him. As Jesus said: 'As the Father has loved me, so I love you' (Jn 15:9). The Spirit gives me the ability 'to know and rely on the love God has for us. God is love. Whoever lives in love lives in God, and God in him' (1 Jn 4:16). There have been many moments, some simple, others more profound and memorable when I have been so vividly aware of that love that it brought tears of joy to my eyes. As St Peter said: 'Though you have not seen him, you love him; and even though you do not see him now, you believe in him and are filled with an inexpressible and glorious joy' (1 Pet 1:8).

Remarkable as it may seem, the Father loves me as if I were Jesus himself endowed with every perfection of divinity. As the 7th Sunday preface of the eucharistic liturgy says, the Father sent his Son Jesus that he 'might see and love in us what he sees and loves in Christ'. The Father says unceasingly to those who have been justified by grace, 'You are my beloved son or daughter in whom I am well pleased' (Mt 17:5). When a person enjoys this Christ-like awareness of God's love, s/he is able to say with his divine Son, who lives within us, 'Abba, Father' (cf. Rm 8:15). As St Paul says in Gal 4:6: 'Because you are sons and daughters, God sent the Spirit of his Son into our hearts, the Spirit who calls out, "Abba, Father".'

Discovering One's Christ-self

Paradoxically, the more we relate to others, the more we discover and relate to our deepest selves. Carl Jung, one of the most introspective of psychologists, stated: 'One is always in the dark about one's personality. One needs others to get to know oneself.'[10] If any of us reflect on our experience we will recognise the truth of this principle. For example, when we think about our friendships we become aware of the fact that we grow in self-awareness through our struggle to grow in intimacy. It confronts us with the limits of such things as our trust, generosity and our ability to receive. In heterosexual relationships, in-depth knowledge of a person of the opposite sex helps one to acknowledge and appropriate either one's male or female potential. Relationships with others also school us in virtues such as patience, forbearance, self-forgetfulness, generosity, compassion, empathy, etc. In spirituality it is much the same, inwardness and relatedness, divine immanence and divine transcendence are interconnected.

As I contemplate God the Father, in and through his Son, I get to know my own divine potential, my Christ-self. Pope John Paul II has adverted to this principle in par. 8 of his encyclical, *Veritatis Splendor*: 'the man who wishes to understand himself should ... draw near to Christ. He must, so to speak, enter him with all his own self ... If this profound process takes place within him, he then bears fruit not only of adoration of God but also of deeper wonder at himself.' In another place the Holy Father says: 'God is present in the intimacy of man's being, in his mind, conscience and heart; an ontological and psychological reality, in considering which St Augustine said of God that he was closer to us than our inmost beings.'[11]

Many of the mystics have spoken about the fact that in getting to know Christ one gets to know him as the intimate guest of one's deepest spiritual self. For example, in the writings of Dame Julian of Norwich we read: 'For our soul is so deeply grounded in God and so endlessly treasured that we cannot come to knowledge of it until we first have knowledge of God, who is the Creator to whom it is united ... It is a great understanding to see and know inwardly, that God who is our Creator, dwells in our soul.'[12] In her *Way of Perfection*, St Teresa of Avila wrote in similar, but more introverted vein: 'Remember how St Augustine tells us about his seeking God in many places and eventually finding him within himself. Do you suppose it is of little importance that a soul which is often distracted should come to understand this truth and to find that, in order to speak to its Eternal Father and to take its delight in him, it has no need to go to heaven … we need no wings to go in search of him but have only to find a place where we can be alone and look upon him present within us.'[13] In the modern era, Thomas Merton once asked during a talk, 'Who am I?' and answered in terms reminiscent of the two great mystics already quoted, 'My deepest realisation of who I am is – I am one loved by Christ … The depths of my identity is in the centre of my being where I am loved by God.'[14]

Scripture often refers to God's glory, that is, God's majesty, presence and power. For example in 2 Cor 3:18 we read: 'And all of us, with unveiled faces, seeing the glory of the Lord, as though reflected in a mirror, are being transformed into the same image from one degree of glory to another.' In his treatise on *Loving God*, St Bernard stressed the importance of not only being consciously aware of the transcendent glory, but also of the way in which that same glory is immanent within believers. Bernard referred to it as 'inner glory'. He said that, objectively speaking, we have such glory in virtue of our creation in God's image (cf. Gen 1:26) and also in virtue of our salvation by the grace of God which abides within us. As Paul said, the love of God has been poured into our hearts by the Holy Spirit (cf. Rom 5:5). He says that these interrelated forms of glory don't do us much good unless we have a conscious awareness of them. He wrote: 'What glory is there in possessing something you do not know you possess?'[15] When we become consciously aware of the divine indwelling, we should not attribute that glory to ourselves but rather to the One who has freely bestowed it upon us. As St Paul said: 'Let him who boasts boast in the Lord' (1 Cor 1:31).

Christ Lives his Life in us
In par 521 of the *Catechism of the Catholic Church*, we are told of another profound effect of the divine indwelling, namely that

Christ lives out his divine-human life in and through us. 'Christ enables us to live in him all that he himself lived, and he lives it in us. By his incarnation, he, the Son of God, has in a certain sense united himself with each person.' Personally, I find that this is one of the most profound and moving statements I have ever read. It needs to be repeatedly reflected upon in a prayerful way until it begins to deliver its deeper meaning and implications. St Irenaeus (130-200) described one of the important consequences of this form of indwelling by stating that Christ sanctified every stage of our lives. I'll paraphrase what he said. Christ came to save all, infants, children, youths, and mature adults. He therefore passed through every age, becoming an infant for infants, thus sanctifying infants; a child for children, thus sanctifying those who are of this age, a youth for youths, becoming an example to youths, and thus sanctifying them for the Lord. So likewise he was a mature adult that he might be a perfect Master for all, sanctifying the mature also. Then, at last, he came on to death, that he might be 'the first-born from the dead, that in all things he might have the pre-eminence,' the Prince of life, existing before all, and going before all.[16] Given these realities, no wonder St John Eudes (1601-1680) was able to say that we must continue to accomplish in ourselves the stages of Jesus' life and to ask him repeatedly to perfect and realise them in us and in his whole church. It is the plan of the Son of God to make us and the whole church partake in the mysteries of his life and to continue and extend them, both in our personal lives and in his whole church.[17]

As we move through the different developmental stages of life, which have been well described by psychologists such as Jung, Piaget, Erickson, Kohlberg, Fowler, Levinson and Gilligan, we can have the faith assurance that we do so in Christ, who went through the very same stages himself. There is nothing in our experience which is alien to him except sin. Even there Paul went so far as to say, 'For our sake he made him to be sin who knew no sin, so that in him we might become the righteousness of God' (2 Cor 5:21). In other words Christ allowed himself to suffer many of the effects of sin as though he had sinned himself, e.g. a certain alienation from God. That was poignantly evident when at the beginning of his ministry he submitted to John's baptism of repentance, and at the end of his ministry when he cried out on the cross, 'My God, my God why have you forsaken me?' (Mt 27:46). So he knows from personal experience what it is like to be human at each of the stages of life. As we go through the same stages we can make an act of faith in the fact that Christ is at work within us by his Spirit to know God's will of love and to carry it out (cf. Phil 2:13). As Ps 37:5 puts it: 'Commit your way to the Lord; trust in him, and he will act.' In other words, by his grace at work within us God will enable us to live Christ's life in the world today, no matter what the inner and outer obstacles may be. As St Paul proclaimed: 'I can do *all things* in him who strengthens me' (Phil 2:13).

Doing Divine Deeds
In one of his writings St John Eudes (1601-1688) quoted a well known Pauline text, 'I make up what is lacking in the sufferings of Jesus Christ for the sake of his body the church' (Col 1:24). He went on to observe that what Paul says about our sufferings can be extended to all our other actions as well. Here is an extended quotation from Eudes's book *The Life and Kingdom of Jesus in Christian Souls*: 'We can say that any true Christian, who is a member of Jesus Christ, and who is united to him by his grace, *continues* and *completes* (my italics) through all the actions that he carries out in the spirit of Christ, the actions that Jesus Christ accomplished during the time of his temporary life on earth. So that when a Christian prays, he continues and fulfils the prayer that Jesus Christ offered on earth. Whenever he works, he continues and fulfils the laborious life of Jesus Christ. Whenever he relates to his or her neighbour in a spirit of charity, then he continues and fulfils the relational life of Jesus Christ. Whenever he eats or rests in a Christian manner, he continues and fulfils the subjection that Jesus Christ wished to have to these necessities. The same can be said of any other action that is carried out in a Christian manner.'[18]

Let's take a practical example to illustrate John Eudes's point. If I have to relate to someone who irritates me I may find it particularly hard to carry out the golden rule by doing to that person what I would like him or her to do to me (cf. Mt 7:12). But, if I make a decision to do so, believing that it is what God wants me to do, while at the same time trusting in the Spirit's help, it will become possible. Not only will I want what is best for the other person, I will have an empathic sense of what it might be. One is reminded in this regard of a difficult relationship in the life of St Thérèse of Lisieux. She felt her vocation was to love as Jesus loves. She wrote in words that are reminiscent of those of John Eudes's teaching: 'I am not just to love my neighbours as myself; *I am to love them as Jesus loves them* (my Italics).'[19] She went on to add: 'Always, when I act as charity bids, I have this feeling that *it is Jesus who is acting in me*; (my italics) the closer my union with him the greater my love for all the sisters without distinction.'[20]

One of the sisters she lived with had the knack of rubbing her up the wrong way at every turn. Thérèse says that every time she met this sister, 'I reminded myself that charity is not a matter of fine sentiments; it means doing things. So I determined to treat this sister as if she were the person I loved best in the world. Every time I met her I prayed for her, offering God all her virtues and merits ... I didn't confine myself to saying a lot of prayers for her ... I tried to do her every good turn I possibly could. When I felt tempted to take her down a peg or two with an unkind retort, I would put on my best smile instead, and try to change the subject ... We used often to meet, outside recreation time, over our work; and when the struggle was too much for me, I used to turn tail and run.'[21] Thérèse tells us that the sister in question never suspected what she really felt about her. She tells us that once at recreation, the sister actually said, beaming all over, something like: 'I wish you would tell me, Sister Thérèse, what it is about me that gets the right side of you? You always have a smile for me whenever I meet you.' Thérèse went on to comment wryly: 'Well, of course, what really attracted me about her was Jesus hidden in the depths of her soul ... I could only say that the sight of her always made me smile with plea-sure – naturally I didn't explain that the pleasure was entirely spiritual.'[22]

The principle that is implicit in Thérèse's account, i.e. relying on the indwelling Spirit to live as Jesus lived, can be applied to any Christian task, such as forgiving offenders, loving the enemy, being patient, kind, etc. I also believe that this principle also applies to the struggle to resist temptation. Scripture tells us that as Christ 'himself has suffered and been tempted, he is able to help those who are tempted' (Heb 2:18). When we are faced with powerful temptation, especially against love, we can be sure that if we have realistic self-awareness, and humble and trusting dependence, 'God is faithful, and he also provides the way to escape, that you may be able to endure it' (1 Cor 10:13).

St Vincent de Paul (1580-1660), a contemporary of Eudes, had a strong sense of what God could do in and through the believer. With the image of the vine and branches obviously in mind (cf. Jn 15:1-12) he said to a young protege: 'Just as a wild stock on which a seedling has been grafted brings forth fruits of the same sort as the seedling, so too with us poor creatures. When our Lord imprints his mark on us and gives us, so to say, the sap of his spirit and grace, we, being united to him as the branches are united to the vine, *we will do what he did when he was on earth* (my italics). I mean to say, we shall perform divine actions and beget, like Saint Paul, being filled with this spirit, children to our Lord.'[23] It is interesting that having said that those who are intimately united to the Lord, 'will do what Jesus Christ did on earth' Vincent goes on to qualify this statement by saying, it refers only to the ability to bring about conversions and new life in Christ. But surely the logic of his statement also implies that believers could, in principle at least, do everything Jesus did, including even healings and miracles. After all, Jesus promised in Jn 14:12, 'Very truly, I tell you, the one who believes in me will do the works that I do and, in fact, will do greater works than these, because I am going to the Father.' The contemporary church has stated in a number of official texts, most recently in an instruction of Cardinal Ratzinger, that some people, both lay and clerical, can be given the ability to heal the sick (cf. 1 Cor 12:9).[24]

Nurturing the sense of indwelling
It is clear from the scriptures that a number of actions tend to nurture the inward sense of the divine indwelling. I will briefly advert to three of them, praying to be filled with the Spirit, reading and praying the scriptures and receiving the Eucharist in holy communion.

It is the Spirit that leads us into the truth about God and about the divine indwelling. Not surprisingly, therefore, in Eph 5:18, St Paul says: 'Be filled with the Spirit.' In the *Summa Theologica* St Thomas asks whether a person can experience more than one in-filling of the Spirit. He responds in the affirmative. The first in-filling initiates the divine indwelling, subsequent in-fillings enable 'a certain renewal by grace.'[25] Then he goes on to explain that the Spirit *lives* in us in a new way in order that we may *do* new things, such as giving ourselves more fully to the Lord, e.g. by being willing to embrace some difficult task, such as donating one's money to the poor or volunteering to go on the foreign missions. So it is important to pray regularly for the in-filling of the Spirit. I try to say the following prayer every morning. 'Father in heaven, your Spirit is a Spirit of truth and love. Pour that same Holy Spirit into my body, my mind and my soul. Preserve me today from all illusions and false inspirations. Reveal your presence, your word, and your will to me in a way that I can understand. And I thank you that you will do this while giving me the ability to respond through Jesus Christ our Lord. Amen.'

To read and pray the scriptures is another wonderful way of nurturing the divine presence within. If Christ abides in people, they, like him, have to be attentive to the revelatory word of God. In Ezek 3:3 the Lord said, in a symbolical way, to the prophet that he should eat and digest the word of God. Jesus said: 'If you make my word your home you will indeed be my disciples' (Jn 8:31). St Paul had something similar in mind when he said: 'Let the word of Christ dwell in you richly' (Col 3:16). One is reminded in this regard of something Francis Bacon wrote: 'Some books are to be tasted, others to be swallowed, and some few to be chewed and digested.' The bible is pre-eminent among the latter. As chapter twelve indicates, we can chew and digest the word of God in different ways, such as paying attention to the liturgical readings and by praying the scriptures on a regular basis by means of *lectio divina*. In Jn 14:25 Jesus says that he will continue to abide in those who keep his word: 'If anyone loves me, he will obey my teaching. My Father will love him, and we will come to him and make our home with him.'

Regular reception of the Eucharist, *the* sacrament of God's love, also nourishes the Christian life. As Jesus says in Jn 6:56, 'Those who eat my flesh and drink my blood abide in me and I in them.' John makes it clear that Christ will only continue to abide in people if, having received him in the Eucharist, they love one another in the way Jesus loves them. He wrote: 'No one has ever seen God; but if we love one another, God lives in us and his love is made complete in us. We know that we live in him and he in us, because he has given us of his Spirit' (1 Jn 4:12-13).

Christ in our Midst

There is a well known, much quoted text in Luke 17:21. It can be correctly translated in two ways. In the *New International Version* the first rendition reads: 'the kingdom of God is within you' which is literally correct because the Greek word *entos* usually means 'within'. The second rendition which is found in many other translations reads: 'the kingdom of God is among you.' It is also correct because the Greek word can also mean 'among,' or 'in the midst' of you. In Col 1:27 there is a similar verse that can be translated in the same two ways. It reads: 'To them God has chosen to make known among the Gentiles the glorious riches of this mystery, which is Christ *in you*, the hope of glory.' The verse can also be read as: ' Christ *among you*, the hope of glory.' From a theological point of view these renditions are complementary rather than opposed. It is precisely because Christ is present in individual persons that he is also present in the community.

The gospels tell us that Jesus taught that he was present in the community of believers. There is the well known saying: 'For where two or three come together in my name, there am I with them' (Mt 18:20). The post-resurrection account of the two disciples on the road to Emmaus makes a similar point. As a gentile, Luke is asking how can those who have never met the earthly Jesus encounter him after his glorification? He answers, the Risen Jesus is encountered in the eucharistic community where believers share their lives in the context of three important realities, the word of God in scripture, inspired preaching and the breaking of bread. In the light of these realities 'their eyes were opened and they recognised him' (Lk 24:31). In other words the eucharistic community discerned the presence of the risen Lord in their midst in a way that made their hearts burn within them (Lk 24:32).

St Paul first came to recognise the indwelling of Jesus in the community of believers when he had his conversion experience on the road to Damascus. Acts 22:7-8 recounts the dramatic moment. 'The Lord asked him: "Saul! Saul! Why do you persecute me?" "Who are you, Lord?" I asked. "I am Jesus of Nazareth, whom you are persecuting," he replied.' From the beginning Paul was aware the Jesus lived in the Christian community. Afterwards, the apostle to the Gentiles used a number of metaphors to express this vivid awareness.

Firstly, Paul referred to the community as the temple of the Lord. This image had its roots in the Old Testament and the gospels. Having stated in 1 Cor 6:19 that each individual's body is a temple of the Spirit, Paul goes on to say to the community: 'For we are the temple of the living God. As God has said: "I will live with them and walk among them, and I will be their God, and they will be my people".' (2 Cor 6:16). Sometime later the author of Eph 2:21-22 observes, in Christ: 'the whole building is joined together and rises to become a holy temple in the Lord. And in him you too are being built together to become a dwelling in which God lives by his Spirit.'

The second great image used by Paul is that of the community as the body of Christ. As he says, Christ 'is the head of the body, the church; he is the beginning and the firstborn from among the dead, so that in everything he might have the supremacy' (Col 1:18). Then addressing himself to the believers Paul says: 'Now you are the body of Christ, and each one of you is a part of it' (1 Cor 12:27-28). The charisms and ministries of the Spirit are the charisms and ministries of Christ who expresses himself in and through the giftedness of the community (cf. Rom 12:4-9; Eph 4:9-13).

Christ's Presence in non-Christians and the Poor

Once we can discern the presence of Christ in our own hearts we will be able to discern that same presence in the hearts of fellow believers. Just as the Lord lives in me, so the same Lord lives in them. We are all children of God, members of the same family of faith, and brothers and sisters of Christ. While Christians should esteem non-Christians, they are neighbours rather than brothers and sisters. This distinction is implied in a number of texts such as: 'Let us do good to all people, and especially to those who are of the household of faith' (Gal 6:10). St Peter said: 'Honour all people. Love your brothers and sisters' (1 Pet 2:17). Therefore it is only Christians who are true brothers and sisters, the others are called *hoi exo*, those who stand outside the family of faith (1 Thess 4:10-12; 1 Cor 5:12, 13; Col 4:5).[26] Tertullian echoed this distinction when he distinguished between two kinds of relationship. One depends on common descent and embraces all people; the other depends on the common knowledge of God and a shared experience of the Holy Spirit.[27]

Ralph Martin has written, Christ has 'made an extraordinary promise to those who are abiding in close union with him, so much so, *that for his disciples*, those who hear them hear him: "And if anyone gives even a cup of cold water to one of these little ones because he is my disciple, I tell you the truth, he will certainly not lose his reward" (Mt 10:42).'[28] Surprisingly, Martin overlooks the existence of anonymous Christians. Because of the notion of baptism of desire, there are many men and women who are secret but unrecognised members of the family of faith because they consciously or unconsciously seek God with a sincere heart. Writing about this the *Catechism of the Catholic Church*, says in par 1260: 'Every person who is ignorant of the gospel of Christ and of his church, but seeks the truth and does the will of God in accordance with his understanding of it, can be saved. It may be supposed that such persons would have desired baptism explicitly if they had known its necessity.' Martin goes on to say that that those who extend the notion of brotherhood and sisterhood to all people, whether they are disciples or not, are seriously mistaken because they are confusing different modalities of divine presence. He says that this propensity probably has its roots in the secularising tendencies of the Enlightenment and the French Revolution which advocated the notion that all people were equal as brothers and sisters because of the common paternity of their Creator.

While there is undoubted truth in what Martin says, it must be acknowledged that it is not of any great practical value, be-

cause one can never be quite sure who is, or who is not a
Christian, albeit an anonymous one. In any case there is another
notable exception which he overlooks. It blurs the distinction he
adverts to, even further. In the parable of the general judgement
in Mt 25:31-46, the judge of the world declares to those gathered
before him that the works of mercy done or not done for those in
need were done or not done for himself, and he calls these poor
people in need 'the least of my brothers and sisters' (Mt 25:40).
As Joseph Ratzinger observes: 'nothing suggests that only the
faithful, only believers in the gospel of Christ, are meant here, as
is the case in a similar text (Mk 9:41), but rather all people in
need, without differentiation.'[29] He goes on to say in a rather
convoluted way: 'Christ sees himself generally represented in
the poor and lowly especially, people who – quite apart from
their ethical quality, but simply through their being lowly, and
the appeal to the love of others that lies in that – make present
the master.'[30] Evidently, Jesus identified himself so much with
the poor and needy, irrespective of their beliefs or behaviour,
that to love them was to love him with them and in them. Of
course, the two notions of divine presence can come together
when those in need are also believing Christians, members of
the household of faith. Some people mistakenly argue that if
Jesus is present with and within anonymous Christians and the
poor and needy, why should we try to evangelise them? We do
so for two reasons. It is a divine commission given to us by
Christ (cf. Mk 16:15; Rom 10:14-17), and it is important to help
those who do not know Christ to consciously acknowledge and
believe in the saving power of the One who is already with them
by the Spirit.

St Vincent de Paul was palpably aware of these truths.
Speaking about him, Bishop Abelly wrote: 'He saw Jesus the
worker in artisans, Jesus the poor one in the poor, Jesus the suffering in the sick and dying. He looked on all states in life, seeing
in each the image of his sovereign Lord who dwelt in the person
of his neighbour. He was moved, in this view, to honour, respect,
love and serve each person as our Lord, and our Lord in each individual. He wanted his followers and all those with whom he
spoke to enter into these same sentiments, to make their charity
toward the neighbour more constant and more perfect.'[31]

A Personal Memory

Some time ago these truths came alive for me when I met a group of travelling people behind St James' Brewery, in the heart of Dublin. When I arrived by car all the children ran to welcome me with affection and noisy excitement. Then I was led to one of the caravans. 'You will be hearing confessions here, father,' the owner said. For nearly an hour I administered the sacrament of reconciliation. I was surprised to find that among the travellers were a few settled people from the nearby flats. As I absolved the people in the name of Christ I had a powerful sense that an umbrella of mercy was not only extended above them as penitents but above me as the confessor. We were, all of us, the recipients of God's amazing grace. Afterwards I said Mass in that same caravan. It was filled to capacity with about twenty people. There was a little blond girl sitting beside me.

When the gospel was read I invited the people to share stories of faith, accounts of how God had helped them when they trusted in him. Many moving testimonies were recounted. A settled woman shared how God had helped her grandchild to recover from a riding accident. She had injured her head as a result of a fall on concrete. A man from the nearby flats recounted, in an amusing way, how he had asked Mary to help him to avoid going to prison, and she had. Finally, the man who owned the caravan told us how, three years before, his daughter had been standing beside the stove in the caravan when her nylon dress had caught fire. Besides being badly burnt, the fabric had melted into her skin. When she was brought to hospital, the doctors said that there was very little hope that she would recover. The family trusted in God, and prayed fervently for the little girl. Against all the odds she recovered. The father completed his testimony by saying, 'Father, thanks be to God, that is my daughter, alive and well, sitting beside you.' What a memorable evening that turned out to be. From beginning to end I had a strong and luminous sense that the Lord was in our midst.

Conclusion

As people become more consciously aware of the indwelling of Christ in the individual person and in the community, they become more aware of the fact that they have to avoid anything in thought, word or deed which would be incompatible with the divine life. Discernment is called for, an ability to recognise what impulses come from the old Adam of our unredeemed human nature, and what impulses come from the new Adam of our redeemed human nature. Are they prompted by the spirit of the world or the Spirit of Jesus? I want to include a long, but relevant, quotation from St John Eudes, which describes this tension very well:

- The spirit of Jesus is a spirit of light, truth, devotion, love, trust, zeal and reverence toward God and the things of God. The spirit of the world is a spirit of error, disbelief, darkness, blindness, mistrust, grumbling, impiety, irreverence and hardness of heart toward God and the things of God.
- The spirit of Jesus is a spirit of humility, modesty, distrust of self, mortification, self-denial, reliability and firmness among those who live with this spirit. On the contrary, the spirit of the world is a spirit of pride, presumption, disordered self-love, frivolousness and irresponsibility .
- The spirit of Jesus is a spirit of mercy, charity, patience, gentleness and of unity toward our neighbour. The spirit of the world is a spirit of vengeance, envy, impatience, anger, calumny and division.
- Finally, the spirit of Jesus is the spirit of God, a holy and divine spirit, a spirit of every type of grace, virtue and blessing. It is a spirit of peace and tranquillity, a spirit that only seeks the interests of God and his glory. On the contrary, the spirit of the world is the spirit of Satan. For Satan is the prince and leader of the world. Thus it follows necessarily that the world is animated and governed by his spirit; an earthly, carnal and animal spirit, a spirit of every sort of sin and malediction, a spirit of unrest and anxiety, of storm and tempest, *a spirit of devastation* (Ps 10:7). It is a spirit that seeks only its own ease, satisfaction and interest.[32]

Any concession to the old Adam grieves the spirit of Christ within us. Therefore, when faced with any decision great or small, Christians should ask themselves the question, 'What would Christ do in these circumstances?' Then relying on the power of God to enable them to transcend the limitations of their human nature, they try to live in a Christ-like manner.

Because they are aware of the loving presence of Christ within themselves, they are able to discern and love that same divine presence in others, especially the poor and the marginalised members of society. This twofold awareness finds expression in the following prayer:

Lord, help me to see and love in others,

especially the poor and needy,

what you are seeing and loving in me. Amen.

CHAPTER TWELVE

Reading and Praying the Scriptures[1]

Tertio Millennio Adveniente was published in order to prepare Catholics for the Jubilee year of 2000. In it Pope John Paul II declared: 'In order to recognise who Christ truly is, Christians *should turn with renewed interest to the Bible,* whether it be through the liturgy, rich in the divine word, or through devotional reading, or through instructions suitable for the purpose and other aids.' I'm firmly persuaded that there will be no genuine long lasting renewal and revival in the contemporary church unless it is rooted in and nourished by the word of God.

All Scripture Focuses on Christ

All the books of the Old Testament, point to Christ and find their fulfilment in him. Jesus himself made this clear to the two disciples on the road to Emmaus. Having poured out their sorrows to their companion, 'Jesus replied: "You foolish men! So slow to believe the full message of the prophets! Was it not ordained that the Christ should suffer and so enter his glory?" Then starting with Moses and going through all the prophets he explained to them the passages throughout the scriptures that were about himself' (Lk 24:25-28).

The gospels record the words and actions of Jesus himself. They are like so many panes in the stained glass window of his humanity. When they are illuminated by the Spirit and contemplated with the eyes of faith, they can become a unique source of revelation. Through them we begin to see what God is like. As Jesus said: 'To have seen me is to have seen the Father' (Jn 14:9). The remaining books of the New Testament record the impact and implications of Christ for the first Christians.

The New Testament authors often speak about the importance of God's word. 'All scripture is inspired by God ...it is something alive and active ... it is the sword of the Spirit ... it can judge the secret thoughts and emotions of the heart ... and is useful for teaching truth, rebuking error, correcting faults, and giving instruction for living' (2 Tim 3:1; Heb 4:12; Eph 6:7; 2 Tim 3:1). No wonder St Jerome once wrote: 'The person who doesn't know the scriptures doesn't know Jesus Christ.'

God's Word is Unique

The world is awash with words, written words, spoken words, and words that are broadcast on radio and TV. But no matter how eloquent and profound they may be, they are merely human words. The bible is unique because it is the only book that contains the inspired and inspiring word of God. However, commenting on contemporary culture, T. S. Eliot observed in *Choruses from the Rock*:

> The endless cycle of idea and action,
> Endless invention, endless experiment,
> Brings knowledge of motion, but not of stillness;
> Knowledge of speech, but not of silence;
> Knowledge of words, and ignorance of the Word.

In Western society words describe pre-existing reality. In the bible, however, God's word is constitutive of reality. It contains the power to effect what it says. As George Montague points out, 'When the Hebrew speaks a word, he is not taking in the outside world and shaping it within himself. Rather he is thrusting something creative and powerful outward from himself into the external world and actually changing that world.'[2] As Is 55:10-11 testifies: 'As the rain and the snow come down from heaven, and do not return to it without watering the earth and making it bud and flourish, so that it yields seed for the sower and bread for the eater, so is my word that goes out from my mouth: It will not return to me empty, but will accomplish what I desire and achieve the purpose for which I sent it.' For example, in Gen 1:3 'God said, "Let there be light," and there was light.' In Jer 49:13 the Lord swears by his own divine authority and faithfulness to act in accord with the divine promises. In a unique way, God has both the intention and the ability to carry out the divine undertakings. Outstanding people of faith said amen to those undertakings. The word is derived from a

Hebrew root '*mn* which means, 'to show oneself firm and stable.' So to say amen to God's word of promise is tantamount to saying 'So be it, it is a fact because God is dependable'[3] As Heb 11 points out, the heroes and heroines of faith in the Old Testament were blessed precisely because they trusted, with unwavering faith, in the sure and certain promises of God. When the Angel Gabriel assured Mary that nothing was impossible to God and promised that Jesus would be conceived by the power of the Holy Spirit, she said, 'let it be to me *according to your word*' (Lk 1:38). Later when Mary visited Elizabeth, her cousin declared: 'Blessed is she who believed that there would be a fulfilment of what was spoken to her from the Lord' (Lk 1:45) .

God's Word in Context

Catholics are not fundamentalists. We don't interpret the bible in a literal, non-historical way. Rather we study the circumstances in which its different books were composed in order to discern the intentions and inspired teaching of its different authors. That is why bible study is important. In *the Dogmatic Constitution on Divine Revelation*, par 12, the Second Vatican Council stated: 'Since God speaks in sacred scripture through men in human fashion, the interpreter of sacred scripture, in order to see clearly what God wanted to communicate to us, should carefully investigate what meaning the sacred writers really intended, and what God wanted to manifest by means of their words.' The document goes on to say that to appreciate the intention of the sacred writers:

1. Attention must be paid to the literary forms of the scripture, and the customary modes of expression at the time of writing.
2. The content and unity of the whole of scripture has to be taken into consideration.
3. Account too must be taken of the harmony between different elements of the faith.
4. All interpretations of scripture must ultimately be subject to the judgement of the Church.

By using reputable works such as the *New Jerome Biblical Commentary*,[4] our understanding of what the sacred writers intended to say can deepen and grow in the way recommended by the Council Fathers. For example, if I'm preparing a homily on the Sunday readings, I usually look up a good commentary, such as Fuller's *Preaching the New Lectionary*,[5] in order to study the background of the text. If there is a parable in the gospel of the day I usually look up Joachim Jeremias's wonderful *Rediscovering the Parables*.[6] Nowadays there are many such books available. Some are very scholarly, others are simpler, some expensive others relatively cheap. In view of the fact that we spend a lot of money on newspapers and magazines in order to keep up to date with the news, we should spend time and money in keeping up to date with the Good News.

One could also attend a scripture course in a theological college or seminary. Many dioceses also arrange bible courses during the year. You might ask a priest in your parish to organise such a course locally. I know of groups of lay men and women who have bible studies in their homes on a regular basis. They use simple resource methods and materials. In my experience most people find scripture study unsettling for a time because it challenges many of their naïve preconceptions. But after a while, it throws an exciting new light on the meaning and implications of the text.

Praying the Scriptures
Scripture study is necessary and good but the experiential sense of divine things comes as a result of prayer.[7] There have been numerous descriptions of this all-important activity.[8] For instance, St Thérèse of Lisieux wrote: 'For me prayer is an uplifting of the heart, a glance toward heaven, a cry of gratitude and of love in times of sorrow as well as of joy. It is something noble, something supernatural, which expands the soul and unites it to God.'[9] Thérèse loved to use the scriptures during her prayer times. She said: 'It is the bible I use mainly; everything I need for my soul is there.'[10] When he declared Thérèse a Doctor of the Church, Pope John Paul II said: 'By her loving concentration on scripture – she even wanted to learn Hebrew and Greek to understand better the spirit and letter of the sacred books – she showed the importance of the biblical sources in the spiritual life, she emphasised the originality and freshness of the gospel, she cultivated with moderation the spiritual exegesis of the

word of God in both the Old and New Testaments.'[11] It is important to believe that God's revelatory word is ever fresh, and new
every day. Rather than seeking to have God's word fit in with
one's pre-existing ideas, it is important to allow the word of God
to challenge and change those ideas. As Is 48:6-7 says: 'From this
time forward I make you hear new things, hidden things that
you have not known. They are created now, not long ago; before
today you have never heard of them, so that you could not say, I
already knew them.'

There are many tried and tested ways of contemplating
God's word in scripture such as empathic scripture prayer, the
Benedictine Method, and paired sharing. Each of us needs a
method that suits his temperament and needs.

Empathic Scripture Prayer

We know from the gospels that Jesus was compassionate and
empathised with the people he met. When reading and praying
the scriptures, Christians can try to empathise with the characters mentioned in the text, especially with our Lord. The
Ignatian method is particularly helpful in this regard. It encourages people to desire to have an intimate knowledge of Jesus
who became incarnate for us, by imagining gospel scenes, hearing what is said by Jesus and others, seeing what is done by
them, sensing what they feel, etc.

Prayerful meditation on scripture needs to begin with a
prayer for inspiration, as Paul said in Eph 1:17, 'May the God of
our Lord Jesus Christ, the Father of glory, give you a spirit of
wisdom and perception of what is revealed.' You could begin
with this prayer adapted from the *Divine Office:*

Stay with me Lord Jesus
Be my companion on my way
In your mercy inflame my heart and raise my hope,
So that, I may recognise you in the scriptures,
Who live and reign with the Father and the Holy Spirit,
God for ever and ever.

Then you might go on to read an account such as Jesus' meeting
with the Samaritan woman at the well of Sychar in Jn 4:7-42.
- *Imagine* the scene, see Jesus and the woman. You might want
  to place yourself in the picture as an onlooker.

- *Hear* what is said by Jesus and the woman.
- *Notice* what they do.
- *Empathise* with what they feel, the woman's emotions, but most important with the emotions of Jesus. Sense what he feels. You might advert to the five characteristics of empathy in chapter two. Notice how Jesus illustrates each one of them.

1. He seems to be aware of her mistrust, loneliness, sense of shame, and longing to be loved, to feel special to someone, to belong.
2. He understands the reasons for her feelings. He senses that she has looked in vain for such love in the arms of a number of men. Instead of finding lasting intimacy she has been ostracised because of her permissive behaviour.
3. He does not judge or condemn her in any way. He shows this by breaking a number of taboos by talking to her, and asking her for a drink.
4. He reflects back his sense of her innermost feelings and desires by talking about living water that will truly satisfy.
5. While he doesn't share the woman's feelings, he responds to them with tenderness, compassion and sensitivity.

You could use this method for other gospel accounts which describe Jesus' interaction with the different people he met. In this way you can get to know who Jesus is and what he is like. Why not select an incident in the gospels and try the proposed methodology.

Lectio Divina

The best known means of paying attention to God's word in the scriptures is the Benedictine method. It is known as the *Lectio Divina,* or sacred reading.[12] It's a personal or communal reading of a scripture passage of any length, received as the Word of God, which through the impulse of the Holy Spirit leads to meditation, prayer and contemplation.[13] A twelfth century writer described its purpose in these words: '*Reading* you should seek; *meditating* you will find; *praying* you shall call; and *contemplating* the door will be opened to you.' Before engaging in the *Lectio Divina,* we ask the Lord to bless our prayer time. There is a succinct prayer that I sometimes say: 'Bright as fire in darkness, sharper than a sword, lives throughout the ages, God's eternal word. May that word dwell richly in my heart and bear the fruit of good works. Amen.' A shorter prayer says: 'I open the scriptures to meet you again. Reveal yourself to me.'

1. Reading

One goes on to select a passage to read. It might come from the liturgy of the day, or the following Sunday, or one could choose a passage that would speak to one's needs at that particular time, such as how to cope with bereavement, anger, temptation, etc. Admittedly, one needs to have a fairly good knowledge of the bible in order to choose such an apt passage. Others buy booklets which contain thematic scripture meditations. The bible societies in different English-speaking countries, such as those in America and Ireland, produce useful materials of this kind. Another book that many people find helpful is *Daily Light*. It has a page of thematically arranged verses, drawn from the Old and New Testaments for every morning and evening of the year. If you are choosing a biblical passage yourself, ideally it should not be too long. Then one goes on to read the verses slowly and attentively. I have found that it is good to read the passage two or three times. St Anselm wrote in the eleventh century, 'The scriptures are not to be read in a noisy situation, but where things are quiet, not superficially and in a rush, but a little at a time.'

2. Meditating

We can usefully begin this section with a succinct definition from the *Catechism of the Catholic Church*. 'Meditation is a prayerful quest engaging thought, imagination, emotion and desire. Its goal is to make our own in faith the subject considered, by confronting it with the reality of our own life.'[14] In Prov 4:20-5:1 we are told how to internalise a scripture text: 'My son, pay attention to what I say; listen closely to my words. Do not let them out of your sight, keep them within your heart; for they are life to those who find them ... Above all else, guard your heart, for it is the wellspring of life ... My child, pay attention to my wisdom, listen well to my words of insight.' I often read a bible commentary as part of my meditative exploration of the passage. It can throw light on the context and the true meaning of the verses.

During the meditative stage, one ponders the meaning of the text, thinks about obscure or difficult points, and tries to see how these truths relate to one's own life and the life of the world about us. For example, one might consider how, regardless of their education and material prosperity, many people in modern society also seem to be harassed and dejected like the woman in the gospel story we already mentioned. Indeed one might reluctantly have to admit that, because of personal unhappiness, emotional problems, addictions or obsessions, one could personally identify with the lonely Samaritan

There are two ways of meditating. If you are reflecting on a doctrinal point, for example, from the letters of St Paul, it can be helpful to repeat a chosen word or sentence, over and over again, while letting its meaning sink into the heart. It is rather like sucking a sweet. You let it dissolve in order to savour its taste and flavour. If you are reflecting on a scriptural incident, such as the one mentioned above, it can be helpful, as Ignatius of Loyola suggested, to imagine it as if you were making a mental video.

- *See* the scene and the people who are mentioned. You may choose to see yourself as one of the characters involved.
- *Hear* what is said. You may want to add to the dialogue that is recorded in the text.
- *Notice* what the characters do.
- Finally, try to *sense* what the people feel. I have found that if the story is about Jesus I can try to empathise with him empathising with the people of his time.

3. Praying

As a person begins to react at a personal level to the text, meditation gives way to prayer. Rational thinking gives way to the disclosure of the feelings and desires that have been evoked by one's reading and reflection. Speaking about this transition, St Vincent de Paul once said that when at nightfall a person wants to illumine a room, what, asks the saint, should be done? 'He takes his flint and steel,' he says, 'strikes a spark and lights his candle. When he has done so, he does not go on striking the flint, he does not go looking about for another flint and steel to strike a light, for he does not need it; the light he has suffices for all his needs.'[15] When inspiration comes, meditation gives way to heartfelt prayer. The pray-er may be moved to offer prayers of contrition, petition, intercession, thanksgiving, praise and adoration. In this connection St Benedict counselled, 'Let the prayer be brief and pure.'

4. Contemplating

In the *Catechism of the Catholic Church* we read: 'Contemplative prayer is the simple expression of the mystery of prayer. It is a gaze of faith fixed on Jesus, an attentiveness to the Word of God, a silent love. It achieves real union with the prayer of Christ to the extent that it makes us share in his mystery.'[16] As a person reads, meditates and prays, there can be moments when these activities give way to a graced sense of God's loving and merciful presence. Speaking about this kind of religious experience St Vincent de Paul wrote: 'It is not the result of human teaching. It is not attainable by human effort, and it is not bestowed on everyone ... In this state of quiet, the soul finds itself suddenly filled with spiritual illuminations and holy affections (i.e. feelings and desires).'[17] I suspect that such experiences are not only religious but at least mildly mystical in nature. The phrase 'religious experience' refers not so much to talk or thought *about* transcendental reality, as conscious, mediated awareness *of* that reality. A religious experience therefore is an experience in which one has intimations of the immediate presence of 'the divine.'

5. Responding

As a result of prayer we begin to see Jesus more clearly and to love him more dearly. This leads to a desire to follow him more nearly in everyday life. It's good to make a resolution that flows from the scripture text, e.g. to be more forgiving. St Vincent de Paul says: 'One of the most important and indeed the most important element of prayer is to make resolutions; we should pay most particular attention to that aspect of prayer and not so much to reflection and reasoning.'[18] On an other occasion Vincent said that such resolutions should be Single, Precise, Definite and Possible. As Jesus observed: 'The seeds that fell in good soil stand for those who hear the message and retain it in a

good and obedient heart, and they persist until they bear fruit'
(Lk 8: 15).

Paired Sharing

There is a simple method which can be used by groups in order
to read and reflect on the scriptures in a prayerful way. It consists of eight steps.

1. Opening prayer for inspiration.
2. One person slowly reads the chosen passage out loud.
   Everyone else listens to the reading.
3. Everyone spends one minute reflecting on what they heard.
4. The passage is again read slowly out loud by another person.
5. Everyone prayerfully reflects on the passage for five minutes. They consider, what did it mean? How does it relate to
   my life and the life of the community?
6. Everyone share in twos for five to seven minutes.
7. The coordinator invites people to share from the floor, either
   what they got from the passage or what their neighbour
   shared with them. (This is an optional step).
8. There is a final prayer of thanksgiving.

Conclusion

When you have completed your time of bible study, meditation
and prayer, you could ask yourself the following four questions.

- When was I most aware of Jesus and / or God the father dur-
  ing my prayer time?
- What did I feel as a result of that sense of awareness?
- What did I notice about Jesus / God that evoked the feelings I
  experienced?
- How did I want to respond to the God who revealed the
  Godself to me in either a prayerful and / or a practical way?

It can be helpful to write down your responses in a prayer journal. When a person engages in this kind of prayer in an ongoing
way it can lead to a gradual transformation of a person's way of
thinking, valuing, feeling and acting.

CHAPTER THIRTEEN

Petitionary Prayer in an Age of Science[1]

Many people today have a problem with the teachings of Jesus about petitionary and intercessory prayer. They are difficult to reconcile with the scientific worldview. They imply that God intervenes in an arbitrary way with the inexorable laws that govern the universe. In this chapter I will suggest that the teachings of Jesus can be interpreted, in a non-reductionist way, within a newly emerging convergence of secular and religious ideas.

Since the advent of the Enlightenment the legitimacy of most traditional understandings of petitionary and intercessory prayer have been challenged. In spite of the fact that Jesus' teaching on prayer is epitomised by the prayer of supplication, some writers seem to be embarrassed by the naïve claims of its pre-critical approach. Whereas Jesus promises in an unambiguous, straightforward manner 'Whatever you ask in prayer, you will receive if you have faith' (Mt 21:22), many contemporary writers say 'yes, but!' and then proceed to enter all sort of caveats which seem to owe more to the Deism of the eighteenth century and afterwards than to the teachings of the gospels. Instead of believing that, on many occasions, our prayers will be answered, they merely see them as a way of relating to a God who is unable to do anything practical to help, lest the autonomy of the secular realm be interfered with. In this worldview the best we can hope for is the grace of willing resignation to the unchanging and unchangeable will of God as expressed in and through the deterministic laws of physics.

For example, Irish Augustinian Gabriel Daly says that, for a variety of reasons, a simple, uncritical view 'of God's action in the world is no longer possible for an increasing number of faithful Christians who find it critically and scientifically unacceptable and spiritually repugnant.'[2] He says that as a result, 'The central theological problem raised by pondering the prayer of petition is the mode or manner of God's presence and action in the world.'[3] It seems evident from a number of observations he makes[4] that he adopts the Enlightenment view of the world, as a closed system governed by the unchangeable laws of physics. As a result, he maintains that believers can no longer expect the God of the gaps to intervene in a 'magical way' in their lives or in the world. They can share their feelings and concerns with the Lord, sense what God feels, and do what they can to bring about the coming of the kingdom, but inevitably, the teaching of Jesus to do with God's willingness to answer prayer has to be reinterpreted within this worldview. Unless the prayer is answered through a fortuitous coincidence or our own graced efforts, we cannot expect anything to happen. While one could agree with Daly's general belief that a *Deus ex machina* view of divine action has to be eschewed, surely one doesn't have to adopt his rather classical, Newtonian view of the natural world and our place in it. As John Polkinghorne has observed, the *Deus absconditus* perspective neither accords with people's experience of prayer and providence, or with the views of scientist-theologians such as Pollard, Barbour, or Peacocke.[5]

Petitionary Prayer: A Philosophical Perspective
There are two main ways of looking at God and the prayers of petition and intercession. Firstly, there is the biblical understanding. The God of revelation is neither unchanging or unmoved by human suffering and need. On the contrary, the Lord is compassionate, slow to anger and rich in mercy (cf. Ex 34:6). The holy One not only prompts prayers in the heart, God answers them as well. The Lord hallows the divine name by means of saving actions in history which are often performed in answer to prayer.[6] Secondly there is a philosophical understanding of prayer. It is rooted in an appreciation of the unchanging nature of divinity. For example, some Greek philosophers argued that God was necessarily apathetic, i.e. unmoved by the sufferings of animals and human beings. So there was no point in offering petitionary prayers because God's perfect and unchanging will could not be influenced by creatures. To maintain that God's will could be affected by prayer, would imply that God could be changed, either for better or for worse. If this were so, God would not be God.

Origen (185-254), one of the great Christian thinkers in the early church, was well aware that, from a philosophical point of view, God was immutable. As a result, he maintained that petitionary prayer was necessarily problematic. Acting as a devil's advocate, he reasoned: 'If everything happens in accordance with the will of God and his decrees stand fast, and nothing of what he wills can be reversed, then prayer is absurd.'[7] Twentieth century philosopher Eleonore Stump has made a similar point. 'If what is requested in a petitionary prayer,' she says, 'results in a state of affairs the realisation of which would make the world worse than it would otherwise be, an omnipotent, omniscient, perfectly good being will not fulfil that request. If what is requested in a petitionary prayer results in a state of affairs the realisation of which would make the world a better place than it otherwise would be, an omniscient, omnipotent, perfectly good being will bring about that state of affairs even if no prayer for its realisation is made.'[8] There seem to be two substantial points implicit here.

Firstly, God will do what is best anyway. Philosophical theologian Keith Ward questions the validity of this assertion. He seems to espouse a dynamic rather than a static view of the world. It stresses becoming rather than being and understands God more as an active verb rather than as a passive noun. Ward maintains that it is not true that God does what is best, for the simple reason that there is no such thing as an absolutely best act.[9] He asserts this because he rejects the Enlightenment notion of a closed universe. He sees it rather as an open, evolving system in which free human beings can choose to play a co-creative part with God in realising the potential implicit in creation. Furthermore he says: 'God always has options for action, options limited by many constraints of structure and human response. In such a system, God may well choose one option – indeed an option may become open to him within the constraints of the system – precisely because a creature who loves God desires it and asks God for it.'[10] If one sees the world in this way it is conceivable that God will act in response to petitionary prayer, though many natural factors will constrain the possibilities.

Secondly, one can argue from a philosophical point of view that God does not need our prayers, since God knows what we want. Indeed Jesus said as much. Before he taught his disciples how to pray, he said: 'Your Father knows what you need before you ask him' (Mt 6:8). Strictly speaking, although our prayers add nothing to God's knowledge or intentions, they do help us to grow in holiness by enabling us to express our dependence on the Creator and to identify with God's benevolent purposes. St Augustine expressed something like this when he wrote: 'He who knows how to give good gifts to his children urges us to ask, seek and knock. It might be puzzling why this should be so, in view of the fact that God is aware of our needs before we ask him, if we did not understand that the Lord our God wants us to ask, not because he needs to be made aware of our wish, for he cannot be unaware of it, but that we may by means of prayer stir up that desire to receive what he is ready to give. His gifts are very great and we are very small and limited in our capacity for receiving.'[11] St Thomas Aquinas articulated a similar point of view when he wrote: 'We don't pray in order to change God's arrangements, but in order to obtain effects that God has arranged will be achieved through the prayers of his chosen people. God arranges to give us certain things in answer to requests so that we may confidently have recourse to him, and acknowledge him as source of all our blessings, and this is all for our good.'[12] As Eleonore Stump has observed, St Thomas seems to espouse an off-putting form of theological determinism which is based on a static and essentialist view of nature.[13]

Ward argues, quite rightly I think, that if one believes in an open, evolving universe, one would have to modify the Augustinian-Thomist understanding of prayer. If it is true that rather than being one definitive act, creation is a continuous series of acts, which are open to new possibilities – often in response to human requests – then it would mean that reasonable and benevolent human requests could, in a qualified sense, affect God's activity. Finally, I'm quite convinced that once one asserts that God is utterly unchanging one cannot argue in a rational way that God responds to our petitions and intercessions. All one can do is assert the fact that the God of Judeo-Christian revelation does react. As Karl Rahner has written, and surely it is a point of crucial importance: 'The immutability of God – which taken in isolation would mean that real prayer is impossible –

forgets that God is 'personally' concerned with our affairs. The immutability of God must not be reduced to a proposition which can be manipulated in the usual categories of human thought. It must be kept open for the truth of the incarnation and crucifixion, for the truth that God 'changes' for the sake of man. This is the only possible source of a dialogical character of prayer.'[14]

Petitionary Prayer: A Scientific Perspective

Ever since the rise of science in the seventeenth century, many Christians have had theoretical problems in understanding how God might respond to their petitions. For example, in the nine-teenth century, Francis Galton (1822-1911), a cousin of Charles Darwin, devised a sophisticated method of statistical correlation to study such things as the influence of petitionary prayer upon the lives of people. Subsequently his findings were published in an article entitled, 'Statistical Inquiries into the Efficacy of Prayer' in the *Forthnightly Review* in 1872.[15] Galton began by looking at the biographies of the royal family, well known theo-logians and missionaries. In spite of the fact that many prayers were offered on their behalf, they did not seem to enjoy any bet-ter health or longevity than any one else. If anything their prospects were poorer. He also pointed out that insurance com-panies did not find that people who were prayed for had any better prospects than those who were not prayed for. Galton himself offered prayers of aspiration rather than solicitation. In other words he desired to have the grace to be conformed to God's inexorable purposes rather than asking that those purposes be changed in any way. He didn't believe that there was any credible evidence to suggest that petitionary prayers improved the physical or material circumstances of people's lives. However he didn't give up praying. As he said: 'A confident sense of communion with God must necessarily rejoice and strengthen the heart, and divert it from petty cares.'

Two points can be made in response to Galton's skepticism about the efficacy of petitionary prayer. Firstly, his research was carried out within the perspective of nineteenth-century science which still espoused a closed, mechanical view of the universe. He had little or no appreciation of how the Spirit of the Lord, which fills the whole creation (cf. Wis 1:7; Jer 23:24), might impinge on the workings of the natural world. The Spirit, as Keith Ward points out, 'acts through the open, law-like, emergent and holistic physical system of the universe in ways that direct it as efficiently as possible towards its intended goal. Such acts *will be physically undetectable*, as they are not the result of physical forces and *they are compatible with the continuance of all known laws of nature* (my italics).'[16] If I understand Ward's argument correctly, he is claiming that the Spirit's interrelationship with matter at the sub atomic level is so fundamental, subtle, and quasi-natural, that its influence would not make a detectable statistical difference at the level at which Galton did his research.

Secondly, one can point to the fact that while the effects of prayer are not statistically verifiable in the way Galton did his research, they have been detected by modern researchers.[17] For instance, in 1993 Dr Daniel Benor published an article entitled, 'Survey of Spiritual Healing Research.'[18] In it he defined healing as 'the intentional influence of one or more people upon another living system without utilising known physical means of intervention.' Needless to say prayer for the healing of people was involved, but prayer for other forms of non-human life was also included. By 1993 investigators had performed 131 controlled trials. Dr Larry Dossey lists them all in his interesting book, *Healing Words: The Power of Prayer and the Practice of Medicine.*[19] Fifty-six of these experiments showed that prayer had statistically significant effects at a probability level of .01 or better. In other words the likelihood that the results were due to chance was less than one in a hundred. Twenty-one studies demonstrated a positive effect at a probability level of .02 to .05, i.e. the likelihood that the results were due to chance was between two and five in a hundred.

Before the modern era people believed that God could act powerfully as one cause among many others, thereby influencing the workings of creation. The Newtonian worldview was that of a closed, self-contained system, governed by subtle, but absolute, universal laws. This understanding resisted the notion that, in response to petitionary prayer, God could intervene in the created world, e.g. to change the weather or to heal a sick body. If change was to come about, it would only happen when human beings used their God-given intelligence to understand and modify the workings of nature in accordance with its inherent, God-given laws and potentials. In this secularised world-view petitionary prayer, as Galton suggested, was a matter of asking God for the grace to help ourselves and resigning ourselves to the outcome. For instance, if someone was sick God had only one way of answering the prayers offered by relatives and friends, i.e. through the best efforts of caring, medical professionals. The relatives did not pray for a 'miracle' in the pre-critical sense of an unmediated, direct, intervention of God in the normal biological processes which were created by God.

We have already adverted to Keith Ward's philosophical distinction between a closed and an open understanding of the universe. Happily the latter view can be reconciled with different facets of current scientific thinking such as Heisenberg's uncertainty principle and chaos theory. The uncertainty, or indeterminacy principle in quantum physics was first articulated in 1927. It states that the world isn't tied down and exactly predetermined. The position and the velocity of sub-atomic particles cannot be simultaneously measured with precision. Indeterminate particles act unpredictably, but within definable parameters of probability. Chaos theory seeks to explore the behaviour of complex systems in producing novel forms of order. It indicates how apparently random phenomena observed in various branches of science result from complex, dynamic underlying principles. At the conclusion of a nuanced and well informed chapter entitled, 'Does God Act in the Physical World?', scientist and theologian, John Polkinghorne writes: 'The God of the atemporal view knows all history and interacts with it in a unified if mysterious fashion. The God of temporal process does not yet know the unformed future and interacts with history as it unfolds, responding to its development in the way so often described anthropomorphically in the bible.'[20] Commenting on this latter understanding Angela Tilby writes: 'The God of this kind of universe is one who accompanies creation through its process, a creative, dynamic God, closer to the God of the scriptures than the kind of God whose mind is investigated by Stephen Hawking.'[21]

An Evolutionary Perspective

Ever since the publication of Darwin's *Origin of Species* (1859) evolutionary theory has made us familiar with the notion of development in nature by means of apparently random mutations. However, Teilhard de Chardin (1881-1955), who was clearly influenced by Darwinian and Hegelian thought, has suggested that there is an obvious *elan* discernible in evolution. It is 'a combination of the play of chance (which is physical) and that of finality (which is psychic)'[22] I first came across the writings of de Chardin in my early twenties. They were a breath of fresh air because they challenged the scientific reductionism which was current at the time. Typically, reductionists try to explain complex subjects such as human consciousness in terms of simpler constituent elements such as the electro-chemical activity of the brain. It seemed obvious to me in the nineteen sixties that such a methodology had to be reversed. Simpler constituent elements, had to be understood in terms of the highest instances of evolution, such as human consciousness, and its pre-eminent activity of loving relationship with the world of people and things, and through both with God.

Having read a number of de Chardin's books I could see that consciousness of a loving kind was the interpretative key to evolution. This potential of the evolutionary process had been implicit from the beginning of creation. Over the past two million years or so, it has become quite explicit in human consciousness. Human beings carry the baton of possibility on behalf of the whole of the natural world in which we are immersed. The propensity of all things to seek self-fulfilment through mutual interconnection, and transcendental connection with God, reaches its highest form of intensity in and through loving human consciousness. De Chardin wrote: 'I believe that the universe is an evolution … I believe that it proceeds towards spirit. I believe that in man, spirit is fully realised in person. I believe that the supremely personal is the Universal Christ.'[23] Rightly or wrongly, Teilhard believed that his Hegelian type vision was intimated in Rom 8:19-23; Col 1:15-20; Eph 1:9-23.

As matter assumes ever more complex outer forms, it can simultaneously sustain more sophisticated types of inwardness. The supreme expression of this interrelationship is to be found in the rational consciousness of human beings which is made possible by the biological sophistication of our brains. As a result, we are in the cockpit of evolution. We can freely choose to cooperate with, and direct, its creative energy or *elan*. De Chardin suggested that evolution always moves forward through its highest achievement which currently is the human capacity to love. De Chardin referred to it as 'amorisation.' Evolution is no longer focused on biological development but rather on socialisation and the creation of what de Chardin named the *noosphere*. It is an interconnected envelope of thought. Currently the expansion of the internet, as a world wide web of shared information, is an example of what de Chardin had in mind. He believed that Jesus stood both at the heart of evolution as its loving centre and at its end as its loving goal. It is he who by his Spirit enables the whole of evolution to move forward and upward toward Omega point, i.e. the consummation of history in the second coming.

Towards an Holistic Understanding
There are four interrelated and hierarchical levels of reality:
- the *geosphere* i.e. the world of matter;
- the *biosphere* i.e. the world of living things;
- the *noosphere* i.e. the world of interconnected human thought;
- the *pneumasphere* i.e. the other three spheres when they are open to God and penetrated by the Spirit.

Human beings participate in the first three spheres because their bodies are material, living and conscious. By means of grace, human beings have a unique ability to participate in the life of God by means of the outpouring of the Holy Spirit into their spirits. As a result the Spirit is present to the three natural spheres in and through Spirit-filled human beings, especially those who are nourished by the Eucharist which is the sacrament of the divine presence hidden in the *geosphere* and the *biosphere*.[24] In Rom 8:19-23 St Paul suggests that we humans are the ambassadors of creation. When we achieve spiritual freedom we do so as an integral part of creation and on creation's behalf. The futility of the natural word is overcome in and through the transcendental awareness of Spirit-filled people.

I suspect that when Ward's and Polkinghorne's somewhat similar notions of an open universe are combined with something like de Chardin's evolutionary perspective, many problems to do with the prayer of supplication become easier to resolve. This point of view accords with the teachings of the gospels. Firstly, Jesus was One who engaged in prayerful deeds of power, notably healing (Acts 10:38). Secondly, he promised his disciples that they would do similar things, e.g. by healing in his name (Mk 16:18). Thirdly, St Paul assures us that, in every generation, the Lord grants the charism of healing to some members of the Christian community (1 Cor 12:9). The Spirit searches everything, e.g. every aspect of a cancer patient's body, mind and soul. It also searches the hidden depths of God and God's benevolent, life-giving purposes (cf. 1 Cor 2:10). As a result, the Lord and giver of Life can act in and through a compassionate healer to influence the sick person's entire being. If the healer prays with a charism of faith (cf. 1 Cor 12:9; 13:2), i.e. a form of expectant trust that is evoked by a revealed awareness of God's purposes, a healing can occur.[25]

Once the material world is brought into relationship with Spirit the lower natural laws of the first three spheres, which are familiar to modern science, are transcended. The spiritual potential hidden in the three natural spheres is actualised as it is elevated to a higher realm which is governed by spiritual laws. For example, the Holy Spirit, acting in and through the human spirit, can override the defects of nature by releasing healing powers implicit within a cancer patient's mind and body, thereby restoring him or her to harmony and peace. What might appear to be a supernatural intervention of God is in fact natural in the sense that it is a revelation of the potential of matter when it is elevated, through relationship with the Spirit to a new level of spiritual potential. In this view of reality the Spirit is at once immanent in nature and transcendent. As St Augustine said so wisely in *The City of God*, 'A miracle is contrary not to nature but to what is known of nature.'[26] It strikes me that if the four interconnected dimensions of reality are understood in this holistic way, inexplicable phenomena such as the well attested levitation of St Joseph of Cupertino and stigmata of Therese Neumann would begin to make some sort of rational sense. They could be seen as examples of the subordination of matter when its higher psycho-spiritual potentials are realised in and through prayerful human self-transcendence.

While I was still at school I read a fascinating book entitled *Man the Unknown*, by Nobel prize winner Alexis Carrel.[27] As a scientist and a doctor he became intrigued by the way in which petitionary prayer could lead to remarkable healings which were inexplicable in terms of the medical science of the early twentieth century. The way in which I have been trying to explain God's activity in the world as a result of prayer, seems to be implicit in the following extended quotation:

> Certain spiritual activities may cause anatomical as well as functional modifications of the tissues and organs. These organic phenomena are observed in various circumstances, among them being the state of prayer. Prayer should be understood, not as a mere mechanical recitation of formulas, but as a mystical elevation, an absorption of consciousness in the contemplation of a principle both permeating and transcending our world. Such a psychological state is not intellectual. It is incomprehensible to philosophers, and scientists and inaccessible to them ... The prayer which is followed by organic effects is of a special nature. It is entirely disinterested. Man offers himself to God ... At the same time, he asks for his grace, exposes his needs and those of his brothers and sisters in suffering. Generally, the patient who is cured is not praying for himself, but for another ... Prayer may set in motion a strange phenomenon, the miracle. Despite their small number, they prove the existence of organic and mental processes that we do not know. They show that certain mystic states, such as that of prayer, have definite effects. They are stubborn, irreducible facts, which must be taken into account.[28]

Carrel wrote his book in the 1930s. Subsequently this openminded agnostic investigated the reported miracles at Lourdes and wrote a book about them, as I mentioned in chapter six. To the best of my knowledge he became a Christian some time later. Since then a number of theorists have suggested novel and controversial ways of understanding these unusual phenomena as manifestations of the potential of reality. For example, in a book about the mind entitled *The Adventure of Self-Discovery*, Stanislav Grof, chief of psychiatric research at Maryland Psychiatric Research Center, has written: 'The new data are of such far-reaching relevance that they could revolutionise our understanding of the human psyche, of psychopathology, and of the therapeutic process. Some of the observations transcend in their significance the framework of psychology and psychiatry and represent a serious challenge to the current Newtonian-Cartesian paradigm of Western science. They could change drastically our image of human nature, culture, history and reality.'[29] Drawing on the writings of quantum physicist David Bohm and neurophysiologist Karl Primbram, science writer Michael Talbot has suggested that the human mind is a hologram, within the greater hologram of the world.[30] Talbot believes that their holographic worldview could be loosely summed up in the words of Indian holy man, Paramahansa Yogananda (1893-1952): 'The world is nothing but an objectivised dream. Whatever your powerful mind believes very intensely comes to pass.'[31] These words seem to be reminiscent of what Jesus said about mountain-moving faith in Mk 11:23.

Conclusion

I feel confident that in this century a new synthesis will be formed, one that will seek to relate the interconnected realms of the material (governed by the laws of physics), the biological (governed by organic laws), the mental (governed by psychological laws), and the spiritual (governed by mystical laws). Just as many scientists currently acknowledge that sickness can be psychosomatic in nature, so in the future they will come to see, with the help of mystical theology and transpersonal psychology that there is such a thing as pneuma-psychosomatic illness. For instance, if a person, who is relating to a cancer patient in a loving way, offers prayer for healing while in a state of openness to the Holy Spirit, that same Spirit can act in the spirit of the sick person to bring about psychosomatic peace. So when Christians engage in petition, or intercession, they are not asking God to override the laws of a closed universe but rather to fulfill the highest, often unrecognised, archetypal potential of an open, evolutionary universe in which God the Father is intimately involved, in and through his adopted sons and daughters.

I am well aware that this chapter is exploratory and in many ways incomplete in so far as it fails to explore either the philosophical or scientific issues involved in any great detail. For example, experts in both areas will have to confirm whether Ward's understanding of the influence of prayer in an open universe is correct or not. Suffice it to say that currently many theologians, philosophers, scientists, and depth psychologists are working in an inter-disciplinary way to articulate a vision of reality which may reconcile the worlds of science and religion in a new way. Hopefully, such a framework of understanding would enable the Christian men and women of tomorrow to make sense of the biblical injunction to disclose their requests to God with expectant faith.

CHAPTER FOURTEEN

Thérèse of Lisieux: A Saint for our Times

People's views of Thérèse can be very different. For example, Karl Rahner wrote: 'I find many aspects of this saint's personality and writings irritating or merely boring. And if I were to explain what I find almost repulsive about them so that you could see why, it certainly wouldn't justify the trouble of doing so.'[1] Just before her death at the age of twenty four, one of her companions said something similar: 'I can't imagine what Reverend Mother will find to say about her once she is gone. It won't be easy for her, I can tell you; for this little sister, charming as she is, has certainly never done anything worth telling.' Others like Pope St Pius X said that Thérèse was 'the greatest saint of modern times'. It would also be true to say that she has been the most popular saint of the twentieth century. Fr P. Marie-Eugene, an eminent Carmelite scholar, wrote: 'St Thérèse of the Child Jesus stands out as one of the great masters of the spiritual life, among the greatest of all times. I should willingly rank her with St Bernard and St Teresa of Avila.'[2] The church confirmed this view when it declared in 1997 that Thérèse was a Doctor of the Church.

For many years now I have found that, like many others, I have been graced with a strong sense of relationship with St Thérèse. About twenty five years ago, an elderly nun in Belfast gave me a first class relic of the Little Flower, a strand of her hair. I have treasured it ever since because it represents intimate contact with the saint. In the mid nineteen eighties I had a memorable dream in which Thérèse appeared to me. I could see a youngish woman. Immediately I thought: 'That's St Thérèse of Lisieux.' She wasn't wearing a Carmelite habit. She seemed to be clothed in a very simple dress made of wool. It was modest, reminiscent of the kind worn by peasants in movies. She had black hair. It was short, as if it were in a bun at the back. Her eye-

brows were black, arched and striking. Her face was oval and
sallow. At first she was seated on the ground. Hovering before
her, at face level, was a lively blue flame. Then she got up and
walked toward me and held out her arms to embrace me and
give me a hug. I was surprised by this. I thought to myself: 'I
didn't think a saint would be as demonstrative as this!' At the
same time it occurred to me: 'What do you think a saint is? This
is a woman of love, she has to express her affection and tenderness.' As Thérèse hugged me, I got a feeling of unworthiness. I
thought: 'She won't be pleased by my shortcomings. No doubt
she will warn me, and tell me I need to repent!' As I looked into
Thérèse's face I didn't sense any disapproval, but I felt she was
saying with her look: 'You are right, your shortcomings can be
tackled.' I began to cry in an agitated way. Then it suddenly occurred to me that she was saying with her eyes: 'Stop this crying,
it's false emotion.' I knew she was right. So I stopped straight
away. Then I woke up filled with a deep sense of peace and joy.

Later that same day I happened to take a book from the shelf,
one I hadn't read. I opened it at random and was really surprised when I saw that it was recounting a consoling dream that
Thérèse had experienced during the time she was suffering from
the dark night of the soul sometime prior to her painful death.
She wrote: 'One Saturday in the month of May, I was thinking of
the mysterious dreams which are granted at times to certain
souls. I said to myself that these dreams must be a very sweet
consolation, and yet I wasn't asking for such a consolation. In
the evening, considering the clouds which were covering her
heaven, my little soul said again within herself that these beautiful dreams were not for her. And then she fell asleep in the midst
of the storm … The Blessed Virgin deigned to smile upon her little flower.' It was then that Thérèse dreamt of meeting the
founders of the Carmelites in France. She said: 'Several months
have passed since this sweet dream, and yet the memory it has
left in my soul has lost nothing of its freshness and heavenly
charms.'[3] I could honestly say, that after all these years, my noc-
turnal encounter with Thérèse has not lost its charm either. In
this chapter I will reflect briefly on some of the aspects of her
spirituality which have impressed me. I felt that the blue flame I
saw burning in front of Thérèse was a symbol of the fact that she

was animated by a mystical spirit of love that is illuminating, and enlivening.

Pre-Carmelite Years

Thérèse Martin, the last of nine children was born in 1873 in the town of Lisieux, Alencon in Normandy, France. Her father was a watchmaker, her mother Zelie Guerin, died when Thérèse was eight years of age. At that point her elder sister Pauline, who was about 19, took over the motherly function. Thérèse says that from the age of four to fifteen she was moody, oversensitive, immature, and inclined to cry a lot, especially following her mother's death. After her first communion Thérèse suffered from a bout of scruples. It was triggered by the legalistic instruction she received from Fr Louis Victor Domin, a distant cousin of Thérèse. Nowadays, a problem like this, especially in a person so young, would be seen as a neurotic condition, a sign of an obsessive compulsive neurosis.[4] Thérèse overcame her scruples when another priest, Fr Pichon, assured her that she had never committed a mortal sin.

At the end of 1882 Pauline left home to join the Carmelites. This seemed to trigger a major crisis in the life of her ten year old sister. Another sister Leoine says that 'it started with violent headaches … At the end of March 1883, she became delirious and had convulsions.'[5] The illness ended completely for the whole of the day on which Pauline received the Carmelite habit. But when she returned home the illness became even more severe. Leoine says that the bouts of illness looked 'like continual attacks of delirious terror, often accompanied by convulsions. Her screeches were frightening, her eyes were full of terror and her face was contracted with pain. Nails in the wall took on terrible forms in her eyes, forms that frightened the life out of her. Often she didn't even recognise us. One evening especially she was terrified when my father approached her with his hat in his hand; to her it looked like some terrible beast.'[6] Leonine says that when Thérèse had convulsions she would try to throw herself off the end of the bed and that family members would have to hold her down. On one occasion when her father and sisters were at Mass Leonie kept an eye on her. She left the room for a few minutes. When she returned, she found Thérèse stretched on the floor, 'She had jumped over the head of the bed,' reported Leonie, 'and fallen between the bed and the wall. She could have killed herself or done herself a serious injury but, thank God, she didn't even have a scratch.'[7] Leonie says that the attacks ended in a miraculous way when she and her sister Marie prayed fervently to our Lady that their sister would be cured. She was. Thérèse herself said later that, at that time, Our Lady had appeared to her. Perhaps her neurotic sense of separation anxiety was lessened when she felt connected in an intimate way to the heavenly mother. However Leonie says that during the following period Thérèse could be badly effected by emotionally charged situations. 'I upset her twice in the months that followed her cure,' she tells us. 'She fell down and remained stretched out for several minutes each time; she went completely stiff all over, but this passed off of its own accord.'[8]

What are we to make of all this? Thérèse's herself thought that she had been afflicted by the evil one. 'It was beyond doubt the Devil's work,' she says.[9] Her sister Marie concurred. She wrote: 'Thérèse was stricken with a strange illness, an illness that certainly came from the devil, who as she says herself in her autobiography, had been given an external power over her.'[10] Perhaps there was a demonic aspect to the whole episode. The evil one can exploit our psychological vulnerabilities, but surely there was also some kind of unconscious cause. I'm no psychiatrist. But the whole thing looks like a psychosomatic illness, of an hysterical nature, that had been prompted by a severe anxiety state. It would have been activated when Thérèse felt abandoned by Pauline, her second mother. It is significant, surely, that the illness ended temporarily when Thérèse was able to see Pauline again on the day of her profession. For example, in a chapter on 'conversion reactions', i.e. the manifestation of bodily symptoms such as a convulsion which is rooted in a psychic conflict, Dr Frank Lake writes: 'These occur when the total infantile experience of loss, or impending loss of life, or of personal being itself, is no longer able to be repressed, but is present as an almost total terror within consciousness. Failure of repression permits both somatic and psychic elements of dread to emerge.'[11] He says that such an hysterical illness is a form of wordless language. It seems to me that his depiction of conversion reactions is a good description of Thérèse's condition.

If Thérèse was partly healed of her anxiety state when Our Lady appeared to her at the age of nine, it is my belief that it was completely cured at midnight Mass, on Christmas day 1886. The over sensitive teenager had a life changing religious experience. Thérèse called it her night of conversion and illumination. 'Charity had found its way into my heart,' she declared, 'calling on me to forget myself and simply do what God wanted of me.'[12] I feel confident in saying that Thérèse had experienced what Pentecostals and Charismatics refer to as baptism in the Spirit. It is a religious experience that releases the graces received in the sacraments of initiation, in a way that inaugurates a new and conscious awareness of the presence and activity of the Lord in one's life. Afterwards, she said that as a result of this spiritual awakening, 'I felt a great desire to work for the conversion of sinners.'[13]

Soon after this breakthrough, she heard how a convicted murderer, called Pranzini, was facing execution. Apparently he had murdered two women and a child in the course of a robbery. Thérèse read in the newspaper how he had spurned the help of a prison chaplain. She said: 'There was every reason to think that he would die impenitent.'[14] Thérèse prayed repeatedly on her own, and later with her sister Celine, for Pranzini's conversion. She makes it clear that she offered her petitions in the expectant faith that 'the abandoned wretch' would eventually repent. Her firm faith was rooted in three convictions. Firstly, she had a heartfelt awareness of the love of God as a result of her spiritual awakening. Secondly she realised that she was praying within the will of God because the Spirit had prompted her to pray for sinners like Pranzini. Thirdly, she also knew that the Lord in his providence had promised to grant such prayers. For example, she would have read 1 Jn 5:14-16: 'This is the confidence we have in approaching God: that if we ask anything according to his will, he hears us. And if we know that he hears us – whatever we ask – we know that we have what we asked of him. If anyone sees his brother commit a sin that does not lead to death (such as the sin against the Holy Spirit) he should pray and God will give him life.' Speaking about her expectant faith, Thérèse declared: 'In my heart, *I felt certain* we shouldn't be disappointed; but by way of encouragement in this practice of praying for sinners, I did ask for a sign. I told God I was sure he meant to pardon the unfortunate Pranzini, and I'd such confidence in our Lord's infinite mercy that I would cling to my belief even if Pranzini didn't go to confession and didn't make any gesture of repentance. Only I would like him to show some sign of repentance, just for my own satisfaction.'[15]

The day after Pranzini's execution, Thérèse read in the *La Croix* newspaper that just before he was guillotined, the condemned man had noticed that a priest was standing nearby with a crucifix.[16] He cried out, 'quick, hand me the crucifix' and kissed it three times. A few seconds later he was beheaded. Thérèse was comforted by the conviction that her prayers had finally been answered. As she testified, 'my prayer was answered, and to the letter.'[17]

Thérèse always had a desire to join the Carmelites. Two of her sisters, Pauline and Marie, had already done so. When she applied she was turned down on the basis that she was too young. Undeterred, she went to Rome as a teenager in order to ask Pope Leo XIII for permission to enter before the canonical age. She got the papal go-ahead. In the event she joined at fifteen.

The Little Way
We will not spend time of the details of her daily life in the Carmel at Lisieux. Suffice it to say that she was professed in 1890, that she became the assistant novice mistress in 1893. Thérèse was prevented from becoming a missioner to China in 1896 because she had developed tuberculosis. Mother Agnes, i.e. her sister Pauline, asked her to write her autobiography, *The Story of a Soul*. In this book and other writings Thérèse outlined her so called 'little way.'

In 1896, Thérèse wrote: 'I want to seek out a means of going to heaven by a little way, a way that is very straight, very short and totally new. We are living now in an age of inventions and we no longer have to take the trouble of climbing the stairs for, in the homes of the rich, an elevator has replaced these very successfully.'[18] Thérèse looked for a spiritual elevator, one that would take her reliably and easily into the presence of God. She believed that she discovered such an elevator when she focused on what her sister referred to as the way of *spiritual childhood*.' It was inspired by two texts in particular: 'Who is the greatest in the kingdom of heaven?' And calling to him a child, he put him in the midst of them, and said, 'Truly I say to you, unless you turn and become like children, you will never enter the kingdom of heaven,' (Mt 18:2-3) and 'I thank you, Father, Lord of heaven and earth, because you have hidden these things from the wise and the intelligent and have revealed them to infants' (Mt 11:25). Thérèse believed that one should depend absolutely upon God the Father in an unquestioning way, and to regard everything that comes from his hand, good and bad alike, as a gift. As she used to say repeatedly, 'Everything is a grace.'

Thérèse was impressed by the fact that Jesus had become a child. As such he had to depend utterly on the loving mercy of God as it was expressed through the caring of Mary and Joseph. She felt that God's love for her as a child of God was utterly gratuitous. She felt that if she remained very little, i.e. utterly dependant on the freely given, undeserved graces of God, then Jesus would carry her in his arms. She said: 'The elevator which must raise me to heaven is your arms, O Jesus! And for this I had no need to grow up, but rather I had to remain little and become this more and more.' Thérèse did not believe that she should remain childish, but rather that she should become ever more childlike, ever more dependant upon the loving mercy of God. She explained: 'To be a child is to recognise our nothingness, to expect everything from God as a little child expects everything from its father; it is to be disquieted about nothing ... To be little is not attributing to oneself the virtues that one practices, believing oneself capable of anything, but to recognise that God places this treasure in the hands of his little child to be used when necessary; but it always remains God's treasure. Finally, it is not to become discouraged over one's faults, for children fall often, but they are too little to hurt themselves very much.'[19]

Thérèse also felt called to become holy, but not by doing extraordinary things or having extraordinary spiritual experiences. 'To attain sanctity,' she wrote, 'it is not necessary to do outstanding works, but to hide oneself and practice virtue in such a way that the left hand does not know what the right hand is doing.'[20] Not surprisingly, one of her companions observed:

'During her life in Carmel, the servant of God passed by unnoticed in the community. Only four or five of the nuns, including myself, got close enough to her to realise the perfection hidden under the humility and simplicity of her exterior.'[21] Sr Marie of the Eucharist made the following observation in a letter to a lay woman called Celine Maudelonde: 'Hers is not an extraordinary sanctity; there is no love of extraordinary penances, no, only love for God ... She saw God in everything, and she carried out all her actions as perfectly as possible. Daily duty came before everything else.' Then Sr Marie went out to highlight the important implications of this approach. 'People in the world can imitate her sanctity, for she has tried to do everything through love and to accept all little contradictions, all little sacrifices that come at each moment as coming from God's hands.'[22]

The Justice and Mercy of God

We have already seen how Thérèse experienced an outpouring of that love at Christmas 1886. Later in her life she wrote about the nature of that love. Nineteenth-century spirituality, with some of its roots in the Jansenism of seventeenth-century French spirituality, spoke a lot about the justice of God. Thérèse's bout of scrupulosity as a child was, in all likelihood, an echo of that intimidating, perfectionistic spirituality. In fact the Carmelites saw themselves as willing victims of divine justice, women who took upon themselves the punishments that should rightfully have been meted out to sinners.[23] Thérèse, however, put the emphasis on God's extraordinary mercy. For example she discussed this subject with an elderly companion Sr Febronie. The latter emphasised the justice of God. Eventually Thérèse said to her, 'If you want divine justice, you will get divine justice. The soul gets exactly what it expects from God.'[24] Implicit in the saint's reply, is the following principle, 'If you look into the eyes of God's mercy expecting only mercy, you will receive only mercy, now and at the hour of your death.' She even composed a parable in order to convey what she wanted to affirm.

A rabbit was eating grass in a field. Suddenly it heard the distant sounds of a bugle blowing, dogs barking and horses galloping. It looked over its shoulder in fear. It could see a king together with his courtiers out on the hunt. Clearly, they had already picked up her scent and were heading in her direction, so the rabbit took off across the fields. Eventually she ran out of energy. Soon the dogs had surrounded her. They snarled with teeth bared. They were waiting for the king, who was already dis-mounting, to slay the rabbit. Then they would pounce. She looked up at the king. His hand was on his sword. He was about to draw it. The rabbit thought to herself: 'If I don't do something quickly, I'm finished!' She decided to use her remaining energy to jump up onto the king's outstretched arm. So she hopped up. With eyes full of desperation and pleading she looked into the eyes of the king. When his gaze met hers something melted in his heart. His sword grip weakened. He began to stroke the rab-bit with his other hand. 'I'm bringing this little creature back to the court,' he said, 'My children can play with it.' Thérèse said that in this parable the rabbit is the soul. The dogs are our sins. They pursue us and threaten to devour us. The king is the Lord. The sword is his justice, which in justice he is entitled to use against us. 'But there is a fatal flaw in the heart of the king,' says Thérèse, 'If you look only into the eyes of his mercy, expecting only mercy, you will receive only mercy.'

Thérèse was so aware of the mercy of God that she some-times envied the great sinners like Mary Magdalen, in so far as they had cause to love much because they had been forgiven much. She composed another story about a father who protects his son, by going ahead of him in order to remove stones in his path. Otherwise he might trip over and injure himself. By engag-ing in this imaginative exercise on the anticipatory love of God, she begins to have a sense of gratitude for God's mercy, similar to that of the great sinners. Then she adds: 'I am that child, the object of the Father's all embracing love, he having sent his Son to redeem, not the righteous but sinners. He wants me to love him because he has forgiven me, not much, but all. He hasn't waited for me to love him as much as Mary Magdalen did, but wanted me to know how he loved me with an ineffably anticipa-tory love, so that I shall love him to the point of madness … Instead of stepping forward with the Pharisee, I confidently re-peat the prayer of the publican. But more than all else, I copy the behaviour of the Magdalen, her astounding or rather her loving audacity which charmed Jesus' heart and seduces mine. Yes I'm

sure that if I had every sin that can be committed on my conscience, I should go, my heart broken with repentance, and
throw myself into Jesus' arms, for I know how much he loves the
prodigal child who returns to him.'[25]

Fr P. Marie-Eugene has suggested that Thérèse's understanding of God's mercy led her to cultivate the 'art of failure.'
She would intend to do some good act but would sometimes fail
to do so, for one reason or another. Apparently, she would then
say: 'If I had been faithful I would have received the reward of
merit by appealing to God's justice. I was unfaithful, I am humiliated, I am going to receive the reward of my poverty and hu-
miliation by appealing to God's mercy.'[26] She believed that she
would be rewarded in times of humiliating failure by God's
merciful love. What a remarkable insight into the loving kind-
ness of the heart of our God. I suspect that Thérèse's failures
were small compared to our own. Nevertheless, the principle
she enunciates remains the same. Indeed, it could be argued that
the greater and the more humiliating the failure the greater the
graces that are lavished upon the grieving heart. God does not
react in accordance with what we deserve but in accordance
with the Divine nature which loves us unconditionally.

As a result of all these insights, Thérèse was able to offer herself to Divine love, rather than Divine justice, in 1895. Sometime
afterwards she said: 'After earth's exile, I hope to go and enjoy
you in the fatherland, but I do not to lay up merits for heaven. I
want to work for your *love alone* ... In the evening of this life, I
shall appear before you with empty hands, for I do not ask you
Lord, to count my works. All our justice is blemished in your
eyes. I wish, then, to be clothed in your own *justice* and to receive from your *love* the eternal possession of *yourself*.'[27] In line
with these sentiments, Thérèse said on another occasion: 'Our
Lord is very just; if he doesn't judge our good actions, he will not
judge our bad ones. For those who offer themselves to love, I
don't think there will be a judgment at all; on the contrary, God
will make haste to reward his own love which he will see in our
hearts. We are only consumed by love in so far as we abandon
ourselves to love.'[28] It would seem that for Thérèse God's justice
was subsumed into the divine mercy, so that they became virtually synonymous.

It has occurred to me over the years that Thérèse's understanding of faith as absolute trust in God's saving grace is close to that of Luther and his followers. Like Luther, she was particularly fond of a verse of St Paul, 'God has pity on whom he wills and he shows mercy to whom he wants to show mercy. The only thing that counts is not what humans do but the mercy of God' (Rom 9:15-16). I suspect that she would have heartily agreed with par 15 of the momentous *Joint Declaration on the Doctrine of Justification by the Lutheran World Federation and the Catholic Church* which was published on the eve of the new millenium. It reads: 'Together we confess: By grace alone in faith in Christ's saving work and not because of any merit on our part, we are accepted by God and receive the Holy Spirit, who renews our hearts while equipping and calling us to good works.' It has also occurred to me that devotion to the divine mercy which was revealed to St Faustina Kowalska, and advocated by her in her diaries, has strong affinities with the teaching of Thérèse. For example, the Lord said to Faustina on one occasion: 'Souls who spread the honour of my mercy I shield through their entire lives as a tender mother her infant, and at the hour of death I will not be a Judge for them, but the Merciful Saviour. At that last hour, a soul has nothing with which to defend itself except my mercy. Happy is the soul that during its lifetime immersed itself in the Fountain of Mercy, because Justice will have to hold on to it.'[29]

The Vocation to love
Like other saints before her, such as Pope Gregory the Great and Ignatius of Loyola, Thérèse put a lot of emphasis on religious desires as a key to discovering one's vocation and the will of God. She wrote in a letter to Marie of the Sacred Heart, 8 September 1896: 'To be a martyr was the dream of my youth. And in the cloisters of Carmel the dream grew with me. But even then I realised that my dream was absurd, because I couldn't limit my desires to a specific kind of martyrdom … I opened St Paul's Epistles in the hope of finding an answer. My eye chanced to fall on the 12th and 13th chapters of the First Epistle to the Corinthians. There I first read that not all can be apostles, prophets, doctors, etc. … This answer did not satisfy my desires

... I read on ... and the Apostle explains how all the most perfect gifts are nothing without love ... At last I found peace ... I realised that love covered every type of vocation, that love was everything, that it embraced all times and places. ... Then in the excess of my delirious joy, I exclaimed: Love is my vocation!'[30] Surely, this is the most sublime passage in the writings of St Thérèse.

In line with her notion of the 'little way', Thérèse believed that love was best expressed in the simple mundane circumstances of everyday life rather than in ostentatious acts of self-denial such as fasting. These small acts of love were the 'little flowers' from which she derived her popular name. She gives a graphic example of what she means. 'There is in the community one sister who has the gift of displeasing me whatever she does. I found her ways, her words, her character, all very disagreeable. And yet she is a holy religious who must be very acceptable to God; so, not wishing to give way to the natural dislike which I felt, I told myself that charity should not consist in feelings, but in works. I then set myself to doing for this sister what I would have done for the person whom I love best. Each time I met her I prayed to God for her, offering up all her virtues and merits. I knew this was pleasing to Jesus.'[31] As we noted in chapter eleven, apparently Thérèse was so successful in disguising her true feelings that the sister in question had no idea of what Thérèse really felt.

Looking into the Void
Paul Tillich pointed out in *The Courage to Be*,[32] that neurotic anxiety is rooted in what philosophers call ontological or existential anxiety. Unlike pathological forms of distress which are often subjective and unrealistic, ontological anxiety is both objective and realistic. It is evoked by contingency, i.e. the awareness that nothing, including myself, is the adequate explanation of its own existence, and that all being including my own is threatened by non-being. Tillich argued that ontological anxiety usually expresses itself in three characteristic ways. Firstly, there is fear of fate and death. It was prevalent in the Greco-Roman world. Secondly, there is fear of guilt and condemnation. It was prevalent around the time of the Reformation. Thirdly, there is a fear of emptiness and meaninglessness. It is prevalent in the

contemporary era, which W. H. Auden referred to as the age of anxiety. Anxiety to do with a sense of meaninglessness is reflected in the arts, e.g. painting, music, and movies. It has many possible causes in the culture. The Reformation desacralised creation which was no longer the sacrament of the Divine presence. Descartes said that the world was a machine. Science studied it, capitalism and technology exploited it in a ruthless manner, thereby severing the umbilical cord of meaning that connected us to the world, to ourselves and ultimately to God. Post-modernist relativism has accentuated this form of nihilism and alienation with its associated feelings of anxiety and loneliness. Jean Paul Sartre expressed the consequences in poignant terms when he wrote: 'I prayed, I pleaded for a sign, I sent heaven messages: no reply. Heaven doesn't even know my name. I kept wondering what I was in God's eyes. Now I know the answer: nothing. God doesn't see me, God doesn't hear me, God doesn't know me. You see the void above our heads? That is God. You see the hole in the ground? That's what God is. You see the crack in the door? That's God too. Silence is God. Absence is God. God is human loneliness.'[33]

I believe that ontological anxiety has tremendous spiritual significance. It is the birthplace of religion as the conscious awareness of transcendence. In biblical terms it is the poverty of spirit that Jesus spoke about, i.e. the place of need in which I discover a heartfelt desire for an absolute, non-contingent meaning, or power beyond myself. In his books *On Religion,* and *The Christian Faith*, Friedrich Schleiermacher asserted that natural religion consisted of two characteristics, a feeling of absolute dependence, i.e. an awareness of contingency, and a sense and taste for the infinite.[34] In this century, Rudolf Otto, a disciple of Schleiermacher, tried to combine the two notions in the phrase 'creature- feeling'. One way or another, when a person faces the anxiety of being a contingent creature, he or she usually begins to long for transcendence. This kind of heartfelt desire, which is rooted in the spirit rather than the psyche, is the *sine qua non* of religious experience. As St Augustine once wrote: 'The person who wandering in the abyss screams out, overcomes the abyss. The scream itself lifts the person above the abyss.'[35] W. H. Auden wrote: 'He is the Truth. Seek Him in the Kingdom of

Anxiety; You will come to a great city that has expected your return for years.'

Tolstoy Anticipated the Temptations of Thérèse
In the nineteenth century Tolstoy experienced ontological anxiety as a result of a crisis of meaning. When he reached the age of 50 he had every reason to feel content. He had a wife, children, a 1,500 acre estate, 300 horses and a reputation as the greatest writer in Russia. And yet he was unhappy. He felt that everything he had, and everything he had achieved, were pointless. He wrote in his diary: 'You can't close your eyes in order not to see that there is nothing ahead but the lie of freedom and happiness, nothing but suffering, real death and annihilation.'[36] He was scared by death, not so much because it marked the end of his life, but because it robbed his life of any meaning it might appear to have.

He was fond of quoting an oriental fable which expressed his feelings. A man who was being chased by a tiger climbed down into a well. At the bottom he could see the gaping jaws of a fierce dragon. Because he was unable to go up or down, the unfortunate man clung to a small bush which was growing out from between the stones. As his strength began to fail him, he noticed that two mice, one white the other black, were nibbling away at the roots of the bush. Before long he would fall to his death. Just then the man noticed that there were two drops of honey glistening on one of the leaves. Having made a supreme effort to draw himself up, he licked the nectar and waited for the end. Life is much the same, thought Tolstoy. It is a sigh sandwiched between two mysteries, the nothingness that preceded our birth and the nothingness which will follow our deaths. If there are drops of honey to be enjoyed such as love of family and literature, they lose their savour when one knows that their meaning is called into question by the annihilation of death.

In his diary, Tolstoy reveals that during his times of depression, 'He thought he heard a sort of distant laughter. Someone was making fun of him, someone who had worked everything out beforehand long ago ... I stood there like an idiot, realising at last that there was nothing and never would be anything in life. And he thinks it is funny!'[37] He was so demoralised by

thoughts like these that he was tempted to end it all by committing suicide. In fact he stopped taking his gun with him when he
went out to hunt, so that, as he said himself, 'I could not yield to
the desire to do away with myself too easily.'[38] Tolstoy's crisis of
faith came to an end when, having been edified by the simple
faith of some peasants he knew, he overcame his rationalistic
doubts and recovered his childhood sense of God. The result
was dramatic: 'Everything came alive, took on meaning. The
moment I thought I knew God, I lived. But the moment I forgot
him, the moment I stopped believing, I stopped living ... To
know God and to live are the same thing.'[39]

Thérèse's Crisis of Faith

Some twenty years after Tolstoy's crisis, Thérèse experienced
the same kind of acute ontological anxiety, i.e. the kind of anxiety that is evoked by the threat of non existence. She endured a
spiritual depression, sometimes known as desolation of spirit or
the dark night of the soul. In her *Autobiography*, she talks, like
Tolstoy, about mocking voices, and how the fear of annihilation
seemed to cancel all sense of meaning.[40] She describes how she
used to get tired of the darkness all around her and how she at-
tempted to refresh her jaded spirits with thoughts of heaven
where her hopes were fixed. But what happened? Her torment
grew worse than ever; the darkness oppressing her seemed to
borrow, from those who lived in it, the gift of speech. She tells us
how she heard it say in mocking tones: 'It is all a dream, this talk
of a heavenly country, bathed in light, scented with delicious
perfumes, and of a God who made it all, who is to be our possession in eternity! ... All right, all right, go on longing for death!
But death will make nonsense of your hopes; it will only mean a
darker night than ever, the night of mere non-existence and annihilation.'[41] Sister of St Augustine reported: 'She admitted
something to me which surprised and confused me. If only you
knew the darkness into which I've been flung! I don't believe in
eternal life; I think, after this life there will be nothing more.
Everything has vanished for me.' But she added afterwards –
and this is the point, *'All I have left is love.'*[42] When I read these
deeply moving words I was reminded of something Carl Jung
had said in his autobiography. 'Man can try to name love,

showering upon it all the names at his command, and still he will involve himself in endless self-deceptions. If he possesses a grain of wisdom, he will lay down his arms and name the unknown by the more unknown ... by the name of God.'[43]

Thérèse also spoke to her companions about other temptations against faith. She said to one: 'If you only knew the frightful thoughts that plague me! Pray hard for me not to listen to the devil as he tries to make me believe his many lies. The arguments of the worst rationalists fill my mind. Why must I have such thoughts when I love God so much? I endure them of necessity, but even while having them, never stop renewing my acts of faith.'[44] On another occasion she added in similar vein: 'The reasoning of the worst materialists is imposed on my mind. Science which makes unceasing advances will eventually explain everything naturally. We shall have the absolute explanation for everything that exists and that still remains a problem, because very many things remain to be discovered yet.'[45] It is not clear what rationalists Thérèse had in mind. There were many of them writing at the time. It is worth remembering that she was living at around the same period as post-Enlightenment unbelievers such as Auguste Comte (1798-1857). He had written: 'In the final, the positive (i.e. scientific) state, the mind has given over the vain search after Absolute notions, the origin and destination of the universe, and the causes of phenomena, and applies itself to the study of their laws – that is, their invariable relations of succession and resemblance.'[46] I don't suppose Thérèse had read Comte's book, but she was certainly echoing its sentiments.

Just as Tolstoy was tempted to commit suicide, so was Thérèse. On one occasion she admitted: 'Oh, if I didn't have the faith, I could never endure all this pain. I'm amazed that atheists don't commit suicide more often ... Yes! What a mercy it is to have faith! If I didn't have faith, I should have killed myself without a moment's hesitation.'[47] One of the sisters said that Thérèse begged prayers because, she said, the pain was enough to make her lose her reason. She asked that all poisonous substances be kept out of her reach because in mind numbing pain, 'no longer knowing what one is doing, one could easily take one's life.'[48]

By 9 June 1897 it was clear that Thérèse hadn't long to live. She was moved downstairs. We can record two typical remarks. On one occasion she said, 'See that candle; when the thief comes to carry me off, that will be put in my hand, but you mustn't give me the candlestick – that's far too ugly!'[49] On another occasion her sister asked her to say something nice to the doctor. She replied, 'That's not my style at all. Let him think what he likes. I only like simplicity. I hate humbug. Believe me, what you ask would be wrong for me to do.'[50] All the while she was receiving the barbaric and ineffective treatments of the day, treatments she suspected were doing her no good whatsoever, e.g. blistering, cauterisation, syrup of slugs, friction with a horse hair glove, etc. She said to her companions: 'Don't be upset, dearest sisters, if I suffer a great deal and if you see no sign of happiness in me when I reach the point of death. Our Lord too died a victim of love, and see what his death agony of love was like! … Our Lord died on the cross in agony, yet this was the finest of deaths for love … The only example, indeed. Dying of love doesn't mean dying in transports of joy.'[51] All through her terrible physical and spiritual suffering, which was particularly bad during the last months of her life, i.e. from July to 30 September 1897, she never lost her trust in love. Her love was to triumph.

On the day she died, 30 September 1897, Thérèse suffered such violent temptations against faith that she was in total darkness. Several hours before her death, perspiration stood out on her forehead. She was agitated, close to despair and asked the sisters to sprinkle holy water on her. Her sister Pauline, i.e. Mother Agnes, was bewildered. She knew Thérèse was a saint, but her dying looked like that of a sinner. She went and prayed before a statue, saying, 'Oh Sacred Heart of Jesus, I beg you, do not let my sister die in despair.'[52] In a way it wasn't surprising that Thérèse was suffering in this way. She had stated in the past that she had asked to die the death of Jesus on the cross. This is how her sister, Mother Agnes described Thérèse's death: 'She sighed, "Mother! Isn't this the agony! … Am I not going to die?" … "Yes, my poor little one, it's the agony, but God perhaps wills to prolong it for several hours." She answered with courage: "Well … All right! … All right! Oh! I would not want to suffer for a shorter time!" And looking at the crucifix: "Oh! I love him!

... My God ... I love you!" Suddenly after having pronounced these words, she fell back, her head leaning to the right.'[53] In a letter written to Leonie shortly after their sister's death, Pauline described what had happened: 'Our angel is in heaven. She gave up her last sigh at seven o'clock, pressing the crucifix to her heart and saying: "Oh I love you!" She had just lifted her eyes to heaven; what was she seeing!'[54]

A Psycho-spiritual Reflection
At this point I'd tentatively suggest that Thérèse's harrowing dark night of the soul was related to the psychosomatic crisis she had endured when she was ten. I have already mentioned that it may have been an acute case of neurotic anxiety which was occasioned by the loss of her mother and then, shortly afterwards, by the loss of Pauline, her second mother, when she joined the Carmelites. Christian psychiatrist Frank Lake has pointed out that so long as the mother is present, the child experiences its being and well being in identification with her. It cannot conceive of life going on without her. Afterwards the experience is split off and repressed in the unconscious, where it continues to exercise a hidden influence. I suspect that this is what happened in Thérèse's case. Dr Lake says that this childhood encounter with the threat of non-being, as a result of abandonment feelings, can link up with Tillich's forms of ontological or existential anxiety.[55]

Like an action replay of her childhood experience, Thérèse lost her father twice. Firstly, two weeks after her profession he slipped into a severe mental illness, probably due to cerebral arteriosclerosis. By and large, this condition prevented Thérèse communicating with him. Secondly, she lost him in a definite way when he died in 1894. It is possible that during her dark night of the soul, Thérèse was tapping into the feelings of meaninglessness and abandonment that had been implicit in her childhood crisis. Now that she was psychologically healthy, similar feelings were resurrected, as ontological anxiety, as a result of losing her beloved father. She had to face the ultimate sense of religious abandonment, abandonment by the Father in heaven. Her suffering was no longer mainly psychosomatic, but mainly spiritual. With Jesus on the cross she could cry out: 'My God, my God, why have you forsaken me?' (Mt 27:46.)

Life after Life
Shortly after Thérèse's death, her autobiography was published.
It became an overnight success as she had predicted and was
translated into many languages. Soon afterwards the process of
preparation for possible beatification and canonisation got
under way. Many of those who knew her, or were influenced by
her, were interviewed. Their interesting testimonies have been
published in a book entitled, *Thérèse of Lisieux by Those Who Knew
Her.*[56] She was canonised on 25 May 1925. In 1929 she was
named patroness of the foreign missions. In 1947 she joined her
beloved Joan of Arc as co-patroness of France. In 1997 she was
declared a Doctor of the Church by Pope John Paul II who said:
'The Pastors of the Church, beginning with my predecessors, the
Supreme Pontiffs of this century, who held up her holiness as an
example for all, also stressed that Thérèse is a teacher of the spiritual life with a doctrine both spiritual and profound, which she
drew from the gospel sources under the guidance of the divine
Teacher and then imparted to her brothers and sisters in the
church with the greatest effectiveness.'[57] Thérèse has the distinction of being the youngest of the 33 saints with the title of
Doctor. She is one of only three women who have been honoured in this way.

A Saint for Postmodern times
When the relics of St Thérèse were brought to Ireland in mid
2001, I visited them in a Carmelite convent. As I approached the
casket, I found myself strangely moved. When I left the oratory,
I met a person whom I had known when we were schoolboys.
Having greeted me, he asked what I felt about the relics. I was
virtually unable to speak. I was so full of emotion that I feared
that I'd burst into embarrassing tears. So I just mumbled a few
words in reply. When I got home, I reflected on the whole experience and asked myself two questions. What exactly did you feel
when you venerated Thérèse's mortal remains? And what was it
that you were aware of, that evoked those feelings?

As I tried to name my emotions I realised that I was grieving
for Thérèse. I felt great compassion for her. I was acutely aware
that this lovely young woman, who was filled with such goodness and idealism, had suffered greatly from an emotional,

physical and spiritual point of view. As I dwelt on this awareness, I became conscious of another surprising fact. I find it easier
to identify with the sufferings of women than I do with those of
men. I feel that women are more sensitive and vulnerable than
men. Because of my tendency to relate to other males in a rather
macho, competitive way, I try to be stoical, like them, about my
sufferings. I first learned to do this on the sports field. If I got injured, e.g. in an aggressive tackle, I'd try to grin and bear with
the pain. Perceptive women often comment on this male
propensity to deny emotional and physical suffering. While I
realise that my attitude to female and male responses to suffering is questionable and stereotypical, nevertheless I must admit
that it is still the way I sometimes instinctively react.

As I reflected on these lines, I felt that my male perspective
sometimes prevents me identifying as fully as I might otherwise
do, with the sufferings of Jesus, a fellow male. But when I was
vividly aware of the suffering of Thérèse, who died such a
painful death, her pain acted like a window. Through it I could
contemplate the suffering of Jesus in a new way. After all, as a
relatively young man, he had died an even more painful death
than Thérèse. Over the years, I have occasionally seen pictures
which depicted the crucified One as a woman hanging upon the
cross. I know that some Christians find such images offensive.
But when I visited the relics of St Thérèse, it was as if I saw her
on the cross, and that through her sufferings I was able to appreciate the sacrificial sufferings of Jesus in a new way. My strong
feelings and tearfulness were evoked by a heartfelt awareness of
the terrible torments endured by Thérèse, and of course by
Christ, out of love for sinners like me. As St Paul wrote so
poignantly, 'I live by faith in the Son of God, who loved me and
gave himself for me' (Gal 2:20).

I have often wondered why so many Catholics have such a
genuine devotion to St Thérèse. I think there are two principal
reasons at least. Firstly, although all saints re-live the mysteries
of Christ's life of sacrificial love, St Thérèse did so to a remarkable degree. She made the life of Christ manifest in a very acces-
sible, human way. Secondly, Karl Stern, a Jewish psychiatrist
who became a Catholic, once observed that God is inclined to
raise up great saints whose prophetic lives challenge the spirit of

the times. For example, during the era dominated by the French Revolution, the Lord raised up John Vianney, the Curé d'Ars, as a model of sanctity. Although he lived around the time when atheistic Reason had been enthroned in Notre Dame Cathedral as a pseudo goddess,[58] Vianney found it hard to pass any of his exams. Nevertheless, in spite of his lack of academic ability, word of his holiness spread throughout France and beyond. As many as 20,000 people a year sought him out for confession, advice and prayer. Stern believes that in the modern age when the power of the atom has been harnessed, God has raised up Thérèse of Lisieux as *the* saint for the times. She renounced the modern will to power, which was advocated by Friedrich Nietzsche, in favour of the will to love, which is expressed by means of the Little Way.

In his encyclical *Faith and Reason* Pope John Paul II has described postmodern culture: 'The currents of thought which claim to be postmodern merit appropriate attention. According to some of them, the time of certainties is irrevocably past, and the human being must now learn to live in a horizon of total absence of meaning, where everything is provisional and ephemeral.'[59] St Thérèse of Lisieux could be the patron saint of such a painful cultural experience. At the end of her life she seemed to be adrift, like many people in contemporary society, upon the dark waters of radical uncertainty. God seems to be silent and absent. But she learned to trust in the Lord with blind faith, without the compass needle of experience to guide her. Thérèse had a cousin, Marguerite-Marie Tostain who was married to an atheist. His challenging arguments caused her to doubt her faith around the same time that Thérèse died. When, later, she read *Story of a Soul* she learned to cope by submitting to God in blind faith and by continuing to act as if she had a dazzling light before her eyes.[60] As Prov 3:5 puts it: 'Trust in the Lord, with all your heart, and do not rely on your own insight.' Many of the people of today have to learn to do this.

CHAPTER FIFTEEN

Give Glory to God[1]

There is a tendency in modern spirituality to focus on self-fulfil-ment rather than self-transcendence.[2] There is also a related dan-ger that we focus on what God can do for us rather than what we can do for God. We need to break free of the gravitational pull of self-absorption to focus our attention on the divine nature. While it is true that God's essence is ultimately unknowable, we can have accurate, if inadequate, mediated intimations of what the reality of God is really like. Over the years the Lord can man-ifest it to us in various ways such as the witness of Spirit-filled people, inspirations in prayer and scripture texts that come alive with meaning. In this reflection I would like to describe some of the wonderful attributes of God that I have come to appreciate over the years. Although there are a countless number of them, I want, in a rather arbitrary way, to mention just six. This is not in-tended to be a systematic, scholarly treatment of the subject, but rather a subjective and impressionistic description of some of the divine qualities I really admire. They all begin with the letter 'g,' namely that God is glorious, great, good, gracious, generous, and the giver of gifts of grace.

God is Glorious

The books of the bible repeatedly speak about the glory of God. In the Old Testament *kabod* was derived from *kabed*, 'to be heavy'. It lends itself to the idea that the one possessing glory is laden with riches, power, position, and honour. Yahweh is asso-ciated, above everyone and everything else, with glory. This magnificence is a manifestation to mankind of God's divine being, nature, presence, power and activity, which is sometimes associated with physical phenomena such as thunder and light-ening. There is a good example of this notion in Ex 33:18-23: 'Then Moses said, "Now show me your glory." And the Lord said, "I will cause all my goodness to pass in front of you, and I will proclaim my name, the Lord, in your presence. I will have mercy on whom I will have mercy, and I will have compassion on whom I will have compassion. But," he said, "you cannot see my face, for no one may see me and live." Then the Lord said, "There is a place near me where you may stand on a rock. When my glory passes by, I will put you in a cleft in the rock and cover you with my hand until I have passed by. Then I will remove my hand and you will see my back; but my face must not be seen."

An associated biblical word for glory is *shekinah*, which literally means 'dwelling'. It was used to describe a visible manifestation of the radiance of God dwelling in the midst of his people. Although the word is not found in the bible, *shekinah* frequently occurs in later Jewish writings. It refers to the instances when God's presence was manifested in a symbolic and numinous way as cloud and light. For example, on Sinai we are informed: 'When Moses went up on the mountain, the cloud covered it, and the glory of the Lord settled on Mount Sinai. For six days the cloud covered the mountain, and on the seventh day the Lord called to Moses from within the cloud' (Ex 24:15-16). When he went to pray in the place of meeting, we are told that: 'As Moses went into the tent, the pillar of cloud would come down and stay at the entrance, while the Lord spoke with Moses. Whenever the people saw the pillar of cloud standing at the entrance to the tent, they all stood and worshiped, each at the entrance to his tent' (Ex 33:9-10). In a favourite text of mine the prophet declares: 'God's glory covered the heavens and his praise filled the earth. His splendour was like the sunrise; rays flashed from his hand, where his power was hidden' (Hab 3:3-4). In the Holy of Holies, the tabernacle in Solomon's Temple, the *shekinah* would rest in the form of a luminous cloud above the altar where it would light up the room.

In the New Testament the word for glory is *doxa*. In secular Greek this means 'opinion' or 'reputation'. In certain places *doxa* refers to human honour, but its chief use is to describe the revealed character and the presence of God in the person and work of Jesus Christ. On other occasions it is used as a form of recognition and of vocalised reverence for the Creator and Judge. With reference to God, it denotes the divine majesty and perfection. God is called the Father of glory. The manifestation of the divine presence in terms of light is an occasional phenomenon, as in the Old Testament. The transfiguration is the sole instance, during the earthly ministry, when Jesus was seen to radiate light.

In Mark 9:2-8 we read, in words reminiscent of the *shekinah* of old: 'After six days Jesus took Peter, James and John with him and led them up a high mountain, where they were all alone. There he was transfigured before them. His clothes became dazzling white, whiter than anyone in the world could bleach them. And there appeared before them Elijah and Moses, who were talking with Jesus. Peter said to Jesus, "Rabbi, it is good for us to be here. Let us put up three shelters – one for you, one for Moses and one for Elijah." (He did not know what to say, they were so frightened.) Then a cloud appeared and enveloped them, and a voice came from the cloud: "This is my Son, whom I love. Listen to him!" Suddenly, when they looked around, they no longer saw anyone with them except Jesus.' Sometime after the resurrection of Jesus, Peter recalled: 'He received honour and glory from God the Father when the voice came to him from the Majestic Glory, saying, "This is my Son, whom I love; with him I am well pleased"' (2 Pet 1:17).

St John experienced God's glory on the island of Patmos (Rev 1:12ff). St Paul had a similar experience of the divine glory as a result of his conversion (Acts 9:3ff). He observes in 2 Cor 4:6: 'For God who said, 'Let light shine out of darkness,' made his light shine in our hearts to give us the light of the knowledge of the glory of God in the face of Christ.' In 2 Cor 3:18, Paul says that Christians can experience and mirror to others the glory they have contemplated in the person of Christ. The fact that he is able to speak of God's glory in terms of riches (Eph 1:18; 3:16) and might (Col 1:11) suggests the influence of the Old Testament upon his thinking. The display of God's power in raising his Son from the dead is labeled glory (Rom 6:4). Then in 1 Cor 12:7 Paul uses a beautiful term *phanerosis* to describe the charisms. It is particularly applicable to the charisms of power such as healing, exorcism and miracle working. It means 'manifestation' or 'epiphany.' In other words, whenever the charisms are exercised they are mini theophanies which disclose something of the glory of the risen Lord.

God is Great

The greatest, most majestic reality I know is the universe. From the minute world of subatomic particles to the myriad galaxies that populate the seemingly endless expanses of space, the grandeur of the cosmos is awe-inspiring and mind-boggling. Apparently there are about one thousand million stars in our galaxy alone, but our galaxy is only one of around a thousand million galaxies. Although there is a countless number of stars the distances between them are truly vast. For example if two grains of pollen were put floating on the surface of the Pacific Ocean, its waters would be as crowded with pollen as space is with stars. As Cardinal Newman once observed, there is only one thought greater than that of the universe and that is the thought of its Creator. Nothing that exists is the adequate explanation of its own existence. It depends on Another, on the One who sustains all animate and inanimate beings in a loving way. God, like creation, is majestic. The word 'majestic' is derived from Latin *magnus* and means great. As Paul observes, God's 'eternal power and deity, has been clearly perceived in the things that have been made' (Rom 1:20). As a result the Psalmist declares: 'Great is the Lord and greatly to be praised ... the Lord is great and a great king, let us worship and bow down' (Ps 48:1; Ps 95:3,6).

In the New Testament, God's greatness is mainly associated with the divine power. In Lk 1:37 the angel Gabriel said to Mary: 'Nothing is impossible with God.' On another occasion Jesus told the disciples that it was as hard for a rich man to enter heaven as it was for a camel to pass through the eye of a needle. 'Those who heard this asked, "Who then can be saved?" Jesus replied, "What is impossible with men is possible with God".' (Lk 18:26-27). For the biblical authors faith is a worldview that attributes to God the power to do the impossible and which invites believers to trust wholeheartedly in the Lord and not to lean on their understanding (cf. Prov 3:5). That power was manifest in Christ's deeds, his exorcisms, healings and mighty miracles. As St Peter said: 'God anointed him with the Holy Spirit and power. He went about doing good works and healing all who were in the grip of the devil, and God was with him' (Acts 10:38).

Paul, the apostle, often talked about the power of God. For

him it was pre-eminently the power of the Holy Spirit which raised Jesus from death to glory and which dwells in the lives of believers. These points are encapsulated in the following verses. 'I pray also that the eyes of your heart may be enlightened in order that you may know the hope to which he has called you ... and his incomparably great power for us who believe. That power is like the working of his mighty strength, which he exerted in Christ when he raised him from the dead and seated him at his right hand in the heavenly realms' (Eph 1:18-20). In another place Paul prays 'that according to the riches of his glory, God may grant you to be strengthened with might, through his Spirit in the inner man' (Eph 3:16). Ironically, for Paul, 'God's power is made perfect in human weakness' (2 Cor 12:9).

God is Good
In the Old Testament we are told on many occasions that God is good. The Psalmist has declared repeatedly, 'The Lord is good, his mercy endures forever' (Ps 106:1, 107:1, 118:1, 136:1). In Exodus 33:18-19 God revealed the divine goodness in a particularly vivid way to his servant Moses. He 'said, "Now show me your glory." And the Lord said, "I will cause all my goodness to pass in front of you, and I will proclaim my name, the Lord, in your presence. I will have mercy on whom I will have mercy, and I will have compassion on whom I will have compassion".' In the New Testament there is an interesting text in Lk 18:18-19 where: 'A certain ruler asked Jesus, "Good teacher, what must I do to inherit eternal life?" "Why do you call me good?" Jesus answered. "No one is good – except God alone".' Unlike the created world which is marred by moral evil and obvious defects – Paul says that creation is made subject to futility and groans in agony (Rom 8:20, 22) – there is no evil in God. God is utterly and uniquely good in nature. In the divine there is no darkness.

All of us experience God's goodness to a greater or lesser extent. People who have undergone a spiritual awakening come into a more personal awareness of the unmerited, unrestricted, and unconditional love of God (cf. Eph 3:16). As a result they have a vivid sense of God's goodness. That heartfelt sense of love is the expression of God's goodness and *vice versa*. A few hours before her death St Thérèse of Lisieux declared: 'My God!

My God! You are so good! Oh yes, you are good, I know it!'[3] On 10 January 1935 Sr Faustina Kowalska, the promulgator of the Divine Mercy devotion, heard the Lord say: 'Everything that you say about my goodness is true; language has no adequate expression to extol my goodness. These words were so filled with power and so clear that I would give my life in declaring they came from God.'[4] God's goodness is also apparent in divine providence, the loving plan and provision of the One who not only cares for the birds of the air and the lilies of the field but for each and every human being. God provides for us inwardly by means of our natural abilities and talents and by means of the in-numerable graces we receive. The Lord also provides for us in an outward way by means of all kinds of opportunities and material benefits.

We can also get an idea of how good God must be when we encounter the exceptional goodness of human beings. For exam-ple, on one occasion St Vincent de Paul was suffering from a bad illness. He tells us that during that time of vulnerability he thought of the goodness of St Francis de Sales, the Bishop of Geneva. He thought to himself, 'If a mere man is so good, what must God be like?' He says that he was sure that his consequent sense of God's infinite goodness assisted his recovery. Some time after Vincent's death, one of his friends, Fr Portail attested: 'Vincent was the most perfect image of Jesus Christ that I have ever known on earth.'

I get a similar impression of the incomprehensible goodness of God when I sense exceptional goodness in people I meet. Some time ago I conducted a retreat for a community of en-closed nuns. Over a number of days I had an opportunity to talk to most of the sisters. Without exception they were admirable women. But I can recall thinking at the time that two or three of them, in particular, were exceptionally good. I was almost moved to tears when I sensed qualities such as their idealism, in-tegrity, humility, dedication and love. More recently I was talk-ing to a lay woman who revealed many secrets about her inner life. Again I was deeply touched by her sheer goodness, her single-minded struggle to serve Christ wholeheartedly. For in-stance, she worked for a Catholic charity where she was poorly paid. When I asked why she wouldn't thinks of getting a similar but better paid job, she replied, 'because I'm happy to work where God has led me, no matter how I'm paid.' I thought to myself, 'If she is so good, in a modern non-pious sort of way, what must God be like?'

God is Gracious
The English word 'gracious' is derived from the Latin word *gratia* which literally means 'pleasing'. The implication is that the Lord is full of goodwill, a desire to please. That goodwill finds expression in such things as God's mercy, compassion, gentleness, mildness, and leniency. Because God is gracious, the Lord wants what is best for all creation and especially for human beings who are made in God's likeness. Not only that, they have been adopted into God's family as a result of being born again by means of baptism and personal commitment to Christ. For example, in the Old Testament God's goodwill is mentioned in Wis 1:13-14 which states: 'God did not make death, and he does not delight in the death of the living. For he created all things so that they might exist; the generative forces of the world are wholesome.' Again in Jer 29:11 we read: 'For I know the plans I have for you,' declares the Lord, 'plans to prosper you and not to harm you, plans to give you hope and a future.' In the New Testament Jesus bore witness to the gracious benevolence of God when he said to the disciples: 'I have come that they may have life, and have it to the full' (Jn 10:10). On another occasion he said: 'I have told you this so that my joy may be in you and that your joy may be complete' (Jn 15:11).

There was a time when I thought that God was more demanding than gracious. One day I was engaged in a prayer exercise proposed by St Teresa of Avila. I was imagining that Jesus was standing in front of me. I tried to notice, as Teresa recommended, that Jesus was looking at me with eyes filled with love and humility. Suddenly I got an inner sense that he was not there primarily to tell me what he wanted. Rather, he had come to me in love, as a servant who wanted to know what I wanted. He desired to satisfy my deepest heart's desire. That newfound awareness was like a spiritual revolution. My image of God changed from one where I saw God as a demanding, hard to please parent, to that of a loving and gracious friend. I have come to realise that because Jesus is loving he wants to do what is best for me. He is forever before me as the Suffering Servant, with a towel wrapped around his waist. He is there to satisfy my deepest, God prompted desires.

God is Generous
Jesus had a profound sense of the generosity of God as the expression of the Father's divine greatness, goodness and graciousness. He spoke about it on a number of occasions. It was this awareness that informed all his teaching on the power of prayers of petition and supplication. In Lk 15:31 the Prodigal Father said to his elder son: 'You are with me always, *all I have is yours.*' In other words, 'if you related to me your loving father in a trusting rather than a dutiful way, you would realise that I'm unstinting in my generosity, there is no good gift I would withhold from you. You could have claimed the ring of my authority, worn the cloak of honour, the shoes of freedom, and killed the fatted calf whenever you liked. But because you don't really know me as I am, you didn't realise how I act. You relate to me in terms of cold, impersonal duty, whereas I relate to you in accord with my heartfelt, unconditional love.' On another occasion Jesus drew attention to the way God's generosity found expression in extravagant giving when he said: 'If you parents, who are evil, know how to give good gifts to your children, *how much more will your Father who is in heaven give good things to those who ask him?*' (Mt 7:11). If imperfect parents often go to great lengths to help their children, how much more will the perfect Father in heaven be willing to do what is best for the children of God?

Some time ago an incident occurred that enabled me to grasp what Jesus might have meant. At about 8.30 pm the door bell rang. When I answered it, a travelling man with a drink problem was standing there. Tom asked me if I would give him some food and drink. Reluctantly, I got a glass of milk and a ham sandwich and brought them to him. I asked him how his family was, because I had met his wife and children on more than one occasion in the past. He told me that his son had nearly died a few days before. Apparently he was crying in the middle of the night. Tom had been awakened. He got up and had a look at his child. He was very ill, so he woke up his wife and said that they would have to bring him to the hospital immediately. I asked why he wanted to go so quickly. The traveller told me that one of his daughters had died a few years before of meningitis. He knew that if his son had the same infection he would need urgent treatment.

Tom and his wife arrived at the hospital at 6.00 am in the morning. By now their son had a strong fever. It didn't take long for the doctors to diagnose that the boy, like his sister before him, was suffering from meningitis. The parents knew from bitter experience that they were facing a life and death situation. By now Tom was so intent on telling me his dramatic story that he stopped eating and drinking. He said with great intensity, 'Father, I really prayed to God for my precious son.' He made a gesture as if he were cradling his boy in his arms. 'I said to God, "Lord I would gladly give my life if you would spare my dear son's life".' He spoke with remarkable tenderness and eloquence. I knew that he had meant every word he said, and that he would have gladly sacrificed his life in order to save his son. In the event, the doctors successfully treated the boy with drugs. Because his parents had got him to the hospital in time, they were able to control the fever. Thankfully, Tom's son recovered completely. But what impressed me was this traveller's great generosity. He was willing to make any sacrifice in order to save his child. I thought to myself, 'If such an imperfect man, with a drink problem, knows how to give good gifts to his son, how much more will the all loving Father in heaven give good things to those who ask for them?'

Later in the New Testament St Paul talked about the generosity of God. In Rom 8:32 he observed: 'If God has given us his Son *would he not give us all things in him*?' In other words, if the Father in his unimaginable goodness has given us Jesus as his greatest gift, why should he withhold any lesser gifts? As St Paul said in another place: 'My God will supply every need of yours according to his riches in glory in Christ Jesus' (Phil 4:19). As Jn 1:16 testifies: 'From the fullness of his grace we have all received one blessing after another.'

God the Giver of Gifts of Grace

God's graciousness and generosity finds expression in the giving of divine gifts. The Lord has poured innumerable graces upon us. There is the gift of existence and life, the gift of health and education. There is the gift of natural talents and life opportunities. There is the inestimable gift of salvation and sanctifying grace. Then there are charismatic and ministerial gifts which are given for our own edification and the up-building of the Christian community. As St Paul wrote: 'Each of us was given grace according to the measure of Christ's gift. Therefore it is said, when he ascended on high he made captivity itself a captive; he gave gifts to his people ... The gifts he gave were that some should be apostles, some prophets, some evangelists, some pastors and teachers, to equip the saints for the work of ministry, for building up the body of Christ, until all of us come to the unity of the faith and of the knowledge of the Son of God, to maturity, to the measure of the full stature of Christ' (Eph 4:7-8; 11-14). It is so important not to take the gifts of God for granted, because if we do we will end up taking the God of the gifts for granted also.

The importance of a sense of appreciation and gratitude was underlined by Jesus in the story of the cure of the ten lepers. We are told that 'then one of them, when he saw that he was healed, turned back, praising God with a loud voice; and he fell on his face at Jesus' feet, giving him thanks. Now he was a Samaritan. Then Jesus said, "Were not ten cleansed? Where are the nine?"' (Lk 17:16). Again in Rom 1:21, St Paul said that reason unbelievers do not acknowledge the existence of the God, and therefore go on to live in an immoral way, is because they do not show gratitude for God's gifts, 'for though they knew God,' comments the apostle, 'they did not honour him as God or give thanks to him, but they became futile in their thinking, and their senseless minds were darkened.'

Our immediate sense of appreciation of the gifts of God, and ultimately of the God of the gifts, is best expressed in the form of worship. The word in English is derived from the Old English *weorth*, meaning 'worth'. Appreciation as worship is a heartfelt awareness of the greatness, goodness and graciousness of the Lord who is the generous giver of countless divine gifts. Ps 95:6

shows how the prayer of appreciation as thanksgiving and praise reaches its point of highest intensity in the form of worship. 'Come, let us bow down in *worship*, let us kneel before the Lord our Maker.'

Conclusion

There is a saying which maintains that things and people act in accordance with their natures. Jesus adverted to this principle on more than one occasion. For example in Luke 6:45 he said: 'The good man brings good things out of the good stored up in his heart, and the evil man brings evil things out of the evil stored up in his heart. For out of the overflow of his heart his mouth speaks.' On another occasion he said: 'A good tree cannot bear bad fruit, and a bad tree cannot bear good fruit. Every tree that does not bear good fruit is cut down and thrown into the fire. Thus, by their fruit you will recognise them' (Mt 7:18-20). This principle also applies to God. The Lord is forever active in accord with the divine nature. If we want to be sure of the mighty promises of God, for example those to do with God's willingness to answer prayers of petition and intercession, we need to be sure of the God of the promises. When we have an inner appreciation of who God is, we will be confident that God will give us what we ask. As Jesus assured us: 'The Father will give you whatever you ask in my name' (Jn 15:16).

Having contemplated and experienced the glory, greatness, goodness, graciousness, and generous giving of God, we are urged by the Spirit to be for others what God is for us. As Paul VI said in par 22 of *Evangelisation in the Modern World*: 'Witness, no matter how excellent, will ultimately prove ineffectual unless its meaning is clarified and corroborated – what St peter used to call accounting for "the hope that is in you".' Clearly, we are called to share in God's attributes and to act accordingly in relationships with others, especially the poor. We are called to witness to the glory, greatness, goodness and graciousness of our God by giving ourselves, our time, gifts and goods in a generous way. As Jesus said to us: 'Give, and it will be given to you. A good measure, pressed down, shaken together and running over, will be poured into your lap. For with the measure you use, it will be measured to you' (Lk 6:38). Later St Paul echoed the words of Jesus when he said: 'It is more blessed to give than to receive' (Acts 20:35). In this way we fulfill the Lord's injunction to bear witness to God (cf. Acts 1:8).

A Prayer
Let us worship God.
The God who is Glorious
The God who is Great
The God who is Good
The God who is Gracious
The God who is Generous
The God who gives us
Gifts of grace, now and forever more. Amen.

CHAPTER SIXTEEN

Atheism and the Father of Lies

This chapter proposes to do three interrelated things. It will begin with a brief description of some key points in the development of philosophical atheism. Then it will go on to indicate how a number of prominent psychologists and a noted sociologist have advocated non-belief. Finally, it will look at Pope John Paul II's theological critique of these forms of unbelief by focusing mainly, though not exclusively, on sections two and three of his encyclical, *Lord and Giver of Life* (1986). At the outset it is worth noting that there are three types of atheism. Irreligious atheists neither believe in God or in naturalistic religious experience. Religious atheists do not believe in God but they advocate the importance of naturalistic religious experience such as nature mysticism. While practical atheists often profess faith in God, in everyday life they act as if there was no deity. The related issue of agnosticism will not be dealt with here.

Philosophy and Atheism

In the seventeenth century, Rene Descartes (1596-1650) adopted a philosophical methodology of radical, universal doubt. He ended up by saying that he could only be certain of one thing. Because he was aware of his rational consciousness, his rational consciousness existed. However, this conclusion left him shipwrecked in his subjectivity, uncertain as to whether his body or the external world existed independently from his mind. To escape from this solipsistic awareness he proposed a version of the ontological argument. It tried to prove that God existed as the undeceiving guarantor of the material existence of both Descartes' body and the external world.

It wasn't long before Immanuel Kant (1724-1804) demonstrated that not only was Descartes' ontological argument philosophically invalid, the limitations of rational consciousness meant that the human mind couldn't attain certain metaphysical knowledge of either the existence or attributes of God. Subsequently, Georg Hegel (1770-1831) side-stepped Kant's critique by abolishing the traditional notion of God's transcendence in favour of a purely immanent, panentheistic understanding of divinity, i.e. everything in the universe is part of God and yet God is greater than the sum of the parts. He maintained that God, like a sleeping giant, was awaking to self-awareness in and through evolving, rational consciousness. Friedrich Schleiermacher (1768-1834) also interpreted religion in largely subjective terms. He said that it was a feeling of absolute dependence, a thirst for the infinite, an intuitive sense of the mediated presence of God in and through the oneness and mystery of created reality. In so far as believers, like the ones already mentioned, became preoccupied with epistemological rather than ontological problems, they unwittingly made the notion of God a function of human subjectivity. In doing so they had implicitly laid the foundations of philosophical atheism.

Many people believe that Ludwig Feuerbach (1804-1872) is the father of modern atheism.[1] He made the implications of extreme philosophical subjectivism explicit. He argued that rather than existing either in a transcendental or immanent way, God was another word for the latent possibilities of human subjectivity. In other words, the notion of God was really a projection of human potential on to an imaginary deity. As long as the projection remained unrecognised and unchallenged, people would remain alienated from their inner freedom and creative capacities. Feuerbach maintained that theology should be converted into anthropology. All statements about God ought to be translated into statements about man. Although, Feuerbach was opposed to belief in God, he seemed to favour a religious type of atheism, one that would retain a sense of wonder and reverence for the natural world. Feuerbach wasn't a great philosopher in the way his immediate predecessors were. Nevertheless he was an influential one. He delineated the main contours of classical atheism. Subsequently other thinkers adopted and adapted his key notion of projection in different ways.

Karl Marx (1818-1883) reacted to the subjectivism of Hegel

and Feuerbach, by adopting a radically materialistic attitude to life. He had a dialectical understanding of social evolution and argued that religion was the opium of the people, an other-worldly projection of their futile hope of heavenly bliss. This false expectation prevented the poor from improving their everyday lives by means of a proletarian revolution. He maintained that belief in God was alien to the best interests of those who were oppressed. If the structural causes of their suffering were to be overcome, belief in God would have to be abolished and the hope of eternal happiness would have to be abandoned. Then the masses would finally be motivated to overthrow the true causes of their alienation and oppression, such as invidious class structures and the private ownership of property. In doing this they would create a communist utopia on earth.

If Feuerbach was the father of modern atheism, Friedrich Nietzche (1844-1900) was its principal prophet.[2] He maintained that Judeo-Christianity was a religion with a slave mentality in so far as its followers advocated values such as poverty of spirit, dependence on God, turning the other cheek, etc. Instead of acknowledging and developing their innate capacity for greatness, Judeo-Christian believers projected their potential, in an alienating way, on to an all powerful, oppressive God. Feelings of unacknowledged inferiority and envy were characteristic of those craven individuals who had abdicated their will to power in this way. Instead of being able to affirm and admire the gifts and talents of strong, successful people, they secretly resented them. But rather than consciously acknowledge their negative attitudes, Jews and Christians metamorphosed them in the form of pseudo virtues such as humility, self-sacrificing love and meekness. Consequently, Nietzche believed that the Judeo-Christian God was incompatible with human growth, magnanimity and greatness.

He also believed that people in Western culture were becoming increasingly aware of this state of affairs. In one of his books a madman runs through the streets proclaiming that 'God is dead.' Nietzche meant this to be a cultural rather than a metaphysical declaration. In other words, the madman was acknowledging the fact that the idea of a Judeo-Christian God was dying in Western culture. It was being recognised as something alien to the dignity and potential of people. Nietzche believed that the coming age of atheism would bring about a renunciation of traditional Judeo-Christian values, the gradual transformation of people and the emergence of superman. Arguably, in doing so, Nietzche anticipated the emergence of neo-pagan spiritualities such as Nazism and the New Age movement.

While many of our contemporaries might not consciously subscribe to the philosophical teachings of religious and irreligious atheists, a sizable number of them are, for all intents and purposes, practical atheists. Although they might pay lip service to belief in God and the value of religion, their actions and values belie their words. In actual fact they serve mammon rather than God. In our capitalistic culture, more and more people are clearly preoccupied by worldly things such as sex, possessions, power, fashion, style and status. In a way it is not surprising. Postmodern culture is nihilistic. It seems to be incapable of affirming any absolute meaning. Cut adrift in a sea of partial and provisional truths, it is understandable that people lead overly extroverted lives devoted to consumerism and the frantic pursuit of fleeting pleasures. They are 'distracted, from distraction by distractions'.

Psychology, Sociology and Atheism

A number of modern psychologists and sociologists – most of them secular Jews – have argued that faith in God and human growth are incompatible. In his book *Positive Philosophy*, nineteenth-century theorist Auguste Comte (1798-1857) described the law of the three Intellectual stages. Let us take an example to illustrate what he meant. Why does a rock fall? The *theological or fictitious stage* up to 500 BC, which is based on revelation, would say, the stone falls because God wills it. The second, *metaphysical or abstract stage* up to 1500 AD, which is based on reason, says the stone falls because it is the nature of heavy objects to fall. The third *scientific or positive stage* after 1500 AD, which is based on observation, replies, the stone falls because of the law of gravity. Comte believed that in the age of science, theology and metaphysics were redundant and irrelevant. He believed that in the final, the positive state, the mind would give up the vain search after Absolute notions such as the origin and destination of the universe, and the causes of phenomena. Instead the mind would apply itself solely to the study of their laws, i.e. their invariable relations of succession and resemblance.

In general terms, Sigmund Freud (1856-1939) subscribed to this point of view. He was well read in philosophy and acknowledged that Feuerbach was his most influential mentor. He accepted his predecessor's contention that the notion of God was a projection of human potential. He tried to explain the psychological dynamics of this anthropological thesis. He used two main arguments.

The first was the historical one. In *Totum and Taboo* (1913) he proposed a curious myth of the primal horde. It seemed to be an interpolation of the oedipal complex which he had detected in some of his patients. He maintained that the sons of a primeval patriarchal chief had to murder him in order to have sexual access to the available females. But their patricide filled them with such feelings of guilt that they agreed to have sex only with women from outside the tribe, to celebrate a totem meal as a sign of their solidarity, and to deify the notion of their late father. As a result, Freud argued that religion was an obsessive, compulsive neurosis, a ritualised way for human beings to control their amoral instinctual desires.

His second argument against belief was a more immediate one. He said that as children matured they asserted their independence by moving away from dependence on their parents, especially their fathers. As they did this, however, they felt alone and frightened in an alien and threatening world. So they projected their need for a caring and protective parental figure on to a great daddy in the sky, namely, God the heavenly Father. By his providence he would provide for them in their needs. Freud believed that such illusory projections had to be recognised and renounced in the name of realism and mental health. Not only did Freud advocate atheism, he was opposed to non-theistic forms of religion. He regarded them as yet another form of escapism.

Besides being a well known psychologist, Erich Fromm (1900-1980) had a doctorate in philosophy. Indeed his philosophical point of view often influenced his psychological writings. As a neo-Freudian with Marxist leanings he focused on the way in which society rather than the unconscious influenced human behaviour. In his book *Psychoanalysis and Religion* (1950), he maintained that there were two forms of religion, authoritarian and humanistic. As far as one can make out, he considered Judaism and Christianity to be authoritarian in so far as they put a great deal of emphasis on the all powerful nature of a transcendent God who had to be obeyed by human beings. He said that the more one stresses the fact that God is the centre of all creativity, freedom, wisdom and power, the more alienated human beings become from these innate potentials in themselves. Consequently, they could only get in touch with the depths of their inner identities and powers, in an indirect way, by means of submission to an omnipotent and omniscient God. While Fromm was opposed to an alienating belief in such a transcendent God, he did advocate a humanistic kind of religion. He interpreted the word God, much as Feuerbach had done, merely as a symbol for the immanent potential of God-like human beings.

Abraham Maslow (1908-1970), a founder of what has come to be known as humanistic psychology, has also advocated non-theistic forms of religious experience. As a result of his research into the psychological dynamics of self-actualised people, he found that they were more likely than less integrated people, to have what he referred to as 'peak-experiences'. These were episodes of oceanic feeling, times of heightened awareness when the normal subject-object dichotomy was overcome as a result of a more all embracing sense of mystical union. However, like Freud and Fromm, Maslow believed that God was nothing other than a projection of the human mind. Like Fromm, however, he advocated a non-theistic form of religious experience akin to Buddhism.

Emile Durkheim (1858-1917) was one of the most eminent sociologists in modern times. He was interested in the nature and role of religion, especially in primitive societies, such as that of the Australian aborigines. He believed that the word God was nothing other than a projection of people's experience of collective unity. They experienced society as a reality, a power that was greater than the sum total of its individual parts. It had many important functions. It facilitated a feeling of belonging which enabled people to have a sense of identity, established norms of behaviour and provided for their human needs, e.g. for protection. Although this awareness of solidarity and effervescent energy is sacred in nature, Durkheim thought that it was a mistake to infer from the experience that God existed.

The Psychology of Atheism

Before ending this section it is worth noting that, in a fascinating lecture entitled, 'The Psychology of Atheism,'[3] Professor Paul Vitz has reversed two of the key arguments Freud used in support of atheism, to provide a psychological critique of philosophical, psychological and sociological non-belief. As he says, thanks to Freud it is easier now to understand the neurotic dimension of unbelief. Firstly, he argues that Freud's theory of the oedipal complex as the root of all neuroses, provides a straightforward rationale for understanding the desire to reject God. Freud often described the deity as a psychological equivalent to the father. As a result, a natural expression of oedipal antagonism against one's earthly father would be a powerful, but unconscious, desire to reject God. Atheism, therefore, could be seen as an illusion caused by an oedipal desire to kill the father and replace him with oneself. Secondly, Freud also argued that if a child or adolescent looses respect for his or her earthly father, as a result of such things as his cowardice, abuse, unfaithfulness, or even premature death, the resulting disillusionment can lead to a complete loss of trust in the goodness and very existence of a heavenly father. Vitz refers to the biographies of many prominent atheists, including Feuerbach, Voltaire, Freud, Marx, Camus, Sartre, Nietzche, and Russell to illustrate how unconscious factors, either unacknowledged oedipal desires or an experience of defective fathering, may have led them to become atheists. He has expanded his argument in a book.[4]

John Paul II on Atheism

Pope John Paul II is well aware of these subversive trends in modern culture. In the course of one of the most important interventions made by any bishop at the Second Vatican Council, he said that the atheist was totally alone. Solitude from God leads to a deep solitude and a profound loneliness. It forces men and women to seek a kind of quasi-immortality in the life of the collective. Twenty or so years later, he stated in par 56 of his en-cyclical *Dominum et Vivificantem,* that atheism is *the* most signifi-cant phenomenon of our time. He proceeded to critique its philosophical, psychological, and sociological forms from a theological perspective. His analysis is informed by a very inter-esting understanding of belief which departs from the more traditional notion of faith as assent to truths authoritatively taught by the church. In par 51 he says: 'Faith, in its deepest essence, is the openness of the human heart to the gift of God's self-communication in the Holy Spirit.' In part two of the en-cyclical he shows that when the Spirit comes upon people, one of the first things it does is to convince them of the nature of sin as unbelief. As Jesus said: 'Unless I go away, the Counsellor will not come to you; but if I go, I will send him to you. When he comes, he will convict the world of guilt in regard to sin … in re-gard to sin, *because people do not believe in me*' (Jn 16:8-9).

Although atheism can be partly explained in human terms, it is significant that the Pope discerns that this irreligious urge of the flesh is ultimately the result of the perverse activity of the evil one. It is worth noting that in 1976, Paul VI invited Karol Wojtyla to conduct the Lenten retreat in the Vatican. In one of his addresses he talked about the way in which the devil's initial temptation of our first parents called the truth of God's word into question, 'Did God really say you were not to eat from any of the trees in the garden?' (Gen 3:1). In saying this, he anticipated his 1986 encyclical on the Holy Spirit. In par 37 of *Dominum Vivificantem* he suggests that contemporary atheism is rooted in the fact that our first parents succumbed to this subversive temptation. As he says: 'It means a certain opening of this free-dom of the human mind and will to the one who is the father of lies.' In par 38 he goes on to state that as a consequence of this dynamic, 'Satan manages to sow in man's soul the seed of oppo-sition to the one who, from the beginning, would be considered as man's enemy, and not as Father. Man is challenged to become the adversary of God!' Later in the same paragraph he adds: 'through the influence of the father of lies … there will be a con-stant pressure on man to reject God, even to the point of hating him.'

The hermeneutic of suspicion

As the Father of illusion and false inspirations, the devil is the originator of the hermeneutic of ultimate suspicion. In par 37 the Pontiff says that the deceiver tries to subvert and undermine the truth about God and God's word. As a result, 'God the Creator is placed in a state of suspicion, indeed of accusation, in the mind of the creature. For the first time in human history there appears the perverse genius of suspicion.' The Pope then goes on to observe that the devil 'seeks to falsify Good itself; the absolute Good, which in the work of creation has manifested itself as the Good which expresses itself … as creative love.' Later on he says in par 38: 'Man will be inclined to see in God primarily a limitation of himself, and not the source of his own freedom and the fulness of good. We see this confirmed in the modern age, when the atheistic ideologies seek to root out religion on the grounds that religion causes the radical alienation of man, as if man were dispossessed of his own humanity when, accepting the idea of God, he attributes to God what belongs to man, and exclusively to man! Hence a process of thought … in which the rejection of God has reached the point of declaring his "death" .'

Critique of Marxism

When the Pope wrote his encyclical in 1986, Marxist materialism still held sway in Eastern Europe and the Union of Soviet Socialist Republics. In par 56 he observed: 'Unfortunately, the resistance to the Holy Spirit which St Paul emphasises in the interior and subjective dimension as tension, struggle and rebellion … reaches its clearest expression in materialism, both in its theoretical form: as a system of thought, and in its practical form: as a method of interpreting and evaluating facts, and likewise as a programme of corresponding conduct. The system which has developed most and carried to its extreme practical consequences this form of thought, ideology and praxis is dialectical and historical materialism, which is still recognised as the essential core of Marxism.'

Critique of Nihilism

Perhaps its worth mentioning, in passing, that in a more recent encyclical, Fides et Ratio (1998), the Pope addressed a current form of unbelief, namely, the nihilism which is often an aspect of postmodern thought. Commenting on it he says, in par 91, that it is quite possible that loss of faith in reason's ability to know the truth is rooted in 'the terrible experience of evil which has marked our age.' Presumably he has wars such as the first and second world wars in mind here. In par 90 he says: 'Many philosophies (including postmodernism) have rejected the meaningfulness of being. I am referring to the nihilist interpretation, which is at once the denial of all foundations and the negation of all objective truth ... and therefore with the very ground of human dignity. This in turn makes it possible to erase from the countenance of man and woman the marks of their likeness to God and thus lead them little by little either to a destructive will to power or to a solitude without hope.'

Having described the origins and dynamics of modern unbelief, the Pope goes on to describe some of its effects. Because he believes that human beings can only discover their deepest identities and meaning in the light of faithful relationship with God, atheism leads to very real problems. 'Without the Creator the creature would disappear,' says the Pope in par 38. 'When God is forgotten the creature itself grows unintelligible.' The ideology of the death of God has the effect, on a theoretical and practical level, of leading to the death of man, i.e. a sudden surge of pessimism which is engendered by postmodern nihilism. This phenomenon manifests itself in what the Pope has subsequently referred to as 'the culture of death'. It is evident in such evils as genocide, abortion and euthanasia.

It is quite clear that the Pope thinks that, rather than diminishing or demeaning people, belief in God enables their true psycho-spiritual potential to be acknowledged and developed. During a debate on *Gaudium et Spes* during the Second Vatican Council, Bishop Karol Wojtyla is reported to have said that the closer human beings come to God, the closer they can come to the depths of their own humanity and to the truth of creation. Christian faith is not alienating; Christian faith is liberating in the most profound sense of human freedom.[5] Sometime later, this view was endorsed in par 22 of *Gaudium et Spes*, which John Paul considers to be the theological lynchpin of Vatican II. Among other things it says: 'It is only in the mystery of the

word, the word made flesh, that the mystery of man truly becomes clear.' As we noted in another chapter, he echoed that
teaching in *Veritatis Splendor* par 8: 'the man who wishes to
understand himself should ... draw near to Christ. He must, so
to speak, enter him with all his own self ... If this profound
process takes place within him, he then bears fruit not only of
adoration of God but also of deeper wonder at himself.'

Christian Apologetics

Not surprisingly, in our secular, postmodern society, the decline
of institutional forms of Christianity has coincided with an increasing incidence of theoretical and practical atheism. A growing
number of people are advocating the importance of non-theistic
forms of spirituality. In Ireland for example, some men and
women are attracted to different non-Christian spiritualities,
e.g. of the New Age and Buddhist variety. While they are religious in orientation they don't necessarily involve belief in a
transcendent deity. Although the proponents of some of these
spiritualities may use the word God in their conversations,
teachings and writings, they often do so in a purely immanent
way, to refer to the god-like potentials of human subjectivity.
The different psycho-technologies employed by these spiritualities are often Pelagian methods of trying to transform consciousness solely by means of human effort.

It would be true to say that Christian apologetics is willing
and able to critique the assumptions of philosophical, psychological and sociological atheism. For example, it can point to the
fact that although some people undoubtedly project the notion
of God on to an illusory deity – the word illusion is used here in
its technical sense to refer to wishful thinking – it doesn't necessarily imply that all religious belief is *ipso facto* a delusion.
Psychological arguments, of whatever kind, about the human
propensity to project illusions can say nothing about the metaphysical existence or non existence of a transcendent God. If
they did, a category error would be involved, i.e. moving from
empirical or phenomenological description to ontological or
philosophical assertion.

Christian apologetics can also demonstrate that any claim
that belief in God inevitably alienates people from their deepest

identities is a caricature of Judeo-Christian teaching. On the contrary, it not only maintains that belief in God helps people to recognise their true identities, dignity and potential in Christ, it also reveals that the transcendent God lives and acts immanently in them by the divine Holy Spirit. There are many texts that make this abundantly clear. We will refer to just one of them. 'God lives in us and his love is made complete in us. We know that we live in him and he in us, because he has given us of his Spirit' (1 Jn 4:12-13).

As a result of the working of the transcendent God within us we know that we are empowered, if necessary, do what Jesus did. In Jn 14:12-14 our Lord promised: 'I tell you the truth, anyone who has faith in me will do what I have been doing. He will do even greater things than these, because I am going to the Father. And I will do whatever you ask in my name, so that the Son may bring glory to the Father.' There is no question in these texts of projecting all one's powers outwards on to God, in a slavish, alienating way. On the contrary, they point to the divinisation of human beings.[6] Tempting though it might be, I don't propose to counter the many other arguments of modern atheism. Suffice it to say, that many of those who advocated unbelief did so because they rejected the stultifying and inauthentic expressions of bourgeois Christianity that were current in their own lifetimes.

Conclusion

In line with the Pope's teaching it is important to remind ourselves that behind the presenting arguments of contemporary atheism lies an irreligious spirit which is prompted by the 'enemy of our souls'. Demonstrations of the existence of God will only be effective to the extent that we firstly discern the possible presence and activity of the 'father of lies'. Ultimately the apparently rational arguments of modern atheism have been prompted by Satan's irrational opposition to God. I have found that the following New Testament text is particularly helpful in assuring Christians that they can combat this form of spiritual oppression. It states: 'For though we live in the world, we do not wage war as the world does. The weapons we fight with are not the weapons of the world (e.g. human philosophy, psychology

or sociology). On the contrary, they have divine power to demolish strongholds (i.e. unbelieving ideas prompted by the father
of lies). We demolish arguments and every pretension (such as
those examined in this chapter) that sets itself up against the
knowledge of God, and we take captive every thought to make
it obedient to Christ' (2 Cor 10:3-5). I have found that there are
two weapons which can be used to good effect in this spiritual
warfare.

Firstly, there is the inspired word of God which, as St Paul
tells us, is the sword of the Spirit (Eph 6:17). It is worth remembering that in his encounters with the philosophers of Athens,
Paul learned to rely solely on the scandalous proclamation of the
saving death and resurrection of Jesus. He testifies in 1 Cor 2:4-5
that his kerygmatic preaching did not rely on the arguments of
secular thought. 'My message and my preaching,' he said, 'were
not with wise and persuasive words, but with a demonstration
of the Spirit's power, so that your faith might not rest on men's
wisdom, but on God's power.' God's power is manifested,
therefore, by the two edged sword of anointed preaching which
is supported by deeds such as loving relationships, works of
mercy, action for justice, healings, exorcisms and miracles. St
Paul says that as a result of experiencing both 'the secrets of his
(the unbeliever's) heart will be laid bare. So he will fall down
and worship God, exclaiming, "God is really among you!"' (1
Cor 14:25).

Prayerful intercession is a second way of helping to open the
eyes, ears and hearts of unbelievers to the revelation of the existence and attributes of God. As 1 Jn 5:16 promises: 'If anyone sees
his brother commit a sin (e.g. of unbelief) ... he should pray and
God will give him life.' In the light of what the Holy Father
teaches, it is advisable to pray a deliverance prayer, one that opposes the oppressive power of rebellious, deceiving and irreligious spirits in order to deliver people from every evil. The in-
tercessor can silently command them, in the name of Jesus
Christ, to yield to the liberating power of God. As scripture assures us, 'for he who is in you is greater than he who is in the
world' (1 Jn 4:4). Taken together these forms of spiritual combat
are a necessary prelude to effective, Christian apologetics of the
rational kind.

CHAPTER SEVENTEEN

Who is an Evangelical Christian?
A Catholic Perspective[1]

The word evangelical can have many different meanings.

1. It can designate certain churches in Europe, especially in Germany, which are Lutheran rather than Calvinistic.

2. It can refer to those Protestants who lay particular stress on salvation by faith in the atoning death of Christ, and who deny that good works and the sacraments have any saving efficacy.

3. The word can also be used to describe a wing of the Church of England which first came to prominence in the eighteenth century.

4. The word evangelical can refer to anyone who believes and proclaims the gospel of Jesus Christ. It also refers to the movement in modern Christianity which transcends denominational boundaries and which emphasises belief to the basic tenets of the faith (cf 1 Cor 15:1-4), while engaging in missionary outreach. Understood in this broad sense, a growing number of Catholics would be happy to refer to themselves as evangelicals.

Because many Protestants in the past seemed to interpret the word evangelical in their own distinctive and restrictive way, they did not think that Catholics were evangelicals. Indeed some of them did not think that Catholics were even Christian. In an effort to distance themselves from Protestantism, many if not most Catholics refrained from using the word evangelical in describing themselves. For example, I have checked a number of standard Catholic reference books only to find that none of them have an entry under the heading 'evangelical'.

However, it would be true to say that this situation has been slowly changing since the Second Vatican Council. More and more Catholic people are reaffirming their evangelical roots. As a result of this emphasis, there has been a growing *rapprochement* between Catholics and evangelical Protestants. Nowadays an increasing number of Catholics, especially those who have been influenced by the Charismatic Movement, are happy to use the word evangelical to describe themselves, if and when it is used in the inter-denominational sense mentioned above. I want to highlight three important characteristics of this understanding of evangelicanism: the primacy of scripture; justification by faith; and the mission to conduct basic evangelisation or evangelism.

The Primacy of Scripture

In the years following the Reformation, Protestants were evangelical in the sense that they based their faith solely upon their understanding of the scriptures. As *The Oxford Dictionary of the Christian Church* observes, Evangelicals have commonly upheld the verbal inspiration and sole authority of scripture, thereby denying that the church has the power to impose its interpretation upon the individual.[2] It could be added that many Evangelicals would also be fundamentalist in their understanding of the sacred text. They would be extremely suspicious of the use of hermeneutics, i.e. the use of historical, archeological and critical methods when interpreting the word of God.

Vatican II stressed the fundamental importance of scripture. In the *Dogmatic Constitution on Divine Revelation,* par 11, we read: 'The books of scripture must be acknowledged as teaching firmly, faithfully and without error that truth which God wanted put into the sacred writings for the sake of our salvation.' Catholics became wary of the obvious dangers implicit in the purely private interpretation of the bible. They could see that the differing interpretations of Protestants led to a proliferation of churches with conflicting beliefs. Recently, I came across an interesting observation on this point by psychiatrist Carl Jung who was a Lutheran. 'Protestantism, having pulled down so many walls carefully erected by the church, immediately began to experience the disintegrating and schismatic effects of individual revelation. As soon as the dogmatic fence was broken down and the ritual lost its authority, man had to face his inner experience without the protection and guidance of dogma and ritual, which are the very quintessence of Christian religious experience.'[3]

Like Evangelical Protestants, Catholics believe that the Holy Spirit can lead the individual believer into the truth of God's word. As a verse of a hymn in the *Divine Office* reads: 'In the scriptures by the Spirit, may we see the Saviour's face, hear his word and heed his calling, know his will and grow in grace.' Ultimately, however, Catholics rely on the teaching authority of the church to discern which interpretations are consistent with the inspired meaning of the text. It is interesting to note that the word dogma is derived from the Greek *dokein*, 'to seem good.' In other words dogma seeks to establish what interpretations are good because they are in accord with divine revelation as traditionally understood by the church, e.g. in the Nicene Creed.

Catholics do not believe in biblical fundamentalism. Speaking about scripture interpretation at the World Catholic Federation for the Biblical Apostolate in 1986, Pope John Paul II said: 'Attention must be given to the literary forms of the various biblical books in order to determine the intentions of the sacred writers. And it is most helpful, at times crucial, to be aware of the personal situation of the biblical writer, of the circumstances of culture, time, language, etc., which influenced the way the message was presented ... In this way, it is possible to avoid a narrow fundamentalism which distorts the whole truth.'

The Catholic Church encourages the faithful to develop a scripture-based spirituality. For example, in par 133 of *The Catechism of the Catholic Church* we read: 'The church forcefully and specifically exhorts all the Christian faithful ... to learn the surpassing knowledge of Jesus Christ by frequent reading of the scriptures. Ignorance of the scriptures is ignorance of Christ.' In par 1177 the *Catechism* recommends Catholics to do this by engaging in the Benedictine *Lectio Divina*. As we noted in an earlier chapter it is a fivefold method of praying the scriptures which involves reading, reflecting, praying, contemplating and living out the word of God. Over the last 25 years or so, an increasing number of Catholics have become more scripture-centred and have made God's word their rule of life.

Justification

Justification by faith is a foundational belief of Evangelical Protestants. Many of them believe that Catholics are not saved because they hope to be justified as a result of their good works. A growing number of Catholic men and women find that this attitude is not only misinformed but hurtful. Clearly, dialogue is needed in order to clear up misunderstandings. For example, following a period of discussion in the North of Ireland an inter-church document was produced. It was entitled: *Evangelicals & Catholics Together in Ireland.* It described areas of conflict (cf. pp 7-8) and of common agreement especially on the all important subject of justification (cf. pp 3-5).

In recent years, the Catholic understanding of the gift of faith has shifted from the post-Tridentine emphasis on *mental assent* to revealed doctrines taught authoritatively by the church, on God's behalf, to the complementary notion of faith as *heartfelt trust* solely in the person, word and saving work of the Lord Jesus. Needless to say, these notions of faith are interdependent. We give mental assent to the revealed truths of God because we place our heartfelt trust in the God of truth, who can neither deceive or be deceived. As a result of this change in focus many Catholics have strongly welcomed and endorsed the recent *Joint Declaration on the Doctrine of Justification* by the Lutheran and Catholic churches. For more on this point see the chapter on St Thérèse of Lisieux. Its teaching, especially in par 15, found an echo in *Evangelicals and Catholics Together in Ireland.* Speaking of the doctrine of justification it says: 'The New Testament makes it clear that the gift of justification is received through faith, "By grace you have been saved through faith, and this is not our own doing, it is the gift of God" (Eph 2:8). Genuine saving faith is always expressed by works of loving obedience, bearing fruits worthy of grace and proving our repentance, just as fruit ever comes from the living root of a good tree.'

In a book entitled *Adventures in Reconciliation* which was published in 1998, twenty-eight Catholics living in Ireland described how, in various ways, they experienced a spiritual awakening.[4] As a result they were utterly convinced that as a result of faith in the justifying grace of Christ they were saved, that Christ lived in their hearts through faith (Eph 3:17) and that in him there is no condemnation (Rom 8:1). While Catholics do not believe that they are saved by the sacraments, they certainly do believe that when the sacraments are received with faith they mediate the freely given, saving and sanctifying grace of Christ, the sole mediator between God and man. That grace is gratefully expressed in, rather than merited by, good works.

Evangelisation Evangelism

The word evangelism is used by Evangelical Protestants primarily in reference to verbal proclamation, i.e. preaching and teaching, which intend to win the world for Christ and to hasten his second coming. It aims to bring sinful individuals to commit their lives to Jesus Christ as their personal Lord and Saviour. Many Evangelical Protestants pray that evangelism will lead to revival, i.e. a sudden and dramatic intervention by God, that will bring about mass conversions similar to those that took place during the Great Awakening in New England 1740-1743.

Catholics have a wider notion of evangelisation. Pope Paul VI expressed its aim in *Evangelii Nuntiandi* par 18: 'If it had to be expressed in one sentence the best way of stating it would be to say that the church evangelises when she seeks to convert, solely through the Divine Power of the message she proclaims, both the personal and collective consciences of people, the activities in which they engage, and the lives and the concrete *milieux* which are theirs.' Whereas the Protestant notion of evangelisation has a clear personal aim, the Catholic notion is wider in scope, and therefore harder to pin down. Catholics pray that evangelisation will lead to a gradual renewal of individuals and society as a graced result of the transforming power of gospel truths and values. I suspect, however, that the Protestant and Catholic understandings of evangelisation/evangelism are complementary rather than opposed to one another

In the document *Catholics and Evangelicals Together*, which I have already mentioned, there is a section entitled, 'We Witness Together' (pp 11-14). It says: 'The teaching of our Lord is unmistakable. The credibility of his mission in the world and in Ireland in particular is dependent upon the unity and love of his disciples as expressed in Jesus' prayer in Jn 17: "May they all be one, as you Father are in me, and I in you, so also may they be one in us, that the world may believe that you sent me." The same connection between unity and witness is strongly echoed in Acts 4:32-36 … All who truly believe in Jesus Christ are brothers and sisters in the Lord and must not allow their differences, however important, to undermine this great truth, or to deflect them from bearing witness together to God's gift of salvation in Christ.'

The Alpha course, which originated in the Evangelical wing of the Church of England, is rooted in the conviction already mentioned. It is currently being used by Catholics and Protestants alike, as they seek to engage in basic evangelisation. A typical session begins with a meal followed by a talk. The presentations are about the basics of Christianity such as, Who is Jesus? Why did Jesus die? How does one pray? The talks are followed by group discussion. The aim of the course is to lead non-believers and inactive Christians to freely and joyfully commit their hearts and lives to the Lord. As was mentioned in the chapter on popular piety, many Catholics would also readily acknowledge that many of their practising co-religionists are sacramentalised but not truly evangelised. While they have received the grace of salvation in the sacraments of initiation they have not fully appropriated that grace by means of a personal, faith-filled adult commitment. As more and more Catholics and Protestants come into this common experience of the Good News of salvation in Christ, Alpha and courses like it will contribute greatly to the on-going search for reconciliation and renewal.

Conclusion

At the beginning of this reflection I suggested that the word Evangelical could be understood in at least four different ways. While Catholics could not identify with the first three interpretations, they could readily identify with the fourth non-denominational one. I believe that many Catholics, like many of their Protestant brothers and sisters, are Evangelicals in so far as they emphasise the primary importance of biblical spirituality and justification by faith. Both of them find expression in basic evangelisation. In this as in other areas of theology, let us stress what unites us rather than what divides.

CHAPTER EIGHTEEN

Charisms and the New Evangelisation[1]

Following his baptism at the Jordan, Jesus did two main things. Acts 1:1 says he began to do and to teach. In other words he *proclaimed* the good news of God's love, especially to the poor, and he *demonstrated* the reality of that good news in two main ways.

Firstly, he related to the people in a welcoming, compassionate, understanding manner which was devoid of judgement or condemnation. He did not dominate them. Instead he came as one who serves. He responded in a humble way to their deepest needs. He longed for their liberation, not only from spiritual bondage but also from the unjust structures of society.

Secondly, he performed deeds of power such as healings, exorcisms and miracles. These signs and wonders were not intended to prove that what Jesus said was true. Rather they were the good news in action, a concrete expression of God's offer of unconditional mercy and love to those who trusted in the Lord. It is interesting to recall that when St John the Baptist was in prison he sent messengers to ask Jesus whether he was the promised messiah. Jesus adverted to his proclamation and demonstration of the good news when he said: 'Go back and report to John what you hear and see: The blind receive sight, the lame walk, those who have leprosy are cured, the deaf hear, the dead are raised, and the good news is preached to the poor' (Mt 11:4-5).

The Commission to Proclaim and Demonstrate the Good News
During his lifetime Jesus instructed the apostles to do the same. Like him, they were to proclaim and demonstrate the coming of the kingdom of God. For example in Lk 9:1-2 we read: 'And he called the twelve together and gave them power and authority over all demons and to cure diseases, and he sent them out to preach the kingdom of God and to heal.' Before his ascension into heaven, the Lord commissioned the apostles to continue to

do the same in the future. In Mk 16:15-19 we read: 'He said to them, "Go into all the world and preach the good news to all creation. Whoever believes and is baptised will be saved, but whoever does not believe will be condemned. And these signs will accompany those who believe: In my name they will drive out demons; they will speak in new tongues; they will pick up snakes with their hands; and when they drink deadly poison, it will not hurt them at all; they will place their hands on sick people, and they will get well".' There are clear indications in the Acts, and especially the earlier epistles of Paul, that the apostles carried out the Lord's instructions. They not only proclaimed the good news, they demonstrated it in deeds of power. As Acts 2:43 testifies, 'Many wonders and signs were done through the apostles.'

There is clear evidence that the charisms were exercised in the early years of Christianity. For example in the fourth century St Hilary wrote in a commentary on Ps 64: 'We who are reborn through the sacrament of baptism have the greatest joy, as we perceive within us the first stirrings of the Holy Spirit, as we begin to understand mysteries; we gain full knowledge of prophecy, speech full of wisdom, security in our hope, gifts of healing and dominion over devils who are made subject to us. These gifts, like drops of liquid, permeate our inner self, and so beginning, little by little they produce fruits in abundance.' It is equally clear that a few centuries later the charisms had all but faded away. Why this happened is not entirely clear. There were a number of possible reasons.

Firstly, there was what sociologist Emile Durkheim referred to as the ritualisation of charism. In other words the church relied solely on official ministries and the administration of the sacraments as means of grace

Secondly, there was a struggle between the institutional and 'charismatic' wings of Christianity. For example, at the end of the second century the Montanists, who were charismatic, were finally condemned as heretics. As a result charisms and charismatics were no longer trusted.

Thirdly, medieval theology, from the time of Pope St Gregory the Great (540-604) onwards was, by and large, unsympathetic to the notion of pre-rational forms of religious experience such as tongues and healings. In the high Middle Ages this tendency was reinforced by St Thomas Aquinas (1225-1274) and some centuries later by the rationalistic worldview of the Enlightenment.

As a result, the charismatic dimension of Christian life was overlooked in favour of the doctrinal and ministerial authority of the institutional church. Priests and people expected the Spirit to be manifested by the witness of lives well lived, works of mercy and in action for justice, but not by unusual charismatic activity. St Thomas Aquinas taught that canonisable saints were the only exception to this rule during their lifetimes and after their deaths. He wrote: 'True miracles cannot be wrought save by the power of God, because God works them ... in proof of a person's holiness which God desires to propose as an example of virtue.' (ST, Q178, A2, obj4)

Charismatic Revival Following Vatican II

For Catholics, all this began to change at the Second Vatican Council. In par 12 of the *Constitution on the Church* and par 3 of the *Constitution on the Laity*, the pope and bishops made ten important points to do with the more unusual charisms.

1. Grace comes to us primarily through sacraments and clerical ministry.
2. Grace also comes through the gifts of the Spirit in general, and the charisms mentioned in 1 Cor 12:8- 10 in particular.
3. The Holy Spirit distributes what are variously referred to as simple and exceptional gifts, among lay people.
4. These gifts are given to build up the church in holiness and to develop people.
5. The charisms are a wonderful means of apostolic vitality.
6. These gifts are to be received with gratitude and consolation.
7. Lay people have a right to exercise their charisms and ministries. This right comes from their baptism and not from the clergy.
8. Lay people have a duty to use their charisms for the good of the church and the world.
9. Bishops and clergy should test the charisms to see that they are genuine and used for the common good.
10. However, the clergy should be careful not to quench the Spirit by an arbitrary use of authority.

Classification of the Charisms

Paul's theology of the gifts is an expression of his experience, not of his reading. So when he listed the charisms in 1 Cor 12:8-10, he probably did so in the light of his personal ministry. I would suggest that they can be classified in the following way:

A. Revelation	B. Proclamation	C. Demonstration
1. The word of wisdom.	1. The gift of prophecy	1. Faith
2. The word of knowledge.	2. Tongue speaking	2. Healings / exorcisms
3. Discernment of spirits.	3. Interpretation of tongues	3. Working of miracles.

According to this classification:

- There are charisms of revelation that enable the believer to know the presence, word and will of the Lord.
- There are charisms of proclamation that enable the believer or preach, teach or share the good news.
- There are charisms of demonstration which manifest the good news, e.g. by means of liberating deeds of power.

While I would have confidence that the three headings are reasonably accurate, scholars differ when it comes to classifying the gifts beneath them. For example, the charism of prophecy could be seen as a gift of revelation or as a gift of proclamation. Notice too how this is a quasi-sacramental view of the charisms, where word and deed together conspire to make the risen Christ present.

The Charisms in 1 Cor 12:8-10 and Evangelisation

It is only when people have experienced an outpouring of the Holy Spirit, that they can expect to exercise one or more of the charismatic gifts mentioned in 1 Cor 12:8-10. They are grace given abilities which equip men and women for acts of service that contribute to the animation, up-building and renewal of the church. They can have a number of good effects, all of which are forms of evangelisation.

Firstly, the charisms can play an important, if not a central role in lay ministry. Lay people are no longer supposed to be the inferior, passive recipients of clerical ministry. Rather, they are called and gifted to be active partners with the clergy in bringing the good news into every aspect of secular life. Current church documents, e.g. par.31 of *The Lay Members of Christ's Faithful People*, use the phrase lay 'apostolate' in preference to lay 'ministry' because, although clerical and lay roles are complementary, they are distinct. One way or another, by using their gifts, lay people evangelise by witnessing to the love of God. As Paul VI has observed: 'The people of our day are more impressed by witness than by teachers, and if they listen to these it is because they also bear witness.'[2]

Secondly, the charisms have an important ecumenical role to play. Happily the Spirit and his gifts have been poured out in all denominations. Through their common exercise, Christians are being drawn closer to Jesus and therefore closer to one another. In an article entitled, 'Ecumenical Origins of the Charismatic Renewal,'[3] Peter Hocken shows clearly that renewal in the Spirit and reconciliation have been virtually synonymous in the Charismatic Renewal. Charisms, as Christians in Northern Ireland and elsewhere recognise, have a unique ability to build bridges of unity.

For example, a Catholic woman in Northern Ireland recently told me that she was doing some shopping in a Protestant area. In one store, she happened to get into conversation with a fellow customer who told her that she was suffering from a painful physical problem. The Catholic woman was touched by what the afflicted woman had shared with her. She asked if she would like to prayed with. The woman answered yes, so they went to a quiet, secluded part of the shop. As the Catholic woman prayed for her Protestant acquaintance she had a strong sense of God's love for her, and the Lord's desire, then and there, to help her by means of his healing power. The prayer lasted for only a few minutes, but it was full of care and conviction. Then the women parted, and returned to their respective homes.

A few days later the Protestant woman returned to the shop. She was looking for information about the person who had prayed for her, because in the interim she had been completely healed. She described what the mysterious stranger looked like. The shop keeper told her, to her complete surprise, that she was a Catholic woman from a nearby town. Later, he contacted his Catholic customer to tell her the good news. Not surprisingly, when a Christian with expectant faith performs a deed of power for a member of another church, not only does it manifest the presence and power of God's kingdom, it also tends to break down the dividing wall of division that sometimes separates Catholics from Protestants and vice versa. In other words it is a powerful means of evangelisation.

Thirdly, the charisms have an important role to play in spreading the good news of Jesus Christ. Many Christians believe that we should go beyond presence evangelisation to engage in what is sometimes known as power evangelisation. As we noted earlier, the former witnesses to the good news mainly by means of loving relationships and liberating action for justice. The latter believes that the charisms of power such as healing, exorcism and miracle working, also have an important role to play. As manifestations of the presence and power of the Lord (1 Cor 12:7) they can be used to revive the faith of the lapsed and to evangelise unbelievers.

In 1979, Francis Mc Nutt gave memorable expression to this point in an article in *New Covenant* magazine: 'A gift of preaching is strengthened by other manifestations of the power of the Holy Spirit. St Paul states that in his sermons he did not depend on arguments that belonged to philosophy but on a "demonstration of the Spirit and power" (1 Cor 2:4). St Thomas Aquinas, in his commentary on this passage, states that the preacher of the gospel should preach as Jesus did, confirming the message either through healings and miracles or by living such a holy life that can only be explained by the power of the Spirit. If I preach the power of Jesus Christ to save and redeem the whole person, people want to see that power made real. They want to see the saving, freeing power of Jesus when we pray that the spiritually sick be given the power to repent, and that the emotionally and physically sick be healed, and may be made better as a sign that the message of salvation and healing are true.' In the remainder of this chapter, we will reflect on the role of the charisms of prophecy, faith, healing and miracles in evangelisation.

Prophecy and Evangelisation
The gift of prophecy (1 Cor 12:10) is the special ability that God gives to some members of the Christian community to receive and communicate an immediate message of God, either to a

group of people or to an individual person, through a divinely inspired utterance. St Thomas Aquinas thought that prophecy was the key to understanding the gifts of the Spirit. He observed in the *Summa Theologica*: 'In a broad sense the subject of prophecy is whatever man knows by God's revelation. It differs from other charisms such as wisdom and knowledge and understanding of speech, the subjects of which man can know by natural reason, though not as perfectly as by God's light ... *Prophecy is knowledge imprinted on the prophet's mind by the teaching of God's revelation* (my italics).'[4] In the *Summa Contra Gentiles*, Thomas described how such knowledge can be imparted by God: 'Now, accompanying this light that we have mentioned which illumines the mind from within, there are at times in divine revelation other external or internal aids to knowledge; for instance, a spoken message, or something heard by the external senses which is produced by divine power, or something perceived internally through imagination due to God's action, or also some things produced by God that are seen in bodily visions, or that are internally pictured in the imagination. From these presentations, by the light internally impressed on the mind, man receives a knowledge of divine things.'[5]

Charismatics talk about a strange gift which they usually refer to as a 'word of knowledge'. Gordon Fee says in *God's Empowering Presence* that it refers to 'a supernatural endowment of knowledge, factual information that could not otherwise have been known without the Spirit's aid, such as frequently occurs in the prophetic tradition.'[6] I was interested to see that Anglican Bishop David Pytches endorses Fee's interpretation. He states that the 'word of knowledge' is a 'supernatural revelation of facts about a person or situation, which is not learned through the efforts of the natural mind, but is a fragment of knowledge freely given by God, disclosing the truth which the Spirit wishes to be made known concerning a particular person or situation.'[7] St Thomas Aquinas and Gordon Fee say, quite rightly I think, that this form of revelation is a form of prophecy. Prophetic revelations can be revealed in many different ways, e.g. in the form of an inner intuition, or a meaningful image.

No wonder that St Paul wrote: 'Earnestly desire the spiritual gifts especially that you may prophesy' (1 Cor 14:1). The

prophetic word has a unique ability to evangelise. Why? In 1
Cor 14:24-25 the apostle Paul answers: 'If all prophesy, and an
unbeliever or outsider enters, he is convicted by all, he is called
to account by all, the secrets of his heart are disclosed; and so,
falling on his face, he will worship God and declare that God is
really among you.'

The Charism of Faith and Evangelisation

Although the charism of faith is a neglected gift it is the key to
the performance of deeds of power. The most important reference to this charism is to be found in 1 Cor 12:9, where Paul says
that to some is given 'faith by the same Spirit.' Commentators
down the centuries are agreed that Paul is not referring to saving faith, but rather to an exceptional form of expectant trust
that leads to deeds of power. For example, St Thomas Aquinas
says in his commentary on 1 Cor 12:9 that the reference to faith is
not to be understood as the theological virtue of faith, i.e. saving
faith, for that is common to all believers.[8] Rather it is to be understood either as the expression of faith, e.g. by means of inspired preaching and teaching, or as a special certitude of faith
that leads to the working of healings and miracles.

Modern scripture scholars would agree with this interpretation. George Montague is representative of their shared opinion
when he writes in his book *The Holy Spirit*, 'The gift of faith in 1
Cor 12:9 does not refer here to the faith that is necessary for salvation (Mk 16:16; Heb 11:6), but rather to a special intensity of
faith for a specific need.'[9] Church of England Bishop David
Pytches accurately describes the charism of faith, in *Come Holy
Spirit*, as 'a supernatural surge of confidence from the Spirit of
God which arises within a person faced with a specific situation
of need whereby that person receives a trans-rational certainty
and assurance that God is about to act through a word or action.'[10]

It seems clear to me that the charism of expectant faith is
evoked by the charisms of revelation such as wisdom, knowledge and prophecy, listed in 1 Cor 12:8, 10. Although I have classified the gift of prophecy as a gift for proclamation, it is rooted
in a revelation of God's purposes. Once God's will is made
known, in the here and now, e.g. by means of an inspiring word

from scripture or a word of knowledge, the recipient has no lingering doubts about the promises of God. Once s/he knows God's existential will, s/he can pray either a prayer of intercession (Mk 11:24) or command (Mk 11:23) with complete assurance. It is not a matter of praying with future hope, *if* what we ask for is in accordance with God's will. Rather, it is a matter of praying with present conviction because we already know that what we ask for *is* God's will. The charism of expectant faith is mainly expressed by means of the charisms of power listed in 1 Cor 12:10 such as healing/exorcism and miracle working,

We have already noted how Jesus proclaimed and demonstrated the good news of God's unrestricted and unconditional mercy and love. We should evangelise in the same way. Inspired preaching and teaching will not be enough. As Paul said: 'The kingdom of God does not consist in (mere) talk but in power' (1 Cor 4:20). We also need to demonstrate the truth of our message in deeds, including deeds of power. Jesus promised, 'Very truly, I tell you, the one who believes in me will also do the works that I do, in fact, do greater works than these' (Jn 14:12). There is clear evidence in the contemporary world that the only Christian groups who are retaining the members they already have, and who are also gaining new members are those such as Pentecostals, Charismatics and Evangelicals, who evangelise by means of inspired preaching and teaching, accompanied by deeds of power. Those deeds, as we have seen, are only made possible by the charism of faith.

The Charism of Healings and Evangelisation
Before he ascended into heaven Jesus said that the proclamation of the gospel would be accompanied by healing. As was noted earlier, in Mk 16:15-18 he said: 'Go into all the world and preach the gospel to the whole creation … And these signs will accompany those who believe … they will lay their hands on the sick, and they will recover.' St Paul was probably adverting to the fulfillment of this promise in 1 Cor 12:10. The apostle was neither referring to the sacrament of the anointing of the sick, which is mentioned in Jas 5:14-15, or to medical healing, but rather to a Spirit-given ability to heal in the way that Jesus did. It is quite likely that the notion of exorcism is included in the charism of

healing. Incidentally, in the Greek of the New Testament, Paul talks about the gift in the plural (cf. 1 Cor 12:10; 28; 29). It can be interpreted in different ways. Firstly, it may be that Paul recognised that one person in the community might be able to heal a particular kind of sickness, e.g. bad backs, while others might be able to heal other ailments such as deafness, skin disease, depression, etc. In that sense there would be different but complementary gifts of healing in the church. Secondly, Paul may have been referring to the fact that many people exercise the gift of healing, in that sense there is a gift of healings. Thirdly, Paul may have been suggesting that the gift of healing is ephemeral rather than permanent. As such, it is new each time it is exercised. I suspect that this latter interpretation is the correct one. In a recent document on healing Cardinal Ratzinger wrote: 'These graces, in the plural, are attributed to an individual (cf. 1 Cor 12:9), and are not, therefore, to be understood in a distributive sense, as the gifts of healing received by those who themselves have been healed, but rather as a gift granted to a person to obtain graces of healing for others. This is given in one Spirit, but nothing is specified about how that person obtains these healings. It would not be farfetched to think that it happens by means of prayer, perhaps accompanied by some symbolic gesture.'[11]

It is interesting to see how St Paul clearly linked the charism of healings with evangelisation. He described his own proclamation of the gospel as characterised by signs and wonders worked by the power of the Holy Spirit: 'For I will not dare to speak of anything except what Christ has accomplished through me to lead the Gentiles to obedience by word and deed, by the power of signs and wonders, by the power of the Spirit' (Rom 15:18-19; cf. 1 Thes 1:5; 1 Cor 2:4-5). Such wonders were not limited to St Paul's ministry, but were also occurring among the faithful. This notion is implicit in these words of Paul: 'Does then the one who supplies the Spirit to you and works mighty deeds among you do so from works of the law or from faith in what you have heard preached?' (Gal 3:5). St Thomas Aquinas said perceptively that the confirmation of what is above reason, i.e. the core truths of Christianity, rests on the exercise of divine power. He observes: 'The grace of healing is distinguished from the working of miracles because it has a special reason for inducing one to the faith, since a person is all the more ready to believe when s/he has received the gift of bodily health through the virtue of faith.'[12]

The Charism of Miracle working and Evangelisation

When the Greek of 1 Cor 12: 10 is literally translated into English it says to some is given 'operations of works of power'. However most translators use the shorter 'the working of miracles'. The word 'miracle' comes from the Latin *miraculum*, meaning a wonder. From a biblical point of view a miracle is a supernatural manifestation of divine power which goes beyond the laws of nature, as we currently understand them, in such a way as to evoke religious awe and wonder in those who witness them. From a theological point of view, St Thomas Aquinas says: 'The knowledge a prophet receives from God, must be communicated to others through the gifts of utterance, and that utterance must be confirmed as believable by the working of miracles: God confirming the message with attendant signs.'[13] In another place he says: 'Two things may be considered in miracles. Firstly, there is the deed that is performed: this is something surpassing the powers of nature ... Secondly, there is the purpose for which miracles are worked, namely, the manifestation of something supernatural.'[14]

In 1 Cor 12:10 Paul is saying that in the Christian community it is possible that a person or persons could be gifted with the ability to perform occasional miracles. To understand his thinking correctly it is important to see this gift in the context of his theology of the community as the Body of Christ. Members of the church are called to proclaim the good news of the outpouring of God's unconditional mercy and love and to demonstrate its presence, not only in the usual ways but also by means of deeds of power, such as miracle working. Like the performance of the other deeds of power, this unusual gift depends, as we have seen, upon the charism of expectant, unhesitating faith (Mk 11:23; 1 Cor 12:9), which may have been evoked in the heart by a revelation of God's purposes.

Modern Catholics have been familiar with the working of miracles in two main ways.

Firstly, they are associated with great saints who performed them during their lives and after their deaths. For example, during his life St Francis of Paola (1416-1507) of Calabria in Italy, was probably the greatest miracle worker the church has ever seen. He cured the sick, raised the dead, and it is said that he crossed the Straits of Messina by standing on his cloak which he laid upon the water. When saints die one or two miracles are required for their canonisation. But when St Charbel Makhlouf (1828-1898), a Maronite hermit in the Lebanon, was declared a saint in 1977, Pope Paul VI revealed that more first class miracles were submitted in support of his cause than for any other saint in history. As far as I can remember there were 1000 of them!

Secondly, there is the charism of miracle working. There is reason to think that these unusual gifts are associated in a special way with the ministry of being an apostle, prophet or teacher. Miracles are sufficiently important to be listed immediately after these primary ministries. I have not seen too many miracles over the years. However I can remember a time when a Polish man and a priest I know well, prayed for a nun who was paralyzed from the neck downwards with Multiple Sclerosis. Following the prayer she recovered. She was able to walk, drive and teach in school. It is very unlikely that it was a matter of profound remission because some twenty years later she has experienced none of the customary relapses and is still OK.

Conclusion

I'm convinced that evangelisation does not have to involve a choice between traditional and charismatic forms of evangelisation. Nowadays many evangelists aim to demonstrate the truth of the gospel proclamation, not just by the witness of transformed lives, but also by the performance of 'signs and wonders' such as healings, exorcisms and occasional miracles. It could be added, in the light of the Pauline theology of ministry, that those who have a ministry of basic evangelisation are more likely to receive the charisms of power than others.

Pope Paul the VI seemed to endorse this point of view when he spoke at the official launch of Cardinal Suenens's influential book, *A New Pentecost?* In the course of his address he departed from his prepared text to say these spontaneous words: 'How wonderful it would be if the Lord would again pour out the charisms in increased abundance, in order to make the church fruitful, beautiful and marvellous, and to enable it to win the attention and astonishment of the profane and secularised world.'[15] There is evidence which indicates that in recent years the charisms mentioned in 1 Cor 12:8-10 have indeed been given to men and women in all the Christian denominations. By and large, Pentecostals and Charismatic groups who evangelise by proclaiming the good news with accompanying charisms such as healing, have been growing fast, while those who do not have tended to decline.

Finally, it is worth recalling a word of caution spoken by John Paul II in par 72 of the encyclical *Catechesis in Our Time*. He is at pains to point out that rather than being an end in themselves, the charisms are merely a means to a more important end. Evangelisation in the Spirit, he observes, 'will be authentic and will have real fruitfulness in the church, not so much according as it gives rise to extraordinary charisms, but according as it leads the greatest possible number of the faithful, as they travel their daily paths, to make a humble, patient and persevering effort to know the mystery of Christ better and better and to bear witness to it.'

CHAPTER NINETEEN

Preaching and Teaching
in a Time of Transition[1]

First, a few comments about the biblical notion of God's word. In Western culture reality is primary, language is secondary and used to reflect it. But in the bible it is the other way around. God's word comes first. It is dynamic. It creates reality because it contains within itself the power of its own fulfillment. Goethe adverted to this point in his great poem. When Faust was translating the first verse of John's gospel he began by writing: 'In the beginning was the Word!,' then he tried, 'In the beginning was the Thought!,' then he went on to, 'In the beginning was the Power!,' Finally he wrote: 'The Spirit is helping me! I see now what I need and write: *In the beginning was the Deed.*'[2]

In the Old Testament the term for word is *Dabar*. It means 'to drive, to get behind, or push.' It can be used as a noun and as a verb. As a noun it is objective. It refers to the word of God which is true in itself. The bible contains that word between its covers. As a verb it is subjective. It refers to the word of God which is true for the individual. It is the revelatory word which is spoken by the Lord to a particular person in specific circumstances. When the Old Testament was translated into Greek, the scholars of the time acknowledged this distinction. When the Hebrew text referred to the word in itself, translators tended to use the Greek term *logos*. When the text referred to the word that is spoken, they often used the Greek term *rhema*. Even if this distinction is arbitrary from a linguistic point of view, it has validity from a theological and experiential point of view. The relationship between *logos* and *rhema* can be expressed in the following statements: *Rhema* takes the eternal *logos* and injects it into time. *Rhema* takes the heavenly *logos* and brings it down to earth. *Rhema* takes the general *logos* and makes it specific. *Rhema* takes a portion of the total *logos* and presents it in the form that a person can assimilate.[3]

St Ignatius of Loyola reminds us in his *Spiritual Exercises:* 'It is not much knowledge that fills and satisfies the soul, but the intimate understanding and relish of the truth.'[4] When people pay prayerful attention to the scriptures, e.g. by means of the Ignatian method or the *Lectio Divina,*[5] they desire that God's word would leap alive off the page into their hearts as an inspired and inspiring word of revelation. Abraham and Mary are the two outstanding exemplars of biblical faith. Their attitude is encapsulated in Is 50:4-5 which says: 'The Sovereign Lord ... wakens me morning by morning, wakens my ear to listen like one being taught. The Sovereign Lord has opened my ears, and I have not been rebellious; I have not drawn back.' They were blessed because they believed that there would be fulfilment of what was spoken to them by the Lord (cf Lk 1:45).

Hearing the Word

Robert Maloney says in his book *He Hears the Cry of the Poor,* that listening to God's word is the basis of all Christian spirituality.[6] The main reason for reading the scriptures is to get to know who God is and what God wants. When St Vincent de Paul was nearing the end of his long and fruitful life in 1656, he appointed a 27 year old priest to be the superior of a community house. Before his departure he invited Fr Durand to his room for some words of encouragement and guidance. Among other things he said that a preacher should be closely united to the Lord: 'Neither philosophy, nor theology, nor learned discourses influence souls. It is essential that Jesus Christ be intimately united with us or we with him; that we operate in him and he in us; that we speak like him and in his Spirit as he himself was in his Father and preached the doctrine taught him by the Father.'[7]

Having talked about the importance of union with Christ, Vincent went on to stress the all-important role of prayer. He said: 'An important task to which you should apply yourself is to remain in close touch with our Lord by means of personal prayer. This is the storehouse where you will find all you need to accomplish the task you are about to assume. When you have a doubt, have recourse to God and say to him: 'Lord, the Father of all inspiration, reveal to me what I must say or do in this case.' ... I not only give you this advice for the difficulties you may experience, but to teach you what you are to say to those in your care … When there is question of doing some good work, say to the Son of God: 'Lord if you were in my place, what would you do on this occasion? How would you teach the people?'[8]

Clearly Vincent was impressed by the fact that Jesus only preached to the people what God had revealed to him in prayer. As he testified: 'I do nothing on my own, but I speak these things as the Father instructed me … What I speak, therefore, I speak just as the Father has told me' (Jn 8:28; 12:50). St Peter echoed these sentiments sometime later: 'If anyone speaks, he should do it as one speaking the very words of God' (1 Pet 4:11). I have sometimes thought that if the priests of Ireland were to preach only those things that had been revealed to them in prayer, a hushed silence would descend upon many of the pulpits and lecterns in the land!

Vincent's advice can be followed in three main ways. Firstly, as people prayerfully reflect on a text they will sometimes recall relevant inspirations that came to them in prayer on previous occasions. Secondly, as they pray the liturgical text/s by means of *Lectio Divina*, there can be graced moments when they feel the Lord is revealing something of the divine presence and will to them. Thirdly, when they get to writing the homily or talk, they can try to ensure that it follows 'The Little Method' of St Vincent de Paul if it seems appropriate. It has three steps: Firstly, preachers and teachers should appeal to the minds of their listeners by dealing with the *nature* of the subject under consideration, whether doctrinal or ethical. Secondly, they should appeal to their emotions by providing *motives* for a personal response. Thirdly, they should appeal to their wills, by providing practical *means* of expressing that response in their everyday lives.

I firmly believe that preaching of the word will only be effective to the extent that Christians live together in unity of mind and heart. Loving relationships in the parish constitute an indispensable interpretative key that opens up the meaning of the scripture. The extent to which the Spirit is present in the united local community is the extent to which the same Spirit will enable us to understand the inspired word of God. As we glean insights from the scriptures and act upon them they will strengthen the bonds of unity. So there is a reciprocal relationship between unity in the locality and insight into God's word. In our local Vincentian community we have found it helpful to read the scriptures for the following Sunday on Monday mornings. We pray and meditate for half an hour, and then go on to spend ten minutes at the end in faith sharing. There are two questions we try to address: what is the word saying? and how can it be preached in a relevant way to the people we serve? I know that some diocesan priests, together with interested lay people, meet once a week and follow a similar methodology.

The Culture in which the Word is Preached

The living word has to be incarnated within the particular circumstances of the age of transition in which we live. We can make three general observations about the contemporary milieu. They augment the observations already made in chapter nine entitled, 'Popular Devotion and Primal piety'.

Western culture has moved from a static to an evolutionary worldview. Each of these outlooks is influenced by a particular perspective. They are referred to nowadays as the *Classical* and the *Historical* points of view.

The classical mentality is deductive. It emphasises universal principles and necessary conclusions. It tends to be abstract and *a priori*. It examines the nature of things and draws conclusions in regard to particular instances depending on whether or not they correspond to stated principles.

The historical mode of thinking emphasises changing circumstances and contingent conclusions. It begins with concrete data, employs an empirical method, stresses hermeneutics, and draws its conclusions inductively from its sources.

Preaching the Word

I suggested in an article entitled 'Models of Evangelisation,' that there are three discernible types operating in the church today.[9] The first, is the didactic/sacramental model. It is head centred, sees faith as assent, and aims at orthodoxy, i.e. right belief. The second is the kerygmatic/charismatic model. It is heart centred, sees faith as trust, and aims at orthokardia, i.e. right experience. The third is the political/developmental model. It is hands centred, sees faith in terms of performance, and aims at orthopraxis, i.e. right action. The essentialist approach of the didactic / sacramental model belongs to classical culture and is, *ipso facto*, increasingly ineffective within the emerging culture of experience. The other two models are existentialist in their approach and therefore better suited to the needs of the times.

I have found that if one adopts any of the models, but especially either of the experiential approaches, the following six points can help one to preach in a more effective manner.

- Firstly, take your human development seriously. Intellectual sophistication is no substitute for emotional maturity. Many of the people we preach to and teach are mature in a psycho-spiritual sense. They need a preacher or teacher who has an experiential understanding of their needs. That depends, in part, on things such as self-awareness, inner healing and empathic skills.
- Secondly, do not neglect your psycho-spiritual welfare. Be sure to foster friendships, leisure, contemplation and sensible exercise and dieting in your life.
- Thirdly, have an in-depth knowledge of your listeners, especially the younger ones, their circumstances, difficulties, concerns, desires, etc. Ideally, personal experience can be augmented by social analysis, i.e. a planned survey of such things as the political, economic, social, and cultural factors affecting the area.
- Fourthly, read the available research on religious trends in contemporary Ireland such as *Values and Social Change in Ireland*, which was published in 1994, and Mícheál Mac Gréil's *Prejudice in Ireland Revisited*, which was published in 1996.
- Fifthly, have a good working knowledge of contemporary popular culture, i.e. the music, films, sports, TV soaps etc., that interest the many readers of the tabloids, e.g. the *Sunday World*.
- Sixthly, have a layman's knowledge of psychology. If one has insights into subjects like self-esteem, stress, addictions and so on, they can often be more useful than familiarity with the finer points of metaphysics.
- Seventhly, support your preaching and teaching with personal witness and testimony. In other words, when you share

with people how the living word has impinged upon your
own life in a liberating and healing way, it can have greater
credibility. As St Francis of Assissi is reputed to have said,
'Preach at all times, and sometimes in words.'

It seems to me that within this evolving context, there is a clear
need for basic evangelisation or re-evangelisation. What is required are well planned programmes which aim to proclaim the
core truths of Christianity. They try to lead people, many of
them nominal Christians, to make a free and conscious commitment to Jesus as Lord and Saviour. As Acts 16:31 and Rom 10:9
make clear, basic evangelisation is the indispensable foundation
stone upon which the edifice of the Christian life, whether of
faith or morals, has to be built. To do otherwise is to build on
sand. In my experience there are four methodologies which are
working well at the moment: The Rite of Christian Initiation of
Adults (RCIA); Cursillo weekends; Life in the Spirit Seminars;
Power to Change and *Alpha* courses. The latter are already proving to be very effective among the lapsed and un-churched in
England and elsewhere, including different parts of Ireland. It is
encouraging to hear that they are evoking a positive response in
universities, prisons and deprived areas. To a greater or lesser
extent, these forms of spreading the good news, especially the
last three, are all examples of the kerygmatic/charismatic approach to evangelisation.

Traditional Catholicism says that when people believe what
the church teaches and behave accordingly, then and only then,
will they will belong in the Christian community. In secular,
post-modern society, where individualism is rampant and social
alienation is common, the order needs to be reversed.
Nowadays people have an overriding desire for a feeling of unconditional belonging. Arguably this is the key to effective evangelisation, especially among young people. Religious people
are, literally, those who are bound together by a common experience of a love that simultaneously connects them to one another,
to their deepest selves and to God. If people have a sense of belonging within a caring Christian community they will be more
open to accept the Christian beliefs that inform that community.
It is only within this loving, faith-filled context that the issue of

right behaviour can be tackled. Ideally, right action should be an expression of a sense of Christian belonging and belief, rather that a dutiful substitute for them both, as it has often seemed to be in the past. I think that Alpha courses really appreciate the importance of this point. Each session begins with a shared meal that fosters a sense of belonging. It is then and only then that the teaching is given.

What will do we do with people who come to personal, committed faith in Christ? There are clear indications that most parishes, especially in the large towns and cities, fail to satisfy people's need for community. The numbers involved are too great and therefore relationships tend to be formal and weak. What many modern day Christians are looking for are smaller groups within the parish, such as prayer, bible, and self-help groups, which can encourage personal relationships, a strong sense of belonging and the promise of spiritual transformation. The cell groups pioneered by Fr Michael Hurley in Ballinteer in Dublin seem to be one way of addressing those needs in an effective way. I think that it goes without saying that parishes in which these groups exist need to be renewed and changed. I believe that Cardinal Roger Mahoney's instruction for his diocese of Los Angles, entitled 'As I Have Done for You: A Pastoral Letter on Ministry' is the best description of what is possible, that I have come across.

Conclusion

To conclude, two important points. Firstly, in his encyclical on evangelisation Pope Paul VI stressed the vital role of the Holy Spirit in preaching. 'The techniques of evangelisation,' he wrote in par 75, 'are valuable, but even though they be perfect, they cannot dispense with the secret action of the Holy Spirit. The most careful preparation by a preacher will be of no avail without him and no discourse will be capable of moving people's hearts unless it is inspired by him. Without him the most skilful plans of sociologists will prove valueless.' Before opening our lips to preach, therefore, we should pray that the Spirit will be at work within us and our listeners. Secondly, St Vincent de Paul used to stress the importance of a simple, unpretentious way of speaking. Evidently, a lot of the preaching in the seventeenth century was above the heads of the people. Some learned and pedantic preachers seemed more intent on displaying how clever they were than in imparting God's word in a clear, down to earth way. He said: 'Use simple words and comparisons, such as those Our Lord used in the sacred scriptures, when you speak to the people … Notice how he spoke in intelligible language … that is how you must speak if you want to be understood by the people to whom you announce the word of God.'

Notes

Introduction
1. For a brief description of postmodernism see chapter nine.
2. It is interesting to note that the word 'symbol' comes from the Greek *symbolon* 'a token', from *syn* 'together', and *ballein* 'to throw'. In other words symbols have a synthetic quality, an ability to bring dispirate elements together. The opposite to the word symbolical is the word diabolical. On this point see chapter three.

Chapter One
1 Adapted from original version 'Maturing as a Priest' published in *Colloque*, no. 32, Autumn , (Dublin: Irish Vincentians, 1995), 141-154.
2 Cf. Myers & Briggs *Gifts Differing* (Palo Alto, CA: Consulting Psychologists Press, 1980)
3 Cf. Bessing, Nogosek & O' Leary, *The Enneagram: A Journey of Self-discovery* (New Jersey: Dimension Books, 1984).
4 Cf. Oldham & Morris, *The Personality Self-portrait* (New York: Bantam, 1990).
5 Pat Collins, *Overcoming Stress* (Dublin: Veritas, 2001).
6 Cf. Pat Collins, 'Dreams: A Christian Understanding,' *Growing in Health and Grace* (Galway: Campus, 1992), 72-86.
7 'True Inspirations and Illusions,' *Conferences of St Vincent de Paul* (Philadelphia: Vincentians Eastern Province, 1963).
8 *The Psychology of Love,* Ed. Sternberg & Barnes, (New Haven: Yale University Press, 1988), 120-122.
9 *Confessions,* IV, 73.
10 Book IV, 77-78.
11 The word 'sexual' is being used in a non-genital sense to refer to male and female attraction which is both physical and emotional.
12 Cf. Pat Collins, *Prayer in Practice: A Biblical Approach* (Dublin: Columba, 2000).
13 (Dublin, Veritas, 1994), 502.
14 *Introduction to the Devout Life* Translated and edited by John Ryan (New York: Harper Torchbooks, 1966), 143.

Chapter Two
1 Shorter version originally entitled 'Loving Empathy', *Spirituality* (July-August 1998), 235-240.
2 (New York: Paulist Press, 1982).
3 *Matthew: New Testament Message 3* (Dublin: Veritas, 1984), 70-71.
4 'Basic Empathy as a Communication Skill', *Initial Training Course for CMAC Personnel* (Dublin: CMAC, 1989), 122.

5 *Clinical Theology* (London: DLT, 1966), 1187.

6 (London: Bloomsbury, 1996), 106-110.

7 (London: DLT, 1992), 75.

8 (London: Signet, 1997).

9 Cf. Diane Papalia & Sally Wendkosolds, *Human Development* (New York: Mc Graw-Hill, 1989), 433.

10 *In a Different Voice* (Cambridge, Mass: Harvard, 1982), 40-45.

11 *Waiting on God* (Glasgow: Fontana, 1951), 71.

12 G. Egan, 'Basic Empathy'.in Initial Training Course for CMAC Personnel (Dublin: CMAC of Ireland, 1989) 125.

13 *About Love* (Chicago: Franciscan Herald Press, 1974).

14 'How Beastly is the Bourgeois Is', *D H Lawrence Selected Poems* (London: Penguin, 1968), 137.

15 Quoted by Peter Gay, *Freud: A Life for our Times* (London: Papermac, 1988).

16 *Thinking Allowed,* Ed Geoffrey Mishlove (Berkley: Council Oak Books, 1992), 357.

Chapter Three

1 Rhoda Tripp, *The International Thesaurus of Quotations* (London, Penguin, 1983), 1036.

2 Cf. Hans Kung, *Eternal Life?* (London: Fount, 1984), 163.

3 Quoted by Barbara Tuchman, 'The Warrior: Julius II', *The March of Folly From Troy to Vietnam* (London: Abacus, 1985), 113.

4 (Baltimore: John Hopkins University Press, 1977).

5 (Stanford: Stanford University Press, 1987).

6 (Baltimore: John Hopkins University Press, 1986).

7 Cf. Michael Prior, *The Bible and Colonialism: A Moral Critique* (Sheffield: Sheffield Academic Press, 1997).

8 Par 1035, (New York: Image Doubleday, 1995), 292.

9 *Crossing the Threshold of Hope* (London: Jonathan Cape, 1994), 186.

10 Bibliomania.com

11 *DS* 1351.

12 *Catechism of the Catholic Church* (Dublin: Veritas, 1994), par 1260.

13 *Uber die Energetik der Seele und Andere Psychologische Abhandlungen* (Zurich: Rascher, 1928), 158.

14 Cf. Pat Collins, 'Me and My Shadow', *Intimacy and the Hungers of the Heart* (Dublin: Columba, 1992), 74-86.

15 Cf. A. A. Anderson, *The New Century Bible Commentary Vol 1: Psalms 1-72* (Grand Rapids, Mich: Eerdmans, 1981), 400.

16 Cf. Pheme Perkins 'Love of Enemies,' *Love Commands of the New Testament* (New York: Paulist Press, 1982), 27-40.

17 *Violence Unveiled,* op. cit., 27.

18 *Violence Unveiled,* op. cit., 27.

19 Quoted by Michael Prior, *The Bible and Colonialism: A Moral Critique* (Sheffield: Sheffield Academic Press, 1997), 62.

20 *The Bible and Colonialism,* op. cit., 59.
21 Cabeza de Vaca, *Adventures in the Unknown Interior of America* (1542)
translated Cyclone Covey, (New Mexico: New Mexico Press, 1983).
22 (London: Penguin Press, 1988), 141.
23 *Modern Ireland 1600-1972,* op. cit., 470.
24 (London: Penguin, 1971), 147.
25 *Summa Theologica* 2a-2ae, xl, 1.
26 *Violence Unveiled,* op. cit., 27.
27 *The Pope in Ireland: Addresses and Homilies* (Dublin: Veritas, 1979), 21.
28 *Violence Unveiled,* op. cit., 268.
29 *Adagia* (1500).
30 (London: Pan, 1967), 269.
31 *Violence Unveiled,* op. cit., 263.

Chapter Four

1 *Intimacy and The Hungers of the Heart* (Dublin: Columba, 1992), 138.
2 *Man's Search for Himself* (New York: Norton, 1953), 241.
3 *Man's Search for Meaning* New York: Pocket Books, 1985), 134.
4 'Envy', *Feelings: Our Vital Signs* (New York: Ballantine, 1980), 137.
5 *Envy: A Theory of Social Behaviour,* (New York: Harcourt, Brace &
World, Inc., 1969).
6 First recorded in *Conversations with Eckermann,* in praise of
Wellington's stand against Catholic Emancipation.
7 *Collected Works,* London, 1910, vol. 7, p. 209.
8 *Gesammelte Werke,* Bern, 1955, Vol. 3, p. 45.
9 Cf. John M. Oesterreicher, *Five in Search of Wisdom* (Notre Dame:
University of Notre Dame, 1967), 111.
10 *One Like Us: A Psychological Interpretation of Jesus* (London: DLT,
1998), 30.
11 Cf. *One Like Us,* op. cit., 29-30.
12 *Summa Theologica,* II-II, 30, 2.
13 (Notre Dame: University of Notre Dame Press, 1983), 306.
14 *Delinquents in the Making,* (New York: Harper, 1952), 149.
15 *Summa Theologiae: A Concise Translation,* ed. Mc Dermott, (London:
Methuen, 1991), 366.
16 *Homin Rom.* 71, 5: PG 60, 448.
17 *The Interior Castle,* part 2. In *A Life of Prayer,* Ed. James Houston,
(Basingstoke: Pickering & Inglis, 1983), 175.
18 Discourses of Gregory Nazianzen, *Divine Office* Vol. 1, Reading 2nd
Jan, (Dublin: Talbot, 1974), 76*.
19 Quoted by Gaylin, *Feelings: Our Vital Signs,* op. cit. 143.
20 'People were laughing Behind a Wall,' *The Poetry of Yevgeny
Yevtushenko: 1953-1965.*

Chapter Five
1 *Religious Life Review* July-Aug 2000, pp. 215-224. Correspondence in
Sept-Oct, and Nov-Dec 2000.

2 Janet Ruffing, 'The 'As if' Relationship: Transference and Counter transference in Spiritual Direction,' *Spiritual Direction: Beyond the Beginnings*, (London: St Pauls, 2000), 155-180.

3 13th Edition of the *Encyclopaedia Britannica* (1926).

4 Cf. Allan Schnarr, 'Safe Touch in Ministry', *Human development* Vol 22, No. 1, (Spring, 2001), 14-15.

5 Cf. John Sanford, *The Invisible Partners*, (New York: Paulist Press, 1980).

6 FreeFone (01) 1800 331 234.

Chapter Six

1 *Spirituality* (Sept/Oct 2001), 294-8.

2 'Psychotherapists or the Clergy' (London: Ark, 1988), 202.

3 *Psychotherapy and Existentialism: Selected Papers on Logotherapy* (London: Pelican Books, 1973), 51.

4 Cf. *Man's Search for Meaning*, (New York: Washington Square Press, 1985), 129-130.

5 Quoted by Edward Hoffman, *The Right to be Human: A Biography of Abraham Maslow*, (Wellingborough: Crucible, 1989), 277.

6 Maltby, Lewis & Day, *The British Journal of Health Psychology* (1999), no. 4. p. 874.

7 *Pass It On* (New York: Alcoholics Anonymous World Services, 1984), 121.

8 Ernest Kurtz, *Not-God: A History of Alcoholics Anonymous* (Center City, Mn: Hazelden, 1991), 125.

9 (London: Hamish Hamilton, 1935), 143-144.

10 Cf. David G. Myers, 'Is Prayer Clinically Effective?' *Reformed Review* 53 (2) (2000), 95-102.; 'On Assessing Prayer, Faith and Health' *Reformed Review*, 53 (2) (2000), 119-126, and http://www.davidmyers.org/religion/faith.tml; Koenig, Larson & Mc Cullough, *Handbook of Religion and Health*, (Oxford: Oxford University Press, 2000); Koenig & Mc Connell, *The Healing Power of Faith* (Simon & Schuster 2001).

11 Robert Eagle, *A Guide to Alternative Medicine* (London: BBC, 1980), 17.

12 David Wulf, *Psychology of Religion: Classic & Contemporary Views* (New York: Wiley, 1991), 171.

13 (London: Routledge, 2000), 157.

14 (New York: Harper/Collins, 1997)

Chapter Seven

1 *Doctrine and Life* (September 2000), 402-407.

2 (New Haven: Yale University Press, 1984), 160-84.

3 (Chicago: University of Chicago Press, 1979).

4 'The origin and development of personal identity through childhood to adult life and its significance in pastoral care.' Second year syllabus, no. 4, *Clinical Theology* (The Clinical Theological Assoc., Hawthornes of

Nottingham Ltd.), 5.
5 *Clinical Theology,* op. cit., 101.
6 (New York: Basic, 1971).
7 'Transitional Objects and Transitional Phenomena' *International Journal of Psychanalysis* 34:2, p. 13.

Chapter Eight
1 *Spirituality* (March-April 2001), 82-5.
2 (Dublin: Veritas, 1998).
3 *A Celtic Quest* (1974).
4 *Patrick, the Pilgrim Apostle of Ireland,* op. cit., 150.

Chapter Nine
1 *The Passing of King Arthur,* l. 407.
2 In Andrew Greely and Connor Ward's 'How 'Secularised' is the Ireland We Live In?' *Doctrine and Life* (Dec. 2000), p. 597, the authors say that currently the figures for weekly Mass attendance are 62% in the cities, 51% in Suburbs, Towns & County seats, and 73% in rural areas.
3 Andy Pollak, 'Poll Shows Church's Moral Authority in Decline,' (Mon. Dec. 16, 1996), 5.
4 Cf. Batson, C. D., Schoenrade, P., Ventis, W. L., *Religion and the Individual* (New York: Oxford University Press, 1993).
5 Cf. Pat Collins, 'Postmodernism and Religion', *Doctrine and Life* (Jan 1999), 22-31.
6 *Faith and Reason* (London: Catholic Truth Society, 1998), par 84.
7 *Faith and Reason,* op. cit. par. 90.
8 Cf. Pat Collins, *Intimacy and the Hungers of the Heart* (Dublin: Columba, 1991), 9-17.
9 *Redemptoris Missio,* par 42.
10 Greely and Ward, op. cit. p. 586. 'The proportions of the Irish people thinking that premarital sex, extra-marital sex, same sex relationships and abortion when there is a strong chance of a serious defect in the child, are always wrong have all declined significantly in the years between 1991 and 1998.'
11 In an article entitled, 'Is Britain's Soul Waking-Up?' in the June 24th 2000 edition of the *Tablet*.
12 *The Secular City: Secularization and Urbanization in Theological Perspective,* (London: SCM Press, 1966).
13 *Fire From Heaven: The Rise of Pentecostal Spirituality and the Reshaping of Religion in the Twenty-First Century* (London: Cassell, 1996), 99-110.
14 Cf. Pat Collins, *Prayer in Practice: A Biblical Approach* (Dublin: Columba, 2000), 18-23.
15 David Barrett, 'Annual Statistical Table on Global Mission: 1995' *International Bulletin on Missionary Research* 19:1 (January 1995), 25.
16 *'Phaedrus,' The Dialogues of Plato* (244) (Oxford: Clarendon Press,

1964) Vol 3, p155.

17 *A Midsummer-Night's Dream* V, i, 7.

18 Paul Tillich, *Love, Power and Justice,* (New York: Oxford University Press, 1980), 36.

19 *Encounter with God: A Theology of Christian Experience* (London: Hodder & Stoughton, 1974), 56.

20 Appendix, Parts 1 & 2, *Encounter With God,* op. cit. 242-245.

21 Cf. George Montague, *The Spirit and his Gifts* (New York: Paulist Press, 1985), 33; David Aune, The Revelatory Trance, in 'Basic Features of Israelite Prophecy', *Prophecy in Early Christianity And The Ancient Mediterranean World,* (Grand Rapids, Mich: Eerdmans, 1983), 86-87.

22 *Encounter with God,* op. cit. p. 35.

23 Cf, Thomas Petrisko, *The Apparitions, Visions and Prophesies of Christina Gallagher.* Published privately in 1995 by the author. In a letter dated 16 Dec 1997, Archbishop Michael Neary of the Archdiocese of Tuam said of Christina Gallagher's claims: 'I find myself obliged to state that no evidence has been presented which might prove beyond reasonable doubt the occurrence of supernatural phenomena of whatever kind in this situation other than that of faith. Mrs Gallagher and her associates retain, of course, the right to believe and state their belief that such have indeed occurred and continue to occur.'

24 On the first occasion, Mary was clothed in a purple dress, her heart pierced by three swords. Her message can be summarised as: 'Prayer, sacrifice, repentance.' During the subsequent appearances, Mary was dressed in white with three roses on her breast. On 7/13, she asked that the 13th of each month be commemorated as a Marian day. Also, a statue of Mary as *Rosa Mystica* was alleged to have shed tears at St John of God parish in Chicago, Il from May 1984 until at least 1992. The phenomenon started after some of the parishioners (including the pastor) visited the original shrine at Montichiari. However, the archdiocesan investigation could not rule out natural causes and decided there was 'no evidence of a miracle.'

25 (London: Paladin, 1979), 171.

26 Carl Jung, 'Jung and Religious Belief,' and 'Letter to Brother Klaus', *Psychology and Western Religion* (London: Ark, 1988), 289, 229.

27 Cf. Samuels, Shorter & Plaut 'Alchemy', *A Critical Dictionary of Jungian Analysis* (London: Routledge & Keegan Paul, 1987), 12-15.

28 *The Passion of the Western Mind* (New York: Ballentine, 1991), 441-442.

29 *The Passion of the Western Mind,* op. cit., 444.

30 For example, on 30 Jan 1991 Christina Gallagher spoke these words which she claimed were revealed to her by God: 'Tell all humanity to prepare themselves. The time has come for the cleansing of all humanity. A great darkness will come upon the world. The heavens will shake. The only light will be through the Son of God and Man. The lightening bolts will flash like nothing the world has ever seen. My hand will

come over the world more swiftly than the wind. Be not afraid.'
31 Fri, 4 May 2001.
32 'The Situation of Faith Today,' *The Practice of Faith: A Handbook of Contemporary Spirituality* (London: SCM Press, 1985), 30.
33 'The Spirituality of the Future,' *The Practice of Faith*, op. Cit., 22.

Chapter Ten
1 Paper read at the annual general meeting of Irish hospital chaplains 24 April 2001.
2 *Clinical Theology: A Theological and Psychiatric Basis to Clinical Pastoral Care* (London: Darton, Longman & Todd, 1966), 327.
3 *Four Quartets* (London: Faber, 1964), 39.
4 *Four Quartets*, op. cit., 39.
5 (New York: Crossroad, 1994), viii.
6 (Kansas: Sheed and Ward, 1995).
7 'Adaptation of guidelines on Theological Reflection' by Anne Brotherton, Director of Field Education, Jesuit School of Theology, Berkley, Spring 1983, printed in *Guidelines for Pastoral Formation* (Dublin: Irish Association for Pastoral Formation, 1991), 27. See also Robert Kinast, *Theological Reflection?* (New York: Paulist Press, 2000).
8 *Method in Ministry*, op. cit..
9 The Greek verb *metanoein* is comprised of *meta* = 'across, over'; *noein* = 'to think'. So *metanoia* literally means 'to change one's mind, way of thinking, or outlook.'
10 Cf. Bernard Lonergan, 'Feelings', *Method in Theology* (London: Darton Longman & Todd, 1972), 30-34. The rational mind is orientated to an understanding of reality, whereas feelings are orientated to the perception of ontic, qualitative, vital, social, cultural, personal and religious values.
11 Pat Collins, 'Spiritual Warfare', *Spirituality for the Twenty First Century*, (Dublin: Columba, 1999), 170-179.
12 Cf. Holland & Henriot, *Social Analysis* (New York: Orbis, 1983).

Chapter Eleven
1 Expanded version of 'A New Prayer', *New Creation,* (Dec 2000), 18-19.
2 Seán Ó Tuama & Thomas Kinsella, *Poems of the Dispossed 1600-1900,* (Dublin: Dolmen, 1981), 191.
3 Quoted by Phillips, Boyden Howes, and Nixon, *The Choice is Always Ours: An Anthology on the Religious Way* (Wheaton, Illinois: Re-Quest Books, 1975), 181.
4 Cf. Karl Rahner & Herbert Vorgrimler, *Theological Dictionary* (New York: Herder and Herder, 1968), 367.
5 'Psychology and Alchemy,' *Collected Works* (1943) Vol 12, p. 14.
6 *Aion, Researches into the Phenomenology of the Self*, Collected Works, Vol. 9, ii, p. 62.
7 Letter dated 22 September 1944, quoted by Gebhard Frei in Victor

White, *God and the Unconscious*, (London: Fontana Books, 1960), 258.

8 Collected Works, IXII, 69-70. Quoted in John Welsh, *Spiritual Pilgrims: Carl Jung and Teresa of Avila*, (New York: Paulist Press, 1982), 192.

9 Letter dated 13 January, 1948, in *God and the Unconscious*, op. cit. 273.

10 *C. G. Jung Speaking*, eds. William Mc Guire and R. F. C. Hull, (Princeton, NJ: Princeton University Press, 1977), 165.

11 *The Holy Spirit in the Life of Church and World*, par. 54.

12 *Julian of Norwich: Showings*, (New York: Paulist Press, 1978), 56.

13 *A Life of Prayer*, (Basingstoke: Pickering & Inglis, 1983), 68.

14 Quoted by John Higgins, *Thomas Merton on Prayer*, (New York: Image, 1971), 59.

15 *The Twelve Steps of Humility and Pride/On Loving God* (London: Hodder & Stoughton, 1985), 86.

16 *Adversus Haerses*, book 2, chapter 22, par. 4.

17 Quotation in *Catechism of the Catholic Church* (Dublin: Veritas, 1994), par 521. Taken from *On the Kingdom of Jesus*, Liturgy of the Hours, Week 33, Friday.

18 *Berulle and the French School: Selected Writings*, ed. W. Thompson, (New York: Paulist Press, 1989), 296.

19 *Autobiography of a Saint: Thérèse of Lisieux*, Trans. Ronald Knox, (London: The Harvill Press, 1958), 266.

20 *Autobiography of a Saint*, op. cit., 266

21 *Autobiography of a Saint*, op. cit. 268.

22 *Autobiography of a Saint*, op. cit., 269.

23 Andre Dodin, *Vincent de Paul and Charity: A Contemporary Portrait of his Life and Apostolic Spirit*, (New York: New City Press, 1993), 82.

24 *Instruction on Prayers for Healing*, Congregation for the Doctrine of the Faith, September 14, 2000, pars. 4 & 5.

25 *ST*, I, Q. 43, A. 6, rep. Obj. 2.

26 Cf. Joseph Ratzinger, *Christian Brotherhood* (London: Sheed & Ward, 1966), 66.

27 *Ap.*, 39, *CCSL*, I, 151.

28 *Unless the Lord Build the House: The Church and the New Pentecost* (Notre Dame: Ave Maria Press, 1975), 30.

29 *Christian Brotherhood*, op. cit. 27-28.

30 *Christian Brotherhood*, op. cit, 28.

31 *The Life of the Venerable Servant of God Vincent de Paul*, Vol 1 (New York: New City Press, 1993), 107.

32 *Berulle and the French School*, op. cit., 305.

Chapter Twelve

1 *New Creation*, (Nov. 1997), 5-8.

2 *Riding the Wind*, (Ann Arbor: Word of Life, 1977), 56-57.

3 Cf. Leon-Dufour, *Dictionary of the New Testament*, (San Francisco: Harper & Row, 1980), 91.

4 Eds. Brown, Fitzmyer & Murphy, (New Jersey: Prentice Hall, 1990).

5 (Collegeville, Minn: Liturgical Press, 1974).

6 (London: SCM Press, 1966).

7 Cf. Jean Laplace, *Prayer According to the Scriptures* (Dublin: Veritas, 1991).

8 Cf. Pat Collins, *Prayer in Practice: A Biblical Approach* (Dublin: Columba, 2000).

9 CTS Pocket Classics, *The Little Way Of St Thérèse of Lisieux: From the Saint's Own Writings,* (London: CTS, 1997), 18.

10 Christopher O' Mahoney, *St Thérèse of Lisieux by those Who knew Her* (Dublin: Veritas, 2001), 39.

11 *Divini Amoris Scientia:* Apostolic Letter of the Holy Father John Paul II for the proclamation of St Thérèse of the Child Jesus and the Holy Face as a Doctor of the Universal Church, par. 9.

12 Michel de Verteuil, *Your Word is a Light for My Steps: Lectio Divina* (Dublin: Veritas, 1997); Mario Masini, *Lectio Divina* (New York: Alba House, 1998).

13 Section 2, *Interpretation of the Bible in the Church* (Pauline Books and Media, 1993).

14 Par 2723, (Dublin: Veritas, 1994), 579.

15 Quoted by Abbé Arnaud D'angel, *St Vincent de Paul: A Guide for Priests,* (London: Burns Oates & Washbourne, 1932), 49.

16 Par 2724, (Dublin: Veritas, 1994), 579.

17 Coste, *Collected Works,* XI, 420.

18 *St Vincent de Paul: A Guide for Priests,* op. cit., 51.

Chapter Thirteen

1 *Milltown Studies,* no. 46 (Winter 2000), 1-13.

2 *Asking the Father* (Dublin: Dominican Publications, 1982), 54-55.

3 *Asking the Father,* op. Cit., 35

4 *Asking the Father,* op. Cit., 39; 52.

5 *Belief in God in an Age of Science* (New Haven: Yale University Press, 1998), 54.

6 John Meier, *Matthew,* New Testament Message 3 (Dublin: Veritas, 1984), 60.

7 Quoted by Friedrich Heiler, *Prayer: A Study in the History and Psychology of Religion,* (Oxford: Oneworld, 1997), 101.

8 'Petitionary Prayer' in the *American Philosophical Quarterly,* 16 (1979), 81-91.

9 'Prayer as Participation in Divine Action' in *Divine Action,* (London: Collins, 1990), 154-169; 'Divine Action as Co-operative Influence' in *God, Faith and the New Millennium: Christian Belief in an Age of Science,* (Oxford: Oneworld, 1998), 104-108.

10 *Divine Action,* op. cit., 159.

11 Letter 130, X, 16-17.

12 Timothy Mc Dermott (ed.) *Summa Theologiae: A Concise Translation,* (London: Methuen, 1991), 402.

13 'Petitionary Prayer' *A Companion to Philosophy of Religion*, ed. P. Quinn, C. Taliaferro (Oxford: Blackwell, 1999), 582.

14 'Prayer' *Encyclopedia of Theology: A Concise Sacramentum Mundi* (London: Burns & Oates, 1975), 1271.

15 No. 12, pp. 125-135.

16 *God Faith and the New Millennium*, op. cit., 106.

17 Cf. chapter six: 'Is Prayer Good for your Health?'

18 *Complementary Medical Research* 4:1, (September 1990), 9-33.

19 (New York: HarperCollins, 1993), 293-323.

20 *Belief in God in an Age of Science*, op. cit., 73.

21 *Science and the Soul: New Cosmology the Self and God* (London: SPCK, 1992), 180.

22 *Activation of Energy* (New York: Harcourt Brace Jovanovich, 1963), 124.

23 *How I Believe*, (New York: Harper & Row, 1969), 3.

24 See Pat Collins *Finding Faith in Troubled Times*, (Dublin: Columba, 1993), 182.

25 See Pat Collins *Expectant Faith* (Dublin: Columba, 1998), 125-127.

26 Book XXI, 8.

27 (London: Hamish Hamilton, 1958) 143-144.

28 *Man the Unknown*, op. cit., 143-144.

29 Quoted by Michael Talbot *The Holographic Universe*, (New York: Harper/Collins, 1991), VII.

30 Holography uses a photographic technique (involving the splitting of a laser beam into two beams) to produce a picture, or hologram, that contains 3-D information about the object photographed. Even if part of the photograph is removed, the entire image can be reproduced, albeit with diminished clarity. In other words, the whole image is contained in each of its parts.

31 *The Holographic Universe*, op. cit., 153.

Chapter Fourteen

1 Quoted by Bernard Bro, *The Little Way* (London: DLT, 1979), 1.

2 *Under the Torrent of His love: Thérèse of Lisieux, a Spiritual Genius* (New York: Alba House, 2000), 7.

3 Letter to Sr Marie of the Sacred Heart, Sept. 8th, 1896, *The Fire and the Cloud: An Anthology of Catholic Spirituality*, ed. David Fleming (London: Geoffrey Chapman, 1978), 309.

4 Cf. Dr Frank Lake, *Clinical Theology: A Theological and Psychiatric Basis to Clinical Pastoral Care* (London: Darton, Longman & Todd, 1966), 158-159.

5 *St Thérèse of Lisieux by Those Who Knew Her: Testimonies From the Process of Beatification*, ed. Christopher O' Mahoney (Dublin: Veritas, 2001), 172.

6 *St Thérèse of Lisieux by Those Who Knew Her*, op. cit., 172

7 *St Thérèse of Lisieux by Those Who Knew Her* op. cit., 172

8 *St Thérèse of Lisieux by Those Who Knew Her*, op. cit., 173.

9 *Autobiography of a Saint* (London: Harvill Press, 1958), 86.

10 *St Thérèse of Lisieux by Those Who Knew Her*, op. cit., 86.

11 Cf. 'Conversion Reactions,' *Clinical Theology*, op. cit., 539.

12 *Autobiography of a Saint*, op. cit., 128.

13 *Autobiography*, op. cit., 128.

14 *Autobiography*, op. cit., 129.

15 *Autobiography*, op. cit., 129.

16 For the full text see *The Little Way*, op. cit., 69-70.

17 *Autobiography*, op. cit., 129.

18 Quoted by Marie-Eugene in *Under Torrents of His Love* (New York: Alba House, 1995), 115.

19 *St Thérèse of Lisieux: Last Conversations* (Washington: Institute for Carmelite Studies, 1977)138-139.

20 Descouvemont & Loose, *Thérèse and Lisieux*, (Dublin: Veritas, 1996), 226.

21 *St Thérèse of Lisieux: Her Last Conversations*, op. cit., 17.

22 *St Thérèse of Lisieux: Her Last Conversations*, op. cit., 281.

23 Cf. Pierre Descouvemont, Helmuth Nils Loose, *Thérèse and Lisieux*, (Dublin: Veritas, 1996), 234-235.

24 *Thérèse and Lisieux*, op. cit., 186.

25 Quoted *The Little Way*, op. cit., 79.

26 *Under the Torrent of His Love*, op. cit., 28.

27 Quoted from 'The Autobiography', in *Catechism of the Catholic Church*, 2011.

28 *The Little Way*, op. cit., 66.

29 George Kosiciki, ed., *Revelations of Divine Mercy: Daily Readings From the Diary of Blessed Faustina Kowalska*, par. 1075 (Ann Arbor: Servant Publications, 1996), 89.

30 Quoted in *The Fire and the Cloud: An Anthology of Catholic Spirituality*, ed. Fleming (London: Geoffrey Chapman, 1978), 311.

31 *The Little Way*, op. cit., 18.

32 (London: Fontana, 1969).

33 Quoted by Bernard Bro, *The Little Way* op. cit., 5.

34 See Hans Kung, 'Friedrich Schleiermacher: Theology at the Dawn of Modernity,' *Great Christian Thinkers* (London: SCM Press, 1994), 155-184.

35 Quoted by Ladislas Boros, *Meeting God in Man* (London: Burns & Oates, 1968), 91.

36 Quoted by Henri Troyat, *Tolstoy* (London: Pelican, 1970), 520.

37 *Tolstoy*, op. cit., 520.

38 *Tolstoy*, op. cit., 521.

39 *Tolstoy*, op. cit., 524.

40 Leo Tolstoy experienced something very similar some 20 years earlier. On this see Pat Collins, *Finding Faith in Troubled Times*, (Columba: Dublin, 1993), 59-60.

41 *The Story of a Soul*, op. cit., 255-256.

42 *The Little Way*, op. cit.,53.

43 *Memories, Dreams, Reflections*, (New York: Vintage, 1965), 354.

44 *The Little Way*, op. cit., 53.

45 Chris O Donnell, *Love in the Heart of the Church: The Mission of Thérèse of Lisieux* (Dublin: Veritas, 1997), 44.

46 Quoted by Flanklin Baumer, *Modern European Thought: Continuity and Change in Ideas 1600-1950* (New York: Macmillan, 1977), 307.

47 *The Little Way*, op. cit., 11.

48 *St Thérèse of Lisieux: Her Last Conversations*, op. cit., 162-163.

49 *The Little Way* op. cit., 10.

50 *The Little Way* op. cit., 11.

51 *The Little Way*, op. cit., 54.

52 Cf. *Under the Torrent of His Love*, op. cit., 56.

53 *St Thérèse of Lisieux: Her Last Conversations*, op. cit., 206.

54 *St Thérèse of Lisieux: Her Last Conversations*, op. cit., 292.

55 *Clinical Theology* (Abridged version) (London: Darton, Longman & Todd, 1986), 13.

56 (Dublin: Veritas, 2001).

57 *Divini Amoris Scientia*, apostolic letter of Pope John Paul II for the proclamation of St Thérèse of the Child Jesus as a Doctor of the universal church, par. 3.

58 Cf. Hans Küng, *Does God Exist?* (London: Fount, 1980), 86.

59 (London: CTS, 1998), par. 91, p. 133.

60 Cf. Christopher O' Donnell, *Love in the Heart of the Church* (Dublin: Veritas, 1997), 184.

Chapter Fifteen

1 *New Creation* (Feb 2001), 5-8.

2 Cf. Joann Wolski Conn & Walter E. Conn, *Self-Sacrifice, Self-Fulfillment or Self-Transcendence in Christian Life?* Vol 3, no. 3, (*Human Development* Fall 1982), 25-28.

3 *St Thérèse of Lisieux: Her Last Conversations*, (Washington: Institute of Carmelite Studies, 1977), 205.

4 George Kosicki Ed., *Revelations of Divine Mercy: Daily Readings from the Diary of Blessed Faustina Kowalska*, (Ann Arbor: Servant Publications, 1996), 39.

Chapter Sixteen

1 Ludwig Feuerbach, 'A Projective Description', *Phenomenology of Religion*, op. cit., 115-137.

2 J. P. Stern, 'Nietzsche', *The Great Philosophers*, ed. Magee (London: BBC, 1987), 234-251.

3 Delivered to the Department of Psychology, New York University and published in the *Telling the Truth Project 1995*, www.leaderu.com/truth/1truth12.html.

4 *Faith of the Fatherless: The Psychology of Atheism* (Dallas: Spence, 1999).
5 George Weigel, *Witness to Hope: The Biography of John Paul II*, (London: Cliff Street Books, 1999), 169.
6 Cf Chapter eleven, 'Christ Within and Among Us'.

Chapter Seventeen
1 *New Creation* (Jan 2001), 9-11.
2 Eds. Cross & Livingstone, (Oxford: Oxford University Press, 1984), 486.
3 From 'The Psychology of Religion' *The Basic Writings of Jung*, Ed. Violet Staub de Laszlo, (New York: The Modern Library, 1959), 486.
4 Eds, Paddy Monaghan & Eugene Boyle, (Guildford, Surrey: Eagle, 1998).

Chapter Eighteen
1 *New Creation* (March 2001), 5-8.
2 *Evangelization Today*, par. 41.
3 *Goodnews*, Special Edition on 25 Years of Charismatic Renewal 1967-1992, 51-53.
4 Timothy Mc Dermott (Ed.), *Summa Theologiae: A Concise Translation* (London: Methuen, 1989), 446.
5 Book 3, ch. 154, [4].
6 (Peabody, Mass: Hendricksons, 1994), 167.
7 *Come Holy Spirit* (London: Hodder & Stoughton, 1985), 99.
8 *St Thomas Aquinas: The Gifts of the Spirit, Selected Spiritual Writings Chiefly From his Biblical Commentaries*, ed. Benedict Ashley, (New York: New City Press, 1995), 32.
9 *The Holy Spirit: Growth of a Biblical Tradition* (New York: Paulist Press, 1976), 152.
10 Op. cit., 109.
11 *Instruction on Prayers for Healing*, Congregation for the Doctrine of the Faith, September 14, 2000.
12 *Summa Theologiae*, II-II Q 111, A 4, reply 3.
13 *Summa Theologiae: A Concise Translation*, Ed. Timothy Mc Dermott (London: Methuen, 1989), 451.
14 *Summa Theologiae*, II-II Q 178, A. 1.
15 Edward O' Connor, *Pope Paul and the Spirit* (Indiana: Ave Maria Press, 1978), 212.

Chapter Nineteen
1 Adapted from *The Furrow*, (Feb 1999), 107-110, and 'St Vincent de Paul on Preaching,' *Intercom*, (Oct 2000), 10.
2 *Faust*, I, 1224.
3 Cf. Derek Prince, *Faith to Live By*, (Ann Arbor: Servant, 1977), 83.
4 Par [2]
5 Cf. Chapter twelve on Reading and Praying the Scriptures.

6 (New York: New City Press, 1995), 13.
7 Louis Abelly, *The Life of the Venerable Servant of God Vincent de Paul* Vol. 3, (New York: New City Press, 1993), 317.
8 Louis Abelly, op. cit. 318.
9 *Doctrine and Life*, (Jan 1998), 31-41.

Index